D1233830

METHODS OF SELF-CHANGE

AN ABC PRIMER

METHODS OF SELF-CHANGE

AN ABC PRIMER

Kjell Erik Rudestam

York University

BROOKS/COLE PUBLISHING COMPANY
Monterey, California
A Division of Wadsworth, Inc.

Printed in the United States of America

10 9 8 7 6 5 4 3 2 1

Library of Congress Cataloging in Publication Data

Rudestam, Kjell Erik.
  Methods of self-change.

  Bibliography.
  Includes index.
  1. Personality change.   2.   Behavior modification.
3. Psychotherapy.   I.   Title.
BF698.2.R83   158'.1   79-25306
ISBN 0-8185-0362-9

Project Development Editor: *Ray Kingman*
Production Editor: *Sally Schuman*
Interior and Cover Design: *John Edeen*
Illustrations: *Lori Heckelman*
Typesetting: *David R. Sullivan Company, Dallas, Texas*

Find a hungry man and feed him a fish.
He won't be hungry.
Find a hungry man and teach him how to fish.
He'll never be hungry.

Talmudic saying

PREFACE

The process of psychotherapy has been described in so many contexts in contemporary society that even the uninitiated student of psychology has some inkling of what goes on behind the closed doors of a therapist's office. Present-day therapists have, in fact, moved beyond existing stereotypes by using increasingly sophisticated techniques to help people resolve both major psychological disturbances and relatively minor problems in living. In the past the field was dominated by a small number of rigidly defined approaches. Today traditional schools of psychotherapy are gradually giving way to approaches that integrate the contributions of different disciplines and draw on a variety of methods to suit the individual client. Many of these methods can be used for initiating self-change, without the assistance of the professional counselor or psychotherapist. This usage ties in with the fact that more and more people want to be directly involved in their own personality growth. Unfortunately, most currently available self-help manifestos are disappointingly narrow and overlook the full range of psychotherapeutic interventions. Consequently, I have written *Methods of Self-Change* to pull together those psychological techniques that offer people the most promise for successful self-change.

Not everything that goes on in formal psychotherapy is amenable to a self-change technology. The nature of the therapist/client relationship is not directly translatable. But a large number of methods taken from several theoretical orientations can be appropriated for self-use. The first chapter of this book presents a simple model for categorizing self-change techniques and for assessing the reader's need for them. Chapters 2, 3, and 4 introduce twenty different techniques, classified as affective, behavioral, or cognitive, according to their respective emphases on feelings, behaviors, or thoughts. I have described each procedure step by step, illustrated them with case examples, and suggested areas of applicability. The final chapter integrates the techniques and discusses their application to four common problem areas: lack of assertiveness, depression, anger, and insomnia. Although the techniques generally derive from successful use with clinical populations, they are often most suitable for everyday problems, including difficulties in interpersonal relationships, feelings of insecurity and distress, and desires for psychological growth and competence.

Methods of Self-Change is intended for anyone who has a commitment to or interest in the self-change process. No academic prerequisites are necessary to understand and benefit from the material. The book is especially appropriate for university and college courses in clinical psychology, counseling, social work, and human relations. Professional therapists or trainees might also profit from the compendium of self-change approaches as prescriptive suggestions for their clients.

A number of friends and colleagues have provided invaluable suggestions and nurturance along the way to completion of the book. I have profited from the reviews of earlier versions of the manuscript by John Brennecke, Mt. San Antonio College; Daniel Fallon, Central YMCA Community College; Alan E. Kazdin, Pennsylvania State University; Richard Lundy, Pennsylvania State University; Dan Perkins, Richland College; Jeanne S. Phillips, University of Denver; James Prochaska, University of Rhode Island; and Kathy West, Portland Community College. Special thanks are due to Rodeen Walderman, to my illustrator, Christine Puffer, and to my editors at Brooks/Cole, Claire Verduin, Ray Kingman, and Sally Schuman. I sincerely appreciate the indefatigable proficiency and marvelous attitude of my typist, Toni Lucente. Finally, I have continuing admiration and appreciation for the help and support given by my editor and wife, Janice.

Kjell Erik Rudestam

CONTENTS

1

THE ABC MODEL
OF SELF-CHANGE
1

2

AFFECTIVE METHODS OF
SELF-CHANGE
19

3

BEHAVIORAL METHODS OF SELF-CHANGE
93

4

COGNITIVE METHODS OF SELF-CHANGE
149

1

THE ABC MODEL OF SELF-CHANGE

RECOGNITION OF A PROBLEM
THE ABC MODEL
IDENTIFICATION OF THE PROBLEM
ASSESSMENT OF THE PROBLEM

In psychology, as in society itself, times have changed. No longer is psychotherapy an esoteric discipline available only to a chosen few: to those wealthy enough to afford it, healthy enough to profit from it, and with enough time on their hands to endure it. We are living in an era in which psychotherapy in all its elaborate guises has become acceptable, if not always available, to a broad spectrum of society. Together with this burgeoning public acceptability of psychotherapy, a growing number of clinicians have realized the wisdom in constantly modifying and updating psychological practices to fit the needs of contemporary clients and their problems.

The demand for professional intervention has far outstripped the availability of competent professional resources. Since it is not possible —nor, perhaps, advisable—for everyone to have his or her own psychoanalyst or psychotherapist, there is a need for effective techniques that we can draw on in the absence of professional mediation. Although there is no limit to the recommendations proferred by newspaper columnists and the well-intended authors of self-help books, advice in this form tends to be directed at the general case rather than the unique individual. The simplistic advice that is usually offered as a panacea for our troublesome feelings and behaviors is simply not sufficient to help us achieve greater satisfaction in our lives. Shrewd aphorisms may not necessarily fit your particular situation. "Haste" does not "make waste" when your house is burning down, and, although a "bird in the hand (may be) better than two in the bush," divorce may indeed be the best recourse for some! The power of the expert clinician lies in his or her ability to assess the unique needs and potentials of the individual and to gear treatment to those special characteristics.

A second limitation to the advice-giving approach is that many of the suggestions offered are simply beyond the ability of the mere mortal to pursue. It is nearly impossible for many people to assiduously follow such advice as "accept yourself," "avoid jealousy," or "live comfortably within your means." This kind of counsel may be useful if it can help you reorganize your way of perceiving yourself or reformulate your values and goals. However, it is *not* worthwhile if you need help in *identifying* the nature of your dissatisfaction or if you want to know exactly *how* to go about achieving

2

your goals. Moreover, we are all quite capable of distorting such messages by reading into them what we wish.

A third disadvantage to popular advice giving (or advice taking) is that it reinforces an unfortunate kind of dependency on caregivers. Ideally, professional intervention not only helps you solve a specific current problem but also provides you with some tools to use in tackling future difficulties by yourself. There is reason to believe that, when people view themselves rather than some external agent as responsible for their growth and change, they are more satisfied with the outcome and the results are more apt to persist.

The following chapters offer a variety of techniques for self-change that are soundly embedded in the practice of psychotherapy. For many of these techniques, there is research evidence to attest to their effectiveness; for others, the scientific evidence is not yet available, but professional clinicians support their power and utility. These methods offer the potential for constructive change in the absence of professional or paraprofessional helpers.

Personal change and growth is more enduring when therapy extends beyond the 50-minute office hour into the arena of the client's own life space. Ultimately you have to feel better and function more effectively not only in the therapist's office but also in your own home. As a result, it is to your advantage to initiate and pursue change in your own environment. Some problems are more difficult than others to alter during the traditional office visit either because they occur infrequently (for example, fighting or stealing) or because they are private and nonobservable (for example, uncomfortable thoughts or sexual problems). In these instances, self-therapy techniques may effectively augment other psychotherapeutic approaches and ensure that change will persist and generalize. Although the professional therapist may possess better methods of observation and a more objective point of view, he or she inevitably has an opportunity to view only a very modest range of your behavior.

At one time Freudian psychology went unchallenged; humans were perceived as puppets, controlled by the twin pressures of the primitive, sexual drives of the libido and the repressive, societal forces of the superego or conscience. However, more recent personality theories have conceptualized the individual as determiner of his or her own fate and controller of his or her universe (see, for example, Mahrer, 1978; Maslow, 1970). Attainment of autonomous self-direction can be facilitated by increasing our understanding of the psychological principles that control our behavior. In so doing, we perpetuate the demand for behavioral science solutions to our very human problems. The creation of a self-change technology reflects this framework by supplying ways and means to modify our own behavior, thoughts, and feelings.

It would be naive to believe that self-change techniques can be an adequate substitute for professional consultation for all problems across the board. They are not. You are encouraged to seek out professional assistance when the going gets tough. Self-therapy techniques, even when they are relatively sophisticated and empirically grounded, are not equivalent to formal psychotherapy with a professionally trained therapist.

Self-therapy has some limitations of its own. For some people, self-change techniques may be used to avoid the potential challenge or threat of a genuine therapeutic relationship. They can be used to show the world "I'm really trying," even if you feel afraid and are reluctant to change. Also, in general, as your discomfort becomes less intense, your motivation to engage in therapy decreases. Self-therapy may have many more dropouts—people who cannot overcome their resistance to change—than formal psychotherapy; self-therapy requires the same, if not more, motivation than the traditional therapy relationship.

On the other hand, the danger of going too deep with self-change techniques—of working on issues that you cannot possibly manage—have surely been overdramatized, perhaps by those who fear some competition to their own business. Karen Horney (1945), the highly regarded post-Freudian psychoanalyst, observed that patients are generally very capable of protecting themselves from insights that they cannot yet handle. In fact, clients seem to know intuitively what should be avoided more often than their therapists do. In self-therapy, the issue is rarely one of going too far; instead, the problem typically is one of not going far enough.

Each of us can benefit from change and growth in numerous directions. The mechanisms for initiating change are available for our use. Unfortunately, there is no easy solution to human suffering, no universal prescription to shake your doubts, erase your difficulties, and transform you into a perfectly functioning, fully actualized person. On the other hand, your situation may not be as bleak as you imagine. Today there are a significant number of psychotherapeutic interventions that can promote change and make a pronounced difference in your life. We each have the ability to play an active, central role in exploring, charting, and experimenting with new behaviors, thoughts, and feelings.

RECOGNITION OF A PROBLEM

The following chapters provide a collection of therapeutic strategies for self-change. They are applicable to problems across a broad range of human functioning: problem behaviors that interfere with your ability to get

along with yourself and with others; self-defeating attitudes and distorted views of the world around you; feelings of discomfort and helplessness. Because these difficulties often interrelate and interact, the strategies can ultimately facilitate major life-style and personality changes.

For most people, professional intervention is the last resort after exhausting other methods for reducing misery and discomfort. People seek the aid of a psychotherapist when there is distress and disruption in their lives and when their habitual, safe ways of living are not working. Most clients are really asking to feel better while staying the same. They are reluctant to risk making substantial personal changes. For some people psychotherapy has become a reflex response to even the most minimal disappointments or stresses. Such receptivity to the use of therapeutic resources reflects favorably on the gradual "destigmatization" of the profession, but it also represents a ridiculous extreme. Indeed, life is filled with sadness, loneliness, and anxiety. And people who live fully, who experience life as an adventure, are most aware of this fact. The only way we can protect ourselves from feelings of sorrow, uncertainty, and disappointment is to live a life of massive denial and distortion, a life that refuses to acknowledge our very humanness. Leslie Farber (1976), well-known psychoanalyst and cultural critic, caricatures our tendency to yearn for Utopian bliss and to promote charismatic gurus and saviors and urges us instead to set realistic limits to our search for control. We can change our eating habits, for example, but not our basic hunger; we can will ourselves to be assertive but not to have courage; we can easily learn to read but not so easily to understand; we can freely lust but not will ourselves to love.

Each of us has some intuitive, probably value-laden, notion about mental health. Freud conceptualized healthy functioning as the ability and freedom to love, work, and play effectively, and in many ways his criteria are still better than most. Perhaps the key characteristic of psychopathology is that it significantly restricts potential actions; that is, the depressed person may be unable to sleep, eat, or relate to others, so that the kinds of potentially rewarding transactions he or she engages in are substantially reduced. The angry person may literally be immobilized by his or her anger. An uptight man cannot assert himself sufficiently to ask for a raise, tell his friends "No," or even meet people he wants to know. Neurotic behavior invariably involves the inability to make choices or take action. A young man cannot complete a task, no matter how skilled he is or how good his intentions are; a woman remains in her house, afraid to venture into the street; a woman strives to win the man who attracts her and, on conquering him, immediately loses interest; a man becomes highly aroused by his lover, only to become impotent once he generates the same sexual passion in her. In each case, and the list is interminable, the individual experiences himself or herself as locked into a particular pattern of behavior. He or she feels stuck and is unable to imagine or engage in alternative forms of action.

By acting in rigid and repetitive ways, we defend ourselves from experiencing some of our most terrifying and risky thoughts and feelings. Psychopathology or neurosis is part of a vicious circle. We try to defend ourselves from stress and tension by erecting patterns to make life tolerable. However, these patterns make us less flexible and adaptable, and we are thrown off balance by new stressors that threaten to unleash our greatest fears. So we clamp down still harder and try to get more control of our lives. There is a continuous conflict between our unexpressed feelings and our maladaptive behavior patterns that can be played out internally, creating somatic aches and pains, or interpersonally, affecting our relationships with others in negative ways. In either case, psychotherapeutic intervention can break up the pattern and create opportunities for growth by increasing the spectrum of alternatives.

Psychopathology can also be related to stress, which appears to be an unavoidable phenomenon in our complex, fast-paced society. There is a physiological response to stress that is virtually identical whether the stressor is physical (viral infection, air pollution, jet lag) or psychological (expulsion from school, family arguments, financial setbacks). The body responds to stress with changes in autonomic nervous activity: increased gastric activity, pulse rate, and blood pressure, and a surge of adrenaline. Once the organism has mastered the particular stressor, the physiological system returns to its normal baseline activity quite rapidly.

A stressor that is concrete, identifiable, and of limited time duration may be easily mastered. In fact, experience in tackling and resolving stress encourages confidence and maturity and provides the individual with valuable problem-solving skills. However, when the stressor is ambiguous, unanticipated, or prolonged in nature, it is less easily resolved. Consequently, the state of physiological arousal may be extended beyond the limits of health. Overpowering, indefinite stress or a slow accumulation of unresolved stress increases the risk of psychosomatic disorders. Since stress involves major autonomic changes, the vital organs and their systems become vulnerable to dysfunction. Cardiovascular disease, arteriosclerosis, arthritis, asthma, migraine headaches, and essential hypertension are just some of the diseases that are believed to be stress related.

Hans Selye (1974), a pioneer in the study of physiological stress, believes that each person has a finite reserve of adaptive energy and that each new stressor takes its toll on the future resistance of the organism. In other words, there is a distinct possibility, if not a probability, that each of us will be victimized by a stress-related disease or condition at some point in our lives. Hypertension (high blood pressure), for example, characterizes fully one-third of the adult population in the United States.

Although we tend to think of stress as related to negative changes in our lives, it can be argued that positive and negative changes are equally stressful. The Social Readjustment Rating Scale (Holmes & Rahe, 1967), for example, can be used to predict your potential for psychophysiological problems (see Table 1-1). The scale includes events that are generally considered positive, such as marriage, outstanding personal achievement, and vacation, as well as "negative" events, such as divorce or financial difficulties. Each life event in the scale is assigned a certain number of "life change units" (LCU's). Theoretically, the more LCU's you accumulate in a short

TABLE 1-1
Social Readjustment Rating Scale

Rank	Life Event	Mean Value
1	Death of spouse	100
2	Divorce	73
3	Marital separation	65
4	Jail term	63
5	Death of close family member	63
6	Personal injury or illness	53
7	Marriage	50
8	Fired at work	47
9	Marital reconciliation	45
10	Retirement	45
11	Change in health of family member	44
12	Pregnancy	40
13	Sex difficulties	39

TABLE 1-1 *(continued)*
Social Readjustment Rating Scale

Rank	Life Event	Mean Value
14	Gain of new family member	39
15	Business readjustment	39
16	Change in financial state	38
17	Death of close friend	37
18	Change to different line of work	36
19	Change in number of arguments with spouse	35
20	Mortgage over $10,000	31
21	Foreclosure of mortgage or loan	30
22	Change in responsibilities at work	29
23	Son or daughter leaving home	29
24	Trouble with in-laws	29
25	Outstanding personal achievement	28
26	Wife begins or stops work	26
27	Begin or end school	26
28	Change in living conditions	25
29	Revision of personal habits	24
30	Trouble with boss	23
31	Change in work hours or conditions	20
32	Change in residence	20
33	Change in schools	20
34	Change in recreation	19
35	Change in church activities	19
36	Change in social activities	18
37	Mortgage or loan less than $10,000	17
38	Change in sleeping habits	16
39	Change in number of family get-togethers	15
40	Change in eating habits	15
41	Vacation	13
42	Christmas	12
43	Minor violations of the law	11

"The Social Readjustment Rating Scale," by T. H. Holmes and R. H. Rahe, *Journal of Psychosomatic Research,* 1967, *11,* 213–218. Copyright 1967 by Pergamon Press, Ltd. Reprinted by permission of the authors and publisher.

period of time, whether from positive or negative events, the more prone you are to psychosomatic difficulties and illness. In one study (Holmes & Holmes, 1970), the vast majority (86%) of subjects who had accumulated over 300 LCU's within a year suffered from serious health problems, as did about half (48%) of those who totaled between 150 and 300 LCU's.

Although stress is not psychopathological per se, self-change techniques can help reduce the destructive potential of the stressors in your life. There are techniques, for example, that can make you more sensitive to the somatic and environmental cues that indicate the presence of stress. Awareness is always an important preliminary step in any self-change procedure. The intensity of stress you experience can be reduced by discovering and changing the factors in your environment and life-style that contribute to your autonomic arousal. Finally, there are a number of self-therapy techniques that can guide you to handle arousing and stressful situations in more adaptive ways. Clearly, self-change techniques are applicable long before the admittedly fuzzy boundary between normal and neurotic functioning is crossed. It pays to develop a set of skills for dealing more effectively with everyday problems and worries before distress seriously affects all areas of life. Consequently, very few of the examples in this book deal with severe emotional disturbance. But even in more extreme cases, in which functioning has become clearly maladaptive and pathological, there are a number of helpful things to do to alleviate pain and alter neurotic behavior patterns.

THE ABC MODEL

Most self-therapy books are theoretical in their approach. The techniques they offer are derived from a particular school or theorist. Followers of Freud, for instance, tend to focus on intrapsychic mechanisms such as unconscious motivation and to provide interpretations of symptoms and dreams. Behaviorists look at overt behavior and offer suggestions for manipulating stimuli and responses, the basic elements that constitute the complex chains of human behavior. Each orientation, from Gestalt and bioenergetics to reality therapy, has its own theoretical and therapeutic bias. The perspective taken in this book, on the other hand, is largely atheoretical. It assumes that useful techniques for self-change can be found in a broad cross-section of personality theories. At the same time, these techniques must be categorized within some useful structure. Figure 1-1 illustrates an ABC approach, where the affective (A), behavioral (B), and cognitive (C) modes of human functioning are represented by the three sides of a triangle within a whole person.

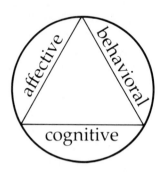

FIGURE 1-1
The well-integrated person is well balanced in all three modalities.

The *affective mode* refers to our feelings and emotions. Some people act as if they are dead at the feeling level. They rarely experience life with any fullness or intensity. They behave mechanically in their relationships. They have difficulty contacting and experiencing their anger, their sexuality, their sadness, and their joy. Other people have difficulties in the opposite direction: they are overwhelmed by their feelings. They cannot control their anger, and they vent it at inappropriate moments or with too much intensity. Perhaps they feel perpetual sadness or, worse, sleepwalk through life, overwhelmed by apathy or depression.

The *behavioral mode* refers to overt actions or behavior patterns that can be confirmed by an observer. Often problems occurring on this level are the easiest to conceptualize. Some people have difficulty controlling their eating behavior, whereas others drink or smoke too much. Many individuals possess annoying habits, such as scratching, nail biting, or perpetual and persistent tardiness. Others suffer from such self-destructive behaviors as getting into barroom brawls with strangers, verbal harangues with their kids, or physical fights with their lovers or spouses. Most of us could improve the way we relate to the opposite sex—how we meet them, how we converse with them, how we are intimate with them.

The *cognitive mode* refers to thinking, reasoning, and planning. These operations occur inside our heads but may also be reflected in our overt behavior. Some people have distorted perceptions of the world. They hear voices that no one else hears, or they expect others always to be nurturant and protective or always to be hostile and rejecting. Others engage in illogical reasoning and fail to solve life problems very effectively. Many people turn rejections and frustrations into catastrophes, and many more harbor a poor self-image or "inferiority complex."

It is important to understand that the affective, behavioral, and cognitive levels are not functionally independent but interrelated aspects of the whole person. At one time it was believed that significant changes in behavior could be obtained only after the individual achieved insight or cognitive understanding. There is now a growing body of evidence to suggest that changes in awareness and self-concept often follow, rather than precede, changes in overt behavior (Bem & McConnell, 1970). Moreover, there is an ongoing, constantly shifting relationship among the three levels, so that either a vicious cycle or a virtuous cycle of change may be established. Take, for instance, the stress of dealing with a separation or divorce. You may feel depressed by the loss of a long-term partner (an affective response), then begin to think of yourself as worthless and hopeless (a cognitive response), and then shun people (a behavioral response) in order to refrain from contaminating or burdening them; this sequence then leads to further feelings of depression and hopelessness and to increased avoidance behavior. This is a vicious cycle. Fortunately, a virtuous cycle can be established in a similar way: a successful experience on the job might lead to feelings of joy (affective) and thoughts of competence (cognitive), leading to increasingly bold moves (behavioral) that, if successful, elicit further positive feelings and thoughts.

Sometimes, however, change in the affective, behavioral, or cognitive realm does not automatically lead to change in the other two areas. Therapeutic movement along the affective or the cognitive dimension, for instance, does not necessarily imply behavioral change. The man who overcomes his fear of the crowds in discothèques may still have to learn to dance to become a social success. Similarly, many clients in psychotherapy are able to amass marvelous insights about their early childhood experiences without modifying their behavior one iota. You can maintain your fear of social gatherings yet push through your anxiety at the behavioral level and function as a bold, outgoing, yet frightened guest. You can pursue such high-risk activities as parachuting and mountain climbing and consistently experience great fear. Likewise, some people learn to function as though they had high self-esteem and persist in the belief that they are fundamentally no good. The fact that the affective, behavioral, and cognitive levels of functioning at times operate relatively independently suggests that a total treatment package may need to consider all three modes in order to be optimally therapeutic (Lang, 1971; Rudestam & Bedrosian, 1977).

It should also be apparent that different people will need to focus more or less on each of the three different levels. The ABC triangle illustrates the need for balance among the affective, behavioral, and cognitive modes for totally effective human functioning. Some individuals are out of balance. They may never be quite in control of their feelings; their behavior may habitually be ineffective or self-defeating; or their thinking may be generally fuzzy or poorly grounded. As you read more about the ABC's of therapeutic change, you will discover which mode or modes are most applicable to your own particular case and the set of techniques on which you may need to concentrate.

The following chapters explain and illustrate a host of self-therapy techniques that focus on either undesirable behaviors, cognitions, or feelings. Affective self-change methods are most relevant to difficulties at the experiential level. Behavioral self-change methods directly attack problem behaviors and may be the most direct approach to altering them. Cognitive self-change methods deal directly with and attempt to modify verbalized and nonverbalized attitudes and thought processes. The techniques may at times be useful for creating changes at the other two levels as well, but they have been categorized according to the primary mode involved—that is, whether they manipulate affective, behavioral, or cognitive variables. The final chapter addresses the task of integrating techniques across modalities in order to facilitate meaningful personality change.

IDENTIFICATION OF THE PROBLEM

Those who are serious about self-change can best begin by confronting two fundamental questions: "What is it I wish to change about myself?" and "How will I know when I've succeeded in bringing about this change?" By and large, you are the person best qualified to judge and define what bothers you. Others may help bring your problems to your attention by offering you feedback, but, if their feedback takes the form of complaints or accusations, you are likely to feel defensive and to deny the validity of their input. In your own mind, however, you probably know when what you do conflicts with the type of life-style you would like to create for yourself. One way to determine whether your behavior, feelings, or thoughts are maladaptive is by considering Karen Horney's (1945) idea of "overdriven strivings." In this conceptualization, your strivings or behaviors are "overdriven" or "neurotic" when they conform to the following three criteria: they are indiscriminant; they are insatiable; and you experience extreme frustration if they are blocked. A behavior is indiscriminant if it is expressed not only in appropriate contexts but also in inappropriate contexts. Seeking approval and admiration from your closest friends and relatives is certainly more adaptive than needing the approval of every shopkeeper, salesperson, and taxi driver you encounter. Insatiability suggests that you are never satisfied, never fully at peace with the fulfillment of a striving. An example is the inability to take pride and satisfaction in an otherwise good performance that has been marred by a single mistake. Horney's final clue to overdriven behavior focuses on the impact of a frustrated goal on your feelings and actions. Whereas being turned down for a date is a minor disappointment for some people, for others it is a devastating experience that is not easily forgotten.

It is considerably more useful to think of your psychological problems along a continuum from more to less severe than to make a global judgment about your craziness or sanity. From this perspective, we all have strengths and we all have weaknesses; problems are relative rather than absolute. Typically, we decide that behaviors are maladaptive and disadvantageous not because they exist per se but because they are too frequent, too long in duration, or too intense or because they occur in the wrong contexts. Crying, for instance, is perfectly acceptable during times of grief. But uncontrollable weeping on the job is pathological. Likewise, someone who is concerned about keeping a clean and orderly household may be valued as a diligent housekeeper. But if he or she polishes the same area several times a day and is never satisfied that it is clean enough, we suspect some kind of psychological disturbance. The problem is not in the cleaning behavior but in the frequency of that behavior.

ASSESSMENT OF THE PROBLEM

Before you can select appropriate self-change techniques, you have to assess how you are currently functioning. First, determine whether your problem is best categorized as affective, behavioral, cognitive, or some combination of the three dimensions. Next, translate your maladaptive thoughts, feelings, or behaviors into a language that allows you to decide if the problem is one of *excess* or of *deficit*; that is, ask yourself whether your difficulty is one of "too much" or "too little." Most problems can be conceptualized in this way. Do I want to stop smoking because I smoke too many cigarettes (a behavioral excess)? Do I want to be able to express my anger (affective deficit)? Do I want to terminate my obsessive, negativistic thoughts (cognitive excess)? Do I want to feel less anxious in social situations (an excess), have fewer arguments with my husband (an excess), accomplish more work in a day (a deficit), or lose several pounds of fat (an excess)? An excess refers to behaviors, thoughts, or feelings that are excessive in frequency, intensity, duration, or inappropriateness, and a deficit refers to behaviors, thoughts, or feelings that do not occur with sufficient frequency, intensity, duration, or appropriateness. By viewing your problems from this perspective you make them less vague and more concrete. In addition, you avoid relying on traditional psychological or psychiatric diagnostic systems that have been criticized as imprecise, unreliable, and unhelpful (Szasz, 1960; Adams, 1964; Schacht & Nathan, 1977). Although this kind of assessment is derived from the behavioral school (Kanfer & Saslow, 1969), the technique can easily be adapted for problems in the affective and cognitive modalities as well.

The next important step in assessing your problem is to consider it in the context of your environment. We tend to label ourselves and others as too nervous, too angry, too critical or too impulsive and to regard assets and limitations as enduring and consistent personality characteristics. Many clients begin by stating that they don't know what's wrong and that they are always tense. Yet even the most anxious person has moments of relative calm. There is considerable evidence to suggest that the difficulties we experience are not constant but depend on moment-to-moment environmental contingencies (Mischel, 1973). In order to better understand your problem, you must explore *when* and *where* your symptoms are most apt to occur. Consider, for example, the young boy who throws a tantrum when he can't readily convince Mother to give him ice cream but who rarely if ever screams and cries when Father is in the house. Why? Presumably these two stimuli, Mother and Father, have different meanings for the child, since he realizes that having a temper tantrum in front of an irascible father may produce a response that differs significantly from the ice cream payment from hard-pressed Mother!

Virtually all human responses are similarly influenced by the situational context. Perhaps you suffer a headache only when there are other people around. Maybe you are apt to eat whenever the television is turned on. Possibly you lose your temper whenever your husband disappoints you. Perhaps you can't sleep the night before an oral recital. These are examples of environmental cues that suggest the presence of problems in living.

The identification and thorough description of a problem, together with an assessment of the environment in which it occurs, is called a "functional analysis of behavior" (Kanfer & Saslow, 1969). A functional analysis includes specifying the *antecedents*, or events that precede the problem, and the *consequences*, or events that follow and result from the problem. The person who chooses fights with his girlfriend, for instance, as a target problem might ask the following questions: Where do the fights occur? When do they take place? What people are present? What events have occurred during the day of the fight? What verbal and nonverbal statements by both my girlfriend and me precede the fight? How does the fight end? What happens subsequently? Answers to these questions may provide useful information regarding the origin and maintenance of the problem as well as hints for reducing or eliminating it. Sometimes the most relevant antecedents and consequences of identified problems are internal states such as thoughts and feelings. For example, the thought "I'm sure all of her previous lovers are more experienced than I am" could be an antecedent to impotence.

The assessment approach for self-change recommended in this book consists of building an adequate understanding of the problem by collecting reliable and accurate information about the problem itself. Sometimes, of course, obtaining accurate observations is not difficult. It is relatively easy to recall how many dates you had in the last month if you have never had a date! It is more difficult, however, to have confidence in a retrospective estimate of the number of hours you slept each night last week or under what circumstances you become agitated, worried, or depressed. In these cases, the ongoing recording is important. Techniques for recording this kind of information will be described in Chapter 3.

In addition to classifying a difficulty as an excess or a deficit and looking for linkages between it and environmental cues, the following questions can help you clarify the problem situation for yourself (Kanfer & Saslow, 1969):

Who objects to your problem? Who supports it? Your answers will give you some idea about the relative ease you will have in eliminating your problem and the kinds of resistance you may encounter.

What ramifications does the problem have for you and for those close to you? What satisfactions will you continue to have if your problem remains? These questions ask you to consider what kind of investment you may have in maintaining things precisely as they are. In spite of the pain you experience there may be certain advantages in not disrupting the status quo.

What consequences would removal of the problem have for you or others? What new problems in living would successful therapy pose for you? These questions ask you to consider what life would be like if you could overcome the problem. Through honest self-inquiry you might discover that new, previously unconsidered difficulties would develop. You may feel some apprehension that adds to your reluctance to change.

Whether or not you initiate a self-therapy program will depend, first of all, on your stated willingness to change (Kanfer & Karoly, 1972). You are more likely to feel motivated when you are in conflict about your present pattern of behavior or when you no longer experience it as meaningful. You may feel highly motivated to change when your current way of acting is painful for you or others. Or you may feel ready when other people support and reinforce your intention to change. One reason why cigarette smoking, for example, is so difficult to eliminate is that friends and acquaintances continually shove cigarettes under the noses of would-be nonsmokers.

On the other hand, you are unlikely to get to the point of expressing a willingness to change when the changes you want to institute are socially unacceptable or when positive support for change is absent. Likewise, your motivation to change will be lower when change is very difficult to initiate or when you have a history of failure in your attempts to alter your behavior.

Once you *intend* to change, your chances of engaging in the requisite steps to reach your goal depend on several other variables. The clearer the plan or contract you make for yourself, the more likely you will be to succeed. The more skillful you become at mastering the techniques of self-therapy, the greater your chances are for meaningful change. Similarly, the more persistent the negative consequences of the behavior you wish to change, the more hopeful the outcome. Finally, the results of your program will depend on the success or failure experiences that you have had in similar situations or that you now begin to encounter as you experiment with self-therapy.

How will you know when you have succeeded with your program for self-change? The more concrete and definable your goals are at the beginning, the easier it becomes to evaluate progress. By staying away from a conception of your psychological problems as "disease" and by stressing the consequences that certain behaviors, thoughts, and feelings have in your life, you will be more open to discovering changes. Think of your self-therapy strategies as an educational process. The ideal time to terminate your program is when changes become intrinsically satisfying or when the support of others can take over and substitute for your deliberate interventions. With few exceptions the environment does bolster healthy, productive behavior by providing positive interpersonal support, assurances of increased competence, and the ability to live a fuller, richer, more symptom-free life. If you can make a solid commitment, get a good start, and receive ongoing positive feedback about the results of your efforts, you are on your way to a successful program of self-change.

REFERENCES

Adams, H. "Mental illness" or interpersonal behavior? *American Psychologist*, 1964, *19*, 191–197.

Bem, D. J., & McConnell, H. K. Testing the self-perception explanation of dissonance phenomena: On the salience of premanipulation attitude. *Journal of Personality and Social Psychology*, 1970, *14*, 23–31.

Farber, L. H. *Lying, despair, jealousy, envy, sex, suicide, drugs, and the good life.* New York: Basic Books, 1976.

Holmes, T. H., & Rahe, R. H. The social readjustment rating scale. *Journal of Psychosomatic Research*, 1967, *11*, 213–218.

Holmes, T. S., & Holmes, T. H. Short-term intrusion into the lifestyle routine. *Journal of Psychosomatic Research*, 1970, *14*, 121–132.

Horney, K. *Our inner conflicts: A constructive theory of neurosis.* New York: W. W. Norton & Co., 1945.

Kanfer, F. H., & Karoly, P. Self-control: A behavioral excursion into the lion's den. *Behavior Therapy*, 1972, *3*, 398–416.

Kanfer, F. H., Saslow, G. Behavioral diagnosis. In C. Franks (Ed.), *Behavior therapy: Appraisal and status.* New York: McGraw-Hill, 1969.

Lang, P. J. The application of psychophysiological methods to the study of psychotherapy and behavior modification. In A. E. Bergin and S. L. Garfield (Eds.), *Handbook of psychotherapy and behavior change.* New York: Wiley, 1971.

Mahrer, A. R. *Experiencing: A humanistic theory of psychology and psychiatry.* New York: Brunner/Mazel, 1978.

Maslow, A. H. *Motivation and personality.* New York: Harper & Row, 1970.

Mischel, W. Toward a cognitive social learning reconceptualization of personality. *Psychological Review*, 1973, *80*(4), 252–283.

Rudestam, K. E., & Bedrosian, R. An investigation of the effectiveness of desensitization and flooding with two types of phobias. *Behavioral Research and Therapy*, 1977, *15*, 23–30.

Schacht, T., & Nathan, P. E. But is it good for the psychologists? Appraisal and status of DSM-III. *American Psychologist*, 1977, *32*, 1017–1025.

Selye, H. *Stress without distress.* New York: New American Library, 1974.

Szasz, T. S. The myth of mental illness. *American Psychologist*, 1960, *15*, 113–118.

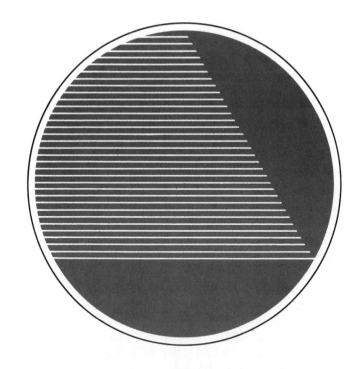

2

AFFECTIVE METHODS OF SELF-CHANGE

SELF-CHANGE TECHNIQUE 1: RELAXATION TRAINING
SELF-CHANGE TECHNIQUE 2: MEDITATION
SELF-CHANGE TECHNIQUE 3: SYSTEMATIC DESENSITIZATION
SELF-CHANGE TECHNIQUE 4: FOCUSING
SELF-CHANGE TECHNIQUE 5: AWARENESS AND FANTASY TECHNIQUES
SELF-CHANGE TECHNIQUE 6: DREAM WORK
SELF-CHANGE TECHNIQUE 7: FLOODING

Psychotherapists historically have been interested in the role of emotion in human experience. The traditional psychoanalytic, psychotherapeutic approach is to uncover repressed feelings, feelings that are out of the patient's awareness and that the patient will go to great lengths to avoid experiencing. Yet, although a central purpose of therapy is to uncover those unpleasant feelings (and the memories with which they may be associated) so that the patient may be free of their effects, the therapeutic technique itself has most often been highly intellectual and cognitive. A verbal, unemotional approach is consistent with the scientific tradition that places a premium on clear reasoning and articulation. It is also consistent with our dominant child-rearing practices: boys don't cry and girls don't show anger. According to societal mores, in fact, any person who expresses feelings of discomfort or pain is in need of assurance, support, and encouragement to help him or her stop emoting.

Perhaps as a result of several decades of emphasis on reasoning, insight, and understanding through psychotherapy, there is currently a focus—on the rebound, if you will—on expressing feelings. In recent years we have seen a flood of experiential therapies that value the expression of feelings for their own sake. Many encounter groups, sensitivity groups, and marathons provide a socially acceptable vehicle for periodic outbursts of emotion. Actually, the idea of provoking emotional crises and dealing with the release of affect has a long history. Temple priests, exorcists, and hypnotists have always been concerned with inducing emotional crises. Freud's psychoanalytic therapy emphasized the importance of guiding the patient to an intense release of affect, called *catharsis*. These feelings were believed to be tied to specific events in the patient's childhood. Many therapists today believe that emotional discomfort can be traced to specific current life experiences in which the patient holds back feelings and that the holding back is often rooted in a childhood experience of being made to feel bad for expressing a feeling.

The goal of the affective therapies is to move from defending against feelings to learning to connect feeling sensations, their meaning, and their expression in an integrated way. The self-change methods presented in this chapter work from two different perspectives. (1) Relaxation, meditation, systematic desensitization, and awareness techniques work directly on reducing anxiety and converting agitation, fear, or anger into relaxation and calmness. (2) Focusing, dream work, fantasy, and flooding techniques, on the other hand, work with heightening and intensifying incompletely experienced affective states until they are tempered and resolved. (See p. 86 for a table of the problem areas with which these techniques are most often and most effectively used.) In both cases, the common core of the affective self-therapy techniques is learning to become more acquainted with and more comfortable with feelings and emotions. Judiciously applied, they can also have the secondary effect of producing lasting behavior change.

The basic underlying principle of this chapter is that feelings cannot be evaluated morally—that is, as "right" or "wrong." Feelings of anger, sadness, fright, and joy simply exist as central components of the human condition. The important therapeutic issues concern a person's understanding of and comfort with his or her own emotional repertoire and the *appropriate* social expression of feelings. Rage reactions, tantrums, crying fits, and infantile screams are not enough. To be able to release pent-up feelings in safe surroundings can bring about a state of increased calm, but the letting go needs to be integrated into a new level of awareness (cognitive understanding) and adult expression (behavioral action) in order to create lasting change.

SELF-CHANGE TECHNIQUE 1:
RELAXATION TRAINING

Relaxation training could justifiably be presented as a "behavioristic" technique, since the most systematic applications of the method have been done by adherents of the behaviorist school of psychotherapy (Wolpe & Lazarus, 1966). Nonetheless, relaxation training is included in this chapter since the technique focuses directly on muscle tension and experienced feelings.

There are at least two major applications of deep muscle relaxation: (1) you can use the procedures on a regular basis as a way of giving yourself a break from an otherwise fast-paced existence, and (2) you can use the procedures as a coping skill that can be used in particularly stressful situations to reduce anxiety and tension. The first application is used by many people who practice yoga. In fact, if you've ever been to a yoga class, the relaxation instructions typically given at the end by the instructor are quite similar to the relaxation training discussed here. And you can train yourself to feel warm and relaxed the way yoga makes you feel much more quickly with deep muscle relaxation training.

It's unusual for people to treat themselves so generously, however. Most yoga devotees, unless they become religiously involved, use relaxation at critical moments in particularly stressful situations or as a way to improve sleep. Relaxation training is more often used as a coping skill, a way of changing anxiety to calm. Relaxation training can be used to soothe stage fright on opening nights, to reduce tension during an exam, to cope with headaches, muscle pains, and insomnia. In fact, relaxation training could be considered a good alternative to using tranquilizing drugs and soporifics.

Many writers have suggested relaxation training procedures of various sorts (Cautela & Groden, 1978; Jacobson, 1938; Marquis & Morgan, 1968; Rosen, 1977; Wolpe & Lazarus, 1966). Most however, incorporate principles similar to those presented here. To learn the technique you must first learn to discriminate those body states that are associated with tension. When you experience anxiety, muscle groups throughout your body become tense. Anxiety and stress affect different people in different places. Some people store tension in the neck; others carry it in the forehead. You need to learn where you store tension in your own body, whether it be in your stomach, neck, legs, head, or other body part.[1] Other signs of tension may include sweating, an increased heart rate, trembling or shaking, and nausea. In relaxation training, you learn to replace muscular tension with an alternative incompatible response like relaxation. After all, you can't be tense and relaxed at the same time.

DEEP MUSCLE RELAXATION

In order to achieve total relaxation, the body is considered in terms of its various muscular components. By alternately tensing and relaxing these muscle groups, relaxation becomes a well-learned and total organismic

---

[1]Some tension may be created by a specific situation. However, there is another kind of body tension that is considered more characterological, deriving from feelings that have been repressed. Wilhelm Reich (1949) called these bodily tensions arising from unexpressed feelings *body armor* and used deep muscle massage as a therapeutic tool. Other therapeutic techniques such as bioenergetics, primal therapy, Gestalt, and Rolfing focus on releasing the feelings maintained by body armor.

response. Read the following relaxation exercise thoroughly before trying it. Get a feel for the tensing positions and the timing involved. When you're ready to begin, make sure you have lots of time and will not be easily distracted. Be sure to choose a place where you will not be disturbed for 20 minutes or so. External distractions and intrusive thoughts are the most common obstacles to total relaxation.

> Begin by sitting back in a comfortable chair with your arms at your sides, your hands on your lap, and your feet flat on the floor. Keep your eyes closed throughout the exercise. When you're feeling comfortable, take two or three slow, deep breaths, noticing the passage of air into and out of your lungs and diaphragm. Now hold out your right arm and make a hard fist with your right *hand*. Notice the tension in your fist as you tighten it. After 5 to 10 seconds of concentrating on the tension, relax your hand. Undo the fist and notice how the tension recedes and sensations of relaxation and comfort take its place. Focus on the difference between the tension and the relaxation. After about 15 to 20 seconds, make a fist of your right hand again, study the tension for 5 to 10 seconds, and relax. Feel the relaxation and warmth. After 15 to 20 seconds, repeat the procedure, this time with your left hand. Be sure to focus only on the muscle group you're tensing and relaxing, and try not to tense the rest of your body at the same time.

> After relaxing your hands, tense and relax your *arms*. Stretch the biceps muscle of your right arm by bending the arm and really tightening the muscle. Allow yourself to focus on the tension for 5 to 10 seconds. Then relax for 15 to 20 seconds and enjoy the sensation of warmth and pleasure that comes as feeling flows through the relaxed muscle. Repeat. Now tense and relax your left biceps muscle. Bend your left arm, tighten the muscle, and hold for 5 to 10 seconds. Study the tension. Now relax and notice the warmth surging through your upper arm. Repeat with this arm. Next examine the tension that comes from your triceps. Straighten your right arm in front of you so that it feels like a bar of iron. After 5 to 10 seconds allow the arm to relax and fall limp at your side. Notice the energy flowing through your arm. Repeat. Now tense and relax your left triceps in the same way. Study the contrast between the tension and relaxation. Enjoy the relaxation. Let it flow through your muscles. Repeat.

> Moving up from the hands and arms we now come to the *neck* and *shoulder* muscles. Hunch your shoulders and study the tension that comes from the tightening of the muscles in that area. After 5 to 10 seconds allow your shoulders to fall and relax.

Experience the sensation of warmth and lightness for 15 to 20
seconds. Repeat the procedure. Now focus on the tension that
develops in the neck muscles by bringing your head forward and
digging your chin into your chest. Feel the way the muscles are
stretched at the back and sides of the neck. Now relax by raising
your neck. Feel the warmth flood the back of your neck. Notice
the difference between tension and relaxation. Repeat.

Next we turn to the *head,* a site where considerable amounts of
tension are often stored. First, tense your *mouth.* Open it as wide
as possible, focusing on the tension. After several seconds allow it
to close to a comfortable, relaxed position. Repeat. Tense your
tongue by pushing it against the roof of your mouth as if you were
trying to push it through the top of your mouth. Study the
tension for 5 to 10 seconds. Now relax. Study the contrast. Enjoy
the warmth of relaxation. Repeat. Now tense your *eyes* by closing
them as tightly as possible for 5 to 10 seconds. Staying with the
tension, study it and then relax and relieve the pressure around
your eyes. Notice the difference; appreciate the difference.
Repeat. Finally, tense your *forehead* by raising your eyebrows as
high as possible until your forehead becomes very furrowed.
Focus on the tension for 5 to 10 seconds. Then lower the
eyebrows and note the feeling of relaxation in your eyes and
forehead. Repeat.

By this time your hands, arms, shoulders, neck, mouth, tongue,
and eyes should be thoroughly relaxed. Pause in the relaxation
procedure by taking two or three deep breaths. Focus on the slow
inhalation and exhalation of air until every last drop of air is
emptied from your lungs and diaphragm. Imagine that when you
exhale you breathe out tension and when you inhale you breathe
in relaxation. Now focus on the *back.* First tense the muscles by
arching your back and pushing your chest forward. Be careful
with this step if you suffer from chronic back problems. Study the
tension in your back for 5 to 10 seconds. Now relax the muscles
and focus on the warm tingling that floods your back. After 15 to
20 seconds, repeat. Now tense your *buttocks* by contracting the
muscles. This raises your pelvic area slightly. Study the tension in
this area. After 5 to 10 seconds relax and focus on the difference.
Repeat.

The *stomach* muscles are a frequent area of tension. Study that
tension by sucking in your stomach, pulling it toward your spine.
Study the tension for 5 to 10 seconds; then relax fully and
completely. Notice and enjoy the difference. Repeat.

Finally, focus on your *legs*. First, tense your thighs by extending your legs in front of you and raising them a few inches off the floor. Focus on the knots of tension in your thighs for 5 to 10 seconds. Study the tension. Then lower your legs and relax thoroughly. Feel the warm flow of energy in your thighs. Repeat. Now relax your calves. Start with your feet flat on the floor; now bend your feet so that your toes are pushed up through the top of your shoes and point toward your head. Feel the tension in the calf muscles. Hold the tension for several seconds, and then relax. Study the warm flow of relaxation as the tension dissipates. Repeat. Finally, relax your feet by digging your toes into the bottom of your shoes. Experience the tension in your feet and in the front of your legs. Study the tension for 5 to 10 seconds. Then relax. Feel the difference. Repeat.

Complete this relaxation exercise by taking two or three deep breaths and feeling the relaxation flow through your body from your arms to your shoulders to your chest to your midsection and through your legs. Each deep and complete inhalation and exhalation of air will increase the depth of relaxation. When you feel ready to open your eyes, count backwards slowly from 10 to 1. With each number, feel yourself becoming more and more refreshed and alert.

By this time the entire tension/relaxation cycle is complete, and you should be experiencing a deep sense of muscular relaxation. Indicators of successful relaxation include a loosening and heaviness in the muscles and limbs, a deeper and more uniform respiration rate, a steadier, less nervous voice, and, perhaps, fluttering eyelids and general sleepiness. You will undoubtedly find that some areas of your musculature are more resistant to relaxation than others. These may be areas where you typically store your tension. You may want to focus on these areas in order to achieve total relaxation. Training is not complete after one session, of course. Try to find 15 minutes in the morning and 15 minutes in the evening to practice relaxation. The procedure as outlined is rather detailed, but, after a few sessions of practicing it in this deliberate way, it should not be necessary to alternately tense and relax each muscle grouping. With a little practice you will begin to focus on the "letting go" portion of the procedure. Once the technique has been mastered initially, the entire procedure can be speeded up by relaxing, without first tensing, all the different parts of the body. You may wish to continue the tension/relaxation process, however, with particularly persistent tension areas.

An abbreviated version of deep muscle relaxation instructions has been proposed by Herbert Benson (1975) in his book *The Relaxation Response*.

These instructions may work well for those who can relax relatively easily and may not need to explore each individual muscle grouping.

> Sit quietly in a comfortable position. Close your eyes. Deeply relax all your muscles. Breathe through your nose. Focus your attention on the exchange of air *in* and *out* through the nose. As you breathe out, say the word "one" silently to yourself. That is, breathe in . . . out, "one"; in . . . out, "one"; and so on.

Relaxation training, like many self-change procedures, is generally practiced in the context of an ongoing therapeutic relationship. The therapist uses his or her voice as a soft, melodic instrument to facilitate the depth of relaxation achieved. Some people may require a soft external voice to hypnotically deliver instructions. For this purpose there are various relaxation tapes commercially available.[2] As an alternative you could record your own, based on the instructions described here, and, via the tape or cassette, be your own therapist in the home. If someone else's voice is particularly effective, you might ask this person to record the tape for you. Although a period of several days of practice using the tape is beneficial, you should eventually stop relying on the tape, in order to maximize the generalizability of the technique. After all, you will probably want to be able to relax at times when the recording equipment is unavailable.

Remember that the first step to being able to relax completely is to distinguish the tension and relaxation patterns of the body. Part of the reason for learning to discriminate tension is so that the presence of tension will become a stimulus that automatically elicits your learned relaxation response. By adopting a cue, or key word, such as "relax" or "calm," to say to yourself, you may be able to set the total relaxation response in motion automatically. You will have reached your goal when you can sit down and in a matter of minutes experience a warm, tingling, utterly relaxed sensation throughout your body. As a self-therapy technique, the relaxation response should be practiced daily. The frequency is much more important than the length of time you spend.

Learning to relax requires training and practice, just like playing tennis or playing the piano. Relaxation is not likely to occur instantly; the skill matures over time. In the beginning, feelings of relaxation may be associated with strange sensations such as tingling in the extremities or feelings of floating and dizziness (Goldfried & Davison, 1976). If you have learned to become tense as a way of coping with pressure, the ebbing of

[2]Muscle-relaxation cassette tapes are available from the author, Dr. K. Rudestam, Department of Psychology, York University. Downsview, Ontario, M3J 1P3, Canada.

tension may be experienced as a frightening loss of control. Such signs are the precursors to relaxation. You may even feel worse at times as you become more aware of tense areas. Such experiences are common and indicative of progress. Like spontaneity, relaxation is not something you can order yourself or others to accomplish. Likewise, you actually acquire greater control over your ability to relax by allowing the sensations to take place, by giving in and letting go. As in dancing or floating on the water, the best performers don't try too hard. If the experience becomes too unpleasant, of course, remember that you have the ability to terminate your training at any point.

OTHER APPROACHES:
BIOFEEDBACK, SELF-HYPNOSIS,
AUTOGENIC THERAPY

There are several other approaches to relaxation training that you can consider. One is biofeedback training, which requires a fair amount of equipment and is illustrated in Figure 2-1. Others are subsumed under the general category of self-hypnosis or autohypnosis. There is considerable theoretical disagreement among psychologists whether hypnosis involves a special trance state with unique properties or is merely a descriptive term which refers to the event of encouraging a person to follow the instructions of a hypnotist to feel relaxed and suggestible (Barber, 1970). In any case, the image of the hypnotized subject as drowsy and loose is similar to the physiological state of the totally relaxed person. As a matter of fact, autohypnotic suggestions are remarkably similar to relaxation instructions.

Another worthwhile approach to total bodily relaxation is "autogenic therapy," which originated at the turn of the century from the sleep and hypnosis research of Oskar Vogt in Berlin (Schultz & Luthe, 1959). Autogenic therapy consists of a series of mental exercises aimed at relaxing both the mind and the body. The recommended setting is similar to training in deep muscle relaxation: a quiet room, reduced lighting, loose clothing, and a relaxed position in a comfortable chair. The proper attitude is one of passive concentration, in which you do not actively try to relax but passively and casually follow the exercises.

Although there are six standard exercises in basic autogenic therapy, only the first two, heaviness and warmth, are especially relevant to achieving a state of relaxation.[3] The first exercise focuses on *heaviness*.

[3]The other four autogenic exercises focus on cardiac regulations, respiration, abdominal warmth, and cooling of the forehead. If you are interested in learning more about autogenic therapy, you can consult Schultz and Luthe's *Autogenic Training* (New York: Grune & Stratton, 1959).

FIGURE 2-1

Biofeedback training is one self-change treatment for stress-related or anxiety-related disorders. Biofeedback techniques have been successful in reducing high blood pressure (essential hypertension), migraine and tension headaches, and other psychosomatic disorders (Sargent, Green, & Walters, 1973; Blanchard & Young, 1974). The biofeedback procedure involves four components (Budzynski & Stoyva, 1969): (1) continuous monitoring of some physiological function, such as heart rate, brain waves, or muscle potential; (2) direct feedback of changes in the physiological response; (3) conversion of the electrical output of the physiological system into an auditory or visual signal that can be identified by the subject; and (4) a way to alter the auditory or visual signal in order to change the physiological response in a desired direction. In the above photograph the subject is hooked up to an electromyographic (EMG) biofeedback device. The machine monitors the electrical activity in his frontalis muscle so that he can learn to reduce the level of tension in that muscle. In this way, biofeedback can be used as an alternative to, or in conjunction with, relaxation techniques to reduce somatic anxiety. (Photo © Joseph Czarnecki.)

Close your eyes and, beginning with your *dominant* arm, slowly
say to yourself "My right (left) arm is heavy." Repeat this phrase
for about 20 seconds. When you have finished this, open your
eyes, breathe deeply, and flex your arms vigorously for about one
minute. Now close your eyes again and repeat the statement "My
right (left) arm is heavy" for 20 seconds more. Pause again for one
minute, open your eyes, breathe deeply, and flex your arms.
Repeat this cycle a third time.

When you have finished this phase, examine your feelings and
impressions and recall those you experienced while you were
engaged in the exercise. This is the appropriate time for attending
to what you felt, rather than during the preceding period of
passive concentration. The entire exercise should take about five
minutes. Should you become distracted during the exercise, stop
and return to it later. The length of time you spend in the exercise
can be very short, but doing it on a regular basis is important.
Try to do it three times a day—after lunch, after dinner, and
before sleep.

It will probably take several days of training with the dominant
arm before you experience a distinct, heavy feeling there. Don't
try to force the heaviness; passively allow it to build. When the
heaviness occurs reliably, do the exercise with your other arm,
proceeding in exactly the same way. Once you have experienced a
distinct heavy feeling in the nondominant arm as well, repeat the
exercise for both arms, saying "Both arms are heavy." After
focusing on both arms for several days, turn to the dominant leg.
Say to yourself "My right (left) leg is heavy"; then gradually move
on to "My left (right) leg is heavy," and eventually suggest "Both
legs are heavy." Don't rush yourself. After many practice
sessions, you will be ready for the summary statement: "My arms
and legs are heavy."

In time the feeling of heaviness in your arms and legs will come
quickly, and the feeling will generalize from your limbs to your entire body.
Once this occurs, it is time to move on to the second autogenic exercise, the
encouragement of *warmth*. After two or three weeks of suggesting heaviness, you may also be experiencing sensations of warmth in your limbs quite
spontaneously. The procedure for instilling warmth is parallel to the procedure for heaviness.

Begin by closing your eyes and suggesting warmth in your
dominant arm by repeating the phrase "My right (left) arm is
warm" for about 20 seconds. Repeat three times with a
one-minute pause between each suggestion. After three

repetitions allow your impressions and feelings during the
exercise to register. When feelings of warmth are distinct in your
dominant arm, move on to your nondominant arm, both arms,
the dominant leg, the nondominant leg, both legs, and both arms
and legs in the same manner as you did for suggesting heaviness.
The final suggestion includes both heaviness and warmth in arms
and legs. By this time you will be saying to yourself "My arms are
heavy . . . my arms are warm . . . my arms are heavy and warm
. . . my legs are heavy . . . my legs are warm . . . my legs are
heavy and warm . . . my arms and legs are heavy and warm."
This entire sequence, which will require approximately three
minutes, should be repeated three times and done three times
each day.

Self-induced states of heaviness and warmth are a good route
to achieving total bodily relaxation. Schultz and Luthe (1959) have indicated that the disciplined application of these standard autogenic exercises can, in addition, be helpful in a variety of clinical cases, including
psychosomatic disorders, sleeping problems, asthma, stuttering, phobias,
and anxiety states.

SOME RESEARCH RESULTS

The utility of self-relaxation with a wide variety of anxiety-related
problems was demonstrated by Sherman and Plummer (1973), who taught
21 university students the principles of deep muscle relaxation using taped
instructions. The students practiced the skill at home, 15 minutes at a time,
twice a day. After two years all but one of the students reported using the
relaxation technique for the following purposes: to reduce tension, to reduce
fatigue, to increase energy and alertness, to relax in general, to prepare for
and take university examinations, to improve quality of sleep, to do better in
interviews, to increase comfort in social situations, to prepare for and
present public speeches, to better deal with feared or stressful situations,
and to control anxiety in general (Sherman, 1975).

In another study, Tasto and Hinkle (1973) worked with three men
and three women who had experienced tension headaches for an average of
1.9 years and at an average rate of 5.5 a week, often lasting several hours
each. The subjects practiced deep muscle relaxation techniques once a day
and also recorded how long they practiced, which encourages staying with
the task. At the first sign of a headache, they ceased whatever activities they
were engaged in and turned to deep muscle relaxation. After three weeks
the headaches had greatly diminished. In a follow-up inquiry two and a half
months later, four of the subjects reported no headaches, and two claimed to

have reduced their pain to an average of one headache a week. They admitted that at the beginning of treatment they had to "consciously pay attention" to relaxing. Only after conscientious practice did the skill become automatic. Eventually the very first signs of an impending headache cued the relaxation response.

ENVIRONMENTAL AND BEHAVIORAL CUES: PRACTICING THE RELAXATION RESPONSE

Once you have mastered the skill of relaxation, begin to pay attention to behaviors or situations that cue feelings of tension and anxiety. You can use these cues to elicit a relaxation response instead. For example, you might check your muscles for relaxation during common environmental or social situations (Marquis & Morgan, 1968). The following behaviors may be indicative of anxiety: reaching for a cigarette, looking at your watch, or biting your fingernails. Taking an examination, conversing with a parent, or attending a party are anxiety associated for many people and are situations in which it may be wise to automatically check for tension. There are undoubtedly other situations particular to you in which you need to learn to relax.

Experiment with your ability to evoke relaxation by exposing yourself to situations that are anxiety provoking for you. At the first indication of anxiety, invoke the relaxation response. Begin with environmental stimuli that provoke low levels of anxiety and then, once you have successfully overcome less formidable situations, *gradually* begin to confront more threatening ones. The process of moving up a hierarchy of more and more anxiety-arousing situations while in a totally relaxed state is a technique known as "systematic desensitization," which will be discussed later in the chapter.

SELF-CHANGE TECHNIQUE 2: MEDITATION

The past few years have seen increased interest in Eastern values and life-styles as an alternative to our fast-paced, "on-the move" Western way of life. Success has traditionally been measured in terms of mobility and achievement, but many people have been forced to acknowledge the legacy of that way of life: general dissatisfaction, cynicism, psychosomatic illness, and even early death from stress. Consequently, more and more people have been attracted to Eastern philosophy and culture, particularly Zen, yoga, and Sufism. Predictably, these complex religions and philosophical systems have been dissected, packaged, and marketed to an American public seeking easy solutions. As a result, the meditative techniques we learn are often abridgments and distortions of well-integrated belief systems.

Nevertheless, these techniques retain their value even when they are not practiced as part of an intact religious discipline. Research suggests that meditation techniques effectively reduce respiration rate, heart rate, oxygen consumption, blood pressure, and other physiological indices of tension (Wallace & Benson, 1972). In general, meditation produces a state of increased physiological relaxation together with a renewed sense of vigor and productivity. In some respects, meditation achieves the same results as deep muscle relaxation. However, instead of focusing on the body and concentrating on releasing physiological tension, meditation techniques emphasize detachment both from physical states and from thoughts and feelings. Muscle relaxation is a skill that can be relied on to reduce anxiety in tension-evoking situations. The benefits of meditation, however, appear to be cumulative rather than immediate.

There are certain general principles that seem to underlie the success of all meditation techniques and that can be incorporated into self-therapy. Most meditation involves a *shift of attention* away from ongoing concerns toward the particular exercise being practiced (Naranjo & Ornstein, 1971). Virtually all meditation exercises consist of paying exclusive attention to the meditation object, which may be an unchanging visual stimulus or your own breathing, or a *mantra*. A mantra is a melodic word or phrase —sometimes the name of a deity, sometimes a syllable with no meaning. Perhaps the most well-known mantra is Om, which is often chanted aloud by groups of people. Another is the Hare Krishna, which is repeated aloud again and again in a group. There is a similarity between meditation with a mantra and Christian prayer, in which intoned prayers are often monotonous and repetitive and also involve the name of the deity (Naranjo & Ornstein, 1971).

In practice, a person can meditate either in solitude or with a group of people engaged in a similar exercise. The meditator typically assumes a comfortable sitting position, either in a chair with feet flat on the floor or Indian style on the floor with the back supported. It is not advisable to lie down to meditate--you might be tempted to fall asleep.

There are many different types of meditation. The most common are Transcendental Meditation, yogic meditation, and zen meditation. Transcendental Meditation (TM) has become extremely popular; it consists of the repetition of a mantra twice a day for about 20 minutes, in order to passively let go of thoughts and associations. As we said, the mantra is a nondescriptive phrase that has neither conscious nor unconscious associations for the meditator. Although the mantra that a person uses in Transcendental Meditation is given to him or her by the trainer and is said to have particular significance for the individual, theoretically almost any melodic word or phrase could be used. For example, the sound "Da-Mi" has no recognizable meaning in English. You can use this sound or one of your own choosing in the following meditation exercise.

> Assume a comfortable position. Concentrate continuously on your sound, repeating it subvocally, slowly and rhythmically, over and over. If your concentration wanders, as it is bound to, gently return to the mantra, repeating it over and over. Perhaps the most significant aspect of the meditation procedure is that you do not work at concentrating on your mantra; instead you adopt a passive attitude and allow the thoughts in your consciousness to move on past you. Let whatever happens happen. If memories, preoccupations, or mental images appear, observe them with detachment, let them slide by, and return to silently repeating your mantra. At first the mantra may mean something to you. After a while you stop thinking of the meaning and get involved with the sound. Eventually the meaning disappears completely and the sound becomes totally compelling and achieves a vibrancy of its own.

Practitioners of TM stress that meditation is a learnable skill, like driving a car. The more you practice, the more proficient you become, until you can proceed undisturbed in spite of surrounding distractions. However, in order to reap the benefits of Transcendental Meditation, you must practice it daily.

In one study, nine highly anxious clients learned a meditation technique similar to Transcendental Meditation (Girodo, 1974). The clients complained of symptoms such as apprehension and worry, trembling, difficulty in breathing, feelings of weakness, sensations of dizziness or faintness, and excessive perspiration. The clients were instructed to sit quietly, with eyes closed, and "passively attend to" the sound "Rama." If other thoughts entered the mind, they were to turn their attention back to the assigned mantra. Each client practiced meditating in this way twice a day for 20 minutes. After about eight weeks, five clients who had suffered from anxiety symptoms for an average of 14.2 months had benefited appreciably from the technique. The other four clients, who had suffered from anxiety problems for an average of 44.2 months, were not helped much by the meditation. (They were appreciably helped later by a flooding procedure,

however, a technique that will be elaborated later in the chapter.) These mixed results for the effectiveness of meditation with severe problems suggest that a technique that is very helpful for one person may not be the treatment of choice for someone else.

TM has been used as a primary form of self-therapy for depression, obsessive-compulsive neurosis, and drug abuse as well as anxiety states. One 25-year-old graduate student suffered anxiety attacks and feared that she was going crazy (Bloomfield, 1976). She had experienced tension, irritability, hyperventilation, apprehension, heart palpitations, chest pain, dizziness, trembling, faintness, and easy tiring for several years. She cried frequently and used excessive amounts of tranquilizers. Regular meditation made a significant difference in her life. She began to relax and feel better, sleep nights, and greet each day with energy. Her improvement was substantiated on psychological tests (including the MMPI) one year after she began practicing TM.

Adherents of yogic meditation maintain that yoga encompasses three different disciplines (Chandhuri, 1975). The ethico-religious discipline is a set of rules for conduct, such as refraining from injuring or killing any living thing and maintaining mental and physical purity. The physical-vital discipline consists of eating a nutritious, well-balanced diet, keeping in close contact with nature, and being kind to the body. The psycho-spiritual discipline involves withdrawing attention from the outside world and re-channeling energy to one specific focus or direction. Theoretically, the focus might be contemplation of bodily activities and behaviors, feelings or internal sensations, mood states such as joy or anger, or objects or thoughts that lead to mood states (Goleman, 1975).

The form of yogic meditation that consists of bringing your mind to one focal point is called *vipassana* by Southern Buddhists. The purpose of vipassana meditation is to experience objects as they are. Sensory stimuli receive scant attention, and sensory perceptions are simply noticed and not allowed to stimulate chain reactions of thought.

> Try to focus on the tip of your nose and note your breath going in
> and out for 15 seconds. Just notice the breath at the tip of the
> nose, not when it moves into your body or when it drifts into
> space (Ram Dass, 1974).

A Buddhist monk in India might be able to do this for a few hours at a time. You may start climbing the walls after a few minutes and find it impossible to keep extraneous thoughts out. In meditation, however, thoughts such as "My leg hurts," "I'd rather play football," "This feels really good," or "What am I doing here?" are unwanted, like a friend who drops by when you are trying to study (Ram Dass, 1974). If you could really meditate on the same point for even 10 seconds, you would be a very enlightened being, according to Eastern thought. Ironically, thoughts of "It's working" are every bit as interfering as thoughts of "It's never going to work."

Detachment from the senses, and, consequently, from needs and wants, is important in the meditative tradition. According to ancient wisdom, if you give up craving or wanting things, you will never suffer because you will never be disappointed. Along the path of vipassana meditation you may experience rapturous feelings, a marvelous state of tranquility and happiness, and clear and incisive perception. Sincere meditators must learn to detach themselves from these experiences, too, and continue to contemplate whatever comes in the same receptive, nonevaluative way. The final point along this meditative path is said to be an indescribably ecstatic state of enlightenment and contentment. Although you may never reach this destination, regular practice of contemplative meditation can bring considerable relief to ongoing tension and distress.

Another form of yogic meditation involves concentrating on an unchanging visual stimulus. An experimental study of this meditation technique was conducted by Deikman (1966), who asked subjects to focus all of their attention on a blue vase placed in the center of a dimly lit room. Subjects were instructed to gaze directly at the vase and to return their attention to the vase whenever it wandered. They were told to concentrate on the vase as a whole, without dissecting or evaluating it. All the subjects reported that the vase began to take on a deeper, more intense blue color and that time passed much more quickly than they thought. Gradually they became better able to ignore distracting stimuli. Each subject regarded the experience as very pleasurable; some even reported experiencing themselves as psychologically merging with the vase itself.

Other visual stimuli used in yogic meditation are specially prepared designs called *mandalas*. Mandalas are circular motifs in which all the lines converge on the center. When you meditate on the mandala, your attention is drawn to its inner circle, the center of the mandala where consciousness changes. The design is intended to induce total mental calm and the feeling of being centered. The experience has been likened to standing on a bridge, looking at the water, and watching your thoughts, feelings, and physical being flow by (Ram Dass, 1974). The Eastern mandala has similarities to the Christian cross.

> To use a visual focus for meditation, select a pleasing, simple object, such as a lit candle or a flower, or a symmetrical design. Sit in a comfortable position, empty your mind of distracting thoughts, and focus exclusively on the visual stimulus. Do not try to analyze, describe, or evaluate the object. Merely allow the image to rest in your awareness. Do not be surprised if the image appears to move or change. Just passively accept the new forms.

In another form of yoga, called *pranayama*, attention is focused on the breathing cycle. Resultant changes in oxygen intake and use lead to physiological changes and, presumably, to changes in awareness. By focusing on breathing, competing processes such as thinking and imagining are shut down, which may explain why Zen and yoga masters are so sensitive to internal body signals. Some yogis are said to have acquired enough breath control to literally stop breathing for a considerable period of time. Although the validity of this astonishing feat is debatable, it is certainly possible to achieve more control over your breathing, which can, in turn, inhibit anxiety responses. Sigmund Freud believed that breathing played a central role in the economy of mental health and saw full and regular breathing as closely allied to the resolution of neurotic conflicts (Lowen, 1967). The following is a well-known Zen meditation and breathing exercise.

> Assume a comfortable position and breathe through your nose. Count each time you exhale, from one to ten, and then count back again from ten to one. As you begin to pay attention to your breathing, you may initially experience a sensation of breathing shallowly and of not getting enough air. This difficulty will pass as you repeat the process of counting to ten and back with your exhalations. You may have difficulty focusing on the breaths and be distracted by irrelevant thoughts and images. If this happens, merely note that your attention has wandered. Do not follow the thoughts; relax and return to the task of breathing. Gradually the task will become "effortless," and you will be able to focus on breathing while concomitantly observing the fears, thoughts, fantasies, and events that are competing for your attention (Shapiro & Zifferblatt, 1976). In time these thoughts may become less disturbing and intrusive, and eventually they may drift away completely.

The use of a Zen breathing exercise is often combined with a mantra to form a complete meditation practice.

> Begin by breathing as slowly and as deeply as you can. Breathe through your nose. Inhale, permitting the air to fill your abdomen, then your middle lung region, and eventually the upper lung area. Hold. After a few moments, exhale by pulling the abdomen in to force air out of the lower lung area and emptying next the middle and finally the upper lungs. Be careful not to breathe too quickly, since this will produce a state of hyperventilation (too much carbon dioxide in the blood), which may cause dizziness and hallucinations. With each exhalation allow your body to sink deeper into relaxation. After a few minutes of concentrated breathing, you are ready to begin focusing on your mantra.

A popular Eastern teacher, Bhaguan Shree Rajneesh (1976), has combined pranayama (breathing) with simple mantras to form Dynamic Meditation. A program of Dynamic Meditation might involve the following instructions.

> In the first stage, breathe deeply and quickly through the nose

for ten minutes, just remembering the incoming and outgoing breath. Let your body be relaxed, and move spontaneously if you wish.

In the second stage, release any energy the breathing has created by any means you wish, including weeping, shaking, dancing, or shouting.

In the third stage, shout the mantra hoo! hoo! hoo! for ten minutes. Raise your arms over your head and jump up and down as you shout, exhausting yourself completely.

In the fourth stage, freeze in whatever position you are in for ten minutes. Stop dead as you are and allow the accumulated energy to penetrate and work deeply within you.

In the fifth stage, dance for ten minutes, celebrating the deep bliss you have experienced.

As a final suggestion, if you can't make much noise where you are, go through exactly the same stages but keep the energy inside and express the sounds through the body silently.

There are still other meditative techniques using different focal stimuli. For example, the repetitive exercise may involve physical movement of the limbs so that awareness is continually directed toward the process of movement. This kind of meditation technique is called a *mudra*. It may consist of as simple an exercise as touching the thumb to each finger of the same hand in succession. Perhaps one of the most dramatic forms of mudra comes from the Sufi tradition: the dance of the whirling dervish. Meditators perform a spinning, repetitive dance while canting significant religious phrases. The trance quality of the dance is induced by the repetitive nature of the exercise—although dizziness might be another significant factor!

Finally, there are concentrative meditational exercises that focus exclusively on riddles or paradoxes called *koans*. These are puzzles with no rational solution. Examples of typical koans are "What is the sound of one hand clapping?" or "Show me your face before your mother and father met." Clearly, no logical answer exists, so that, after all attempts at conceptualization, reasoning, and verbal associations are exhausted, the meditator must return to the object of meditation itself, the koan.

Regardless of the particular mode of meditation, whether internal or external stimuli are used, the process of focused attention can effectively produce a state of nonresponsivity to the external world. Each meditative technique aims to "quiet" the mind by creating a state of consciousness separate from normal waking experience. Experimental psychologists have noted an analogous phenomenon in researching what happens in the central nervous system of a person who focuses all of his or her attention on a single stimulus continuously. Their experiments have found that, when the input of visual stimulation is severely restricted, consciousness of the external world is temporarily turned off (Cohen & Cadwallader, 1958).

In behavioral technology, as we shall see in the next chapter, it is the *content* of the observations that is most important; in experiential self-therapy, the *process* of observing counts most. Alan Watts (1972) expressed it this way: "Zen meditation is a trickily simple affair, for it consists only in watching everything that is happening, including your own thoughts and your breathing, without comment."

As you can see, there are many potentially helpful meditative techniques, and the therapeutic benefits of developing meditative skills are multiple (Shapiro & Zifferblatt, 1976). Try to discover which procedures are most beneficial for you. Meditation is a powerful method for achieving relaxation. You can use it to desensitize yourself to troublesome thoughts and worries that are on your mind. Increased relaxation and the achievement of an "empty mind" will, in turn, help you be better prepared to handle stress situations that occur in the course of daily life.

SELF-CHANGE TECHNIQUE 3: SYSTEMATIC DESENSITIZATION

Systematic desensitization is one of the more highly regarded therapy techniques emanating from the behaviorist tradition. We include it here with the affective methods of self-change because it employs deep muscle relaxation and physiological cues for anxiety.

According to its founder, Joseph Wolpe (1958), the principles of systematic desensitization require that one response, generally relaxation, be substituted for the unwanted response, generally anxiety. Systematic desensitization involves a combination of deep muscle relaxation and a hierarchy of items known to elicit the anxiety response. If you can learn to relax in situations that have previously elicited anxiety, you will be able to cope more adequately and not feel overwhelmed. Generally speaking, desensitization is appropriate for persistent avoidance responses to innocuous events, situations, and memories. For example, disorders that are most amenable to this kind of treatment include: isolated phobias (irrational fears) of many sorts (of heights, driving, animals, insects, exams, water, flying, doctors, crowds, and the like), speech disorders, insomnia, and sexual problems. Arnold Lazarus (1971) adds that desensitization can be used effectively to reduce painful associations from the past as well as in the present. For instance, memories of your mother criticizing your performance in the past may continue to agitate you in the present.

Systematic desensitization is one of the most thoroughly researched techniques available for self-therapy. There is abundant research supporting its effectiveness with both single and multiple fears (see, for example, Paul, 1969a, b). Cure rates are especially high for circumscribed fears and somewhat lower for more generalized phobias and "free-floating" anxiety. The more you can move beyond complaints such as "I'm always tense or anxious—I don't know what's wrong" and pinpoint the source of your anxiety or avoidance behavior, the more straightforward the treatment. With desensitization you can deal with a specific fear without changing your entire personality or risking that successful treatment will result in a new fear or symptom somewhere else.

> To select a target behavior, try to isolate specific situations or events that make you feel anxious or frightened. It is also important to consider whether your anxiety is warranted and appropriate or irrational and inappropriate. For instance, you may be terrified to fondle your best friend's pet tarantula, but this seems like a rather adaptive fear and one that is not apt to restrict your life-style too much. Or you might be afraid of driving in your boyfriend's sports car at 100 miles per hour, again not an unreasonable cause for distress. On the other hand, there is nothing inherently dangerous about touching most small animals, meeting people, or taking elevators. The appropriate behavior for this technique is one in which the anxiety you feel is disproportionate to the risk involved. The fear may have been learned or "conditioned" through a single traumatic episode or through a series of less severe experiences or observations. Realize, however, that learning to reduce an avoidance response is no substitute for skill training. For example, your fear of taking exams may be a realistic appraisal of your lack of preparedness. Becoming more comfortable with writing exams will not ensure that you will successfully complete them unless you have already acquired the requisite knowledge. Likewise, the frightened pilot might use desensitization to reduce his fear of flying, but he will need skill training to improve his piloting.

SECONDARY GAINS OF SYMPTOMS

It is also important to consider what advantages, or secondary gains, you derive from your phobic reaction. For example, a woman was afraid to drive a car by herself and regularly called on a friend to drive her across town. She could not imagine asking her friend to accompany her on cross-town excursions without using her driving phobia as a reason. The secondary gain of this woman's fear of driving is that it fulfilled her need for companionship. In fact, her friend's cooperation actually helped encourage the symptom. A man's fear of heights may ensure that he is never the one who has to change the light bulbs or paint the ceiling. A child's fear of the dark may provide her with a reason to go sleep with her parents. If a symptom has too many gains—such as increased support and attention from others or reduced responsibilities and duties—it will be difficult to eliminate.

THE HIERARCHY OF FEARS

As part of the assessment procedure you need to identify the specific cause of your phobic reaction. Lazarus (1971) cites an example of a man who was afraid to go to the barber and get his hair cut. Although this may seem like an elemental fear, there are many aspects to the situation that may camouflage the real source of anxiety. Is the man afraid of the haircut itself? Is he afraid of the physical contact with another male? Is he afraid of sharp objects, like the scissors being used to cut his hair? Or does he fear the scrutiny of other customers? It is important that you accurately identify your primary fear.

When you have identified your primary fear, the next step is to arrange anxiety-evoking stimuli into a hierarchy.

Rank the thoughts or situations that you have identified as fearful from the least anxiety arousing to the most anxiety arousing. You could begin by simply listing on index cards situations in which you experience undue anxiety. Then order the items according to severity. Or you could begin with the general anxiety-evoking theme (for example, fear of dogs), then establish two extremes (petting a doberman, thinking about a dachshund) and work toward the middle by generating items and distributing them along the scale. You may want to use a scale from 1 to 100 to rate the degree of your fear or anxiety for each situation. It is important that your hierarchy have some items that are relatively low in anxiety. If you have a fear of spiders, you may be less likely to panic at a picture of a spider than at the merest hint of a live spider in the house. Hierarchies may range from 8 to 20 items in length.

Here is an example of a hierarchy of a woman with a fear of heights and a penchant for hiking:

Degree
of fear

5   I am standing on the balcony on the top floor of an apartment tower.

10   I am standing on a stepladder in the kitchen to change a light bulb.

15   I am walking on a ridge. The edge is hidden by shrubs and tree tops.

20   I am sitting on the slope of a mountain, looking out over the horizon.

25   I am crossing a bridge 6 feet above a creek. The bridge consists of an 18-inch-wide board with a handrail on one side.

30   I am riding a ski lift 8 feet above the ground.

35   I am crossing a shallow, wide creek on an 18-inch-wide board, 3 feet above water level.

40   I am climbing a ladder outside the house to reach a second-story window.

45   I am pulling myself up a 30° wet, slippery slope on a steel cable.

50   I am scrambling up a rock, 8 feet high.

55   I am walking 10 feet on a resilient, 18-inch-wide board, which spans an 8-foot-deep gulch.

60   I am walking on a wide plateau, 2 feet from the edge of a cliff.

65   I am skiing an intermediate hill. The snow is packed.

70   I am walking over a railway trestle.

75   I am walking on the side of an embankment. The path slopes to the outside.

80   I am riding a chair lift 15 feet above ground.

85   I am walking up a long, steep slope.

90   I am walking up (or down) a 15° slope on a 3-foot-wide trail. On one side of the trail the terrain drops down sharply; on the other side is a steep upward slope.

95   I am walking on a 3-foot-wide ridge. The slopes on both sides are long and more than 25° steep.

100   I am walking on a 3-foot-wide ridge. The trail slopes on one side. The drop on either side of the trail is more than 25°.

A shorter hierarchy was constructed by a man who had a fear of riding in elevators. The items on his list are arranged from least anxiety arousing to most anxiety arousing.

I am in an elevator with a group of people.
I am in an elevator with two other people.
I am in an elevator with one other person.
I am in an elevator alone.
I am in an elevator with a group of people, and the elevator temporarily stops.
I am in an elevator with two other people, and the elevator temporarily stops.
I am in an elevator with one other person, and the elevator temporarily stops.
I am in an elevator alone, and the elevator temporarily stops.

The list hierarchically organizes fears that revolve around a common theme. In the first case, all the items relate to a fear of heights, although the settings range from balconies to bridges to ladders to ridges. In the second case, the theme is more unidimensional. As you draw up your list, try to include many manifestations of the feared situation. Organize the items from those that generate very little anxiety to those that generate a great deal. You might want to arrange your hierarchy along either the temporal or the spatial dimension. Fear of an upcoming dentist appointment, for example, might be more intense as the fated day approaches (one month before, two weeks before, one week before, two days before, one day before, morning of, on the way to the office, sitting in the waiting room, being called, sitting in the dental chair. . .). You move closer to the fear-eliciting event in both space and time. If you have more than one phobia, it is a good idea to sort different sources of anxiety into different hierarchies rather than incorporate more than one theme into the same hierarchy.

THE ROLE OF DEEP MUSCLE RELAXATION

The second component of systematic desensitization is deep muscle relaxation. Anxiety or fear responses have physiological effects, most often in the form of muscle tension. Theoretically, systematic desensitization focuses on supplanting the anxiety response with the antagonistic response of relaxation. Although hypnosis or drugs can be used to induce the relaxation response, most people can learn deep muscle relaxation readily, without such external aids. Many techniques for relaxation have already been discussed (Self-Change Technique 1). In one study, 20 pregnant women were successfully desensitized to the pain of childbirth by using autogenic training to learn to relax (Kondas & Scetnicka, 1972). Their anxiety hierarchies consisted of 20 items, including having the obstetrical exam, leaving home for the hospital, receiving injections, feeling uterine contractions, being in the labor ward, and experiencing the phases of childbirth.

The crucial next step in desensitization is to pair the relaxation response with each item in the hierarchy without generating anxiety. When pairing the anxiety stimuli with the relaxation response, systematic desensitization normally relies on imagery rather than on real-life anxiety-arousing events. There is evidence that, when you relive a fearful situation in your imagination, you generate a state of physiological arousal somewhat similar to what you would experience if you were actually in the situation. Theoretically, then, if you learn to relax while thinking about and vividly imagining the anxiety stimuli, the reduction in anxiety will generalize to the actual situation. If the technique is going to be effective, you must be able to visualize the items in your hierarchy and experience each stimulus event vividly. Although recent evidence challenges the necessity of muscle relaxation and hierarchy construction for successful desensitization (Richardson & Suinn, 1973; Nawas, Mealiea, & Fishman, 1971), this third component is very important.

> Practice your imagery by creating a pleasant environment for yourself in fantasy. Imagine lying on the beach with the sun shining full upon you and the sound of waves gently lapping the shore lulling you to sleep. Or imagine a mountain retreat, a flower garden, or any other relaxing setting. By creating a pleasant scene, you not only practice your imagery ability but also provide yourself with a refuge to which you can return during desensitization to restore your sense of relaxation and calm.

In a therapy setting, a therapist vividly describes each anxiety-arousing scene to you and instructs you to turn your mental images on and off. For use as a self-therapy approach, you may want to tape-record instructions and descriptions of the scenes in your hierarchy; or you may prefer to simply generate them on your own as you proceed. The critical ingredient in the intervention is the repetition of each scene in the absence of anxiety.

> Sit in a comfortable position with your eyes closed, and relax. Once you are deeply relaxed, imagine the first scene in your

hierarchy as clearly as possible. Stay with that scene for 8 to 10 seconds if you do not experience any anxiety. If you *do* experience anxiety, *immediately* terminate the scene, and relax deeply and completely. This may be facilitated by invoking the pleasant scene you practiced previously. If you are able to imagine the setting for 8 to 10 seconds without experiencing anxiety, stop imagining the stimulus, relax, and then imagine the scene again, repeating the procedure. It is very important that you not proceed if you feel at all anxious, since you may unwittingly reinforce the anxiety response to the stimulus rather than replace it with relaxation. Do not expect to be able to complete the entire hierarchy at a single setting. Because you do not proceed with the second item until you have mastered the first, it is reasonable to expect that you will conquer only one or two items per day. It may be tempting to "cheat" by not visualizing the scene clearly or by suppressing the anxiety you feel. But remember that the treatment's effectiveness depends on your following the instructions faithfully.

If you are unable to master a particular item after several tries, this is probably due to one of three things: (1) You may not be sufficiently relaxed. Be sure to relax completely before you begin *and* before moving on to your second exposure to the same item or to the next item in your hierarchy. (2) You may be jumping too far ahead in your hierarchy. The item may be particularly anxiety-arousing, and you may need to master items that are less intense first. Rearrange your hierarchy so that other, less threatening items precede the one with which you are having difficulty. (3) You may not be visualizing the image properly. Practice the imagery exercise until you can visualize your scene in full. It is also important that you terminate each item completely after each brief exposure.

Be sure to end each session with a success experience by returning to an item that you have successfully completed. Also try to begin each new session with an item you have negotiated successfully. This procedure will not only provide continuity between sessions but also help to determine whether there is any residual anxiety with an item or whether there has been a relapse.

As with many psychotherapy approaches, it is better to practice systematic desensitization frequently for short periods of time than to do it infrequently in long, intense sessions. Try to restrict each desensitization session to about 20 minutes; and allow plenty of time for relaxation. In fact, you should be spending more time relaxing than imagining the items on your hierarchy. Once you are able to imagine a scene for 20 seconds without any attendant anxiety, you have achieved success. If you have more than one hierarchy, you can move freely between or among them. Try for small increments of progress when you are working on several fears concurrently.

IN VIVO DESENSITIZATION

Obviously, it is not enough to be able to tolerate your fantasies of fearful stimuli while relaxing in the safety of your living room; your goal is to tackle anxiety-arousing situations in the real world with more success. You can generalize the effects of self-therapy appreciably by exposing yourself to a particular event or situation *after* you have desensitized yourself to it in imagery. For instance, if you have successfully completed a hierarchy relating to your fear of the dark, it is time to test yourself in a real-life situation. Be sure that you follow the same principles in behavior as you did in imagination. Relax thoroughly and remain in the situation for a short period of time. It is important that you try this only with items you have successfully completed. If you skip ahead to items you have not completed in imagery, you may reinforce your avoidance response and fear.

When desensitization is practiced in real life rather than in imagery, it is called *in vivo desensitization*. With some fears it is possible to bypass imagery training completely and to directly confront the hierarchy in vivo. There is reason to believe that exposure to the actual phobic stimulus may be superior to imagery-based treatment (Barlow, Leitenberg, Agras, & Wincze, 1969; Sherman, 1972). The strategy requires you to systematically increase the duration or intensity of the stimulus while controlling the arousal of anxiety. However, use of this technique is limited to hierarchies over which you have some environmental control. For instance, if you have a fear of knives, you could arrange to expose yourself gradually to sharper and larger knives while in a state of relaxation. Or, if your fear is of the dark, you could gradually reduce the light in your bedroom at night until you can tolerate a pitch-black room. In vivo desensitization might be difficult, however, if your fear is of public speaking; you might find it impossible to structure situations in which you can gradually approach the podium or make the audience larger or more threatening. In such a case, you would probably have to desensitize yourself in imagery first and then, once you have conquered your phobia, confront a real-life audience.

The value of in vivo desensitization for treating a fear of water (aquaphobia) has been demonstrated by Sherman (1972). College students who could not swim and were afraid of water activities followed a hierarchy of 26 behaviors that were increasingly stress inducing. The item at the bottom of the hierarchy (least stress inducing) was walking over to the ladder at the shallow end of the pool; higher on the list were items such as dunking oneself and, ultimately, diving headfirst off the diving board. Each student was told to move slowly up the hierarchy, performing each behavior with minimal anxiety, and was instructed not to proceed with an item if he or she was upset. After one hour of in vivo practice, the students were able to complete most of the hierarchy. Some of the group began the treatment with imaginal desensitization to the items before attempting them in real life. This combination of treatments was effective, but it appeared that the in vivo exposure was the important change ingredient.

Another common problem that has been shown to be amenable to desensitization treatment is fear of flying. In one case, a 28-year-old woman had developed a fear of airplanes and of flying, after experiencing considerable air turbulence (Karoly, 1974). As her jet bumped along in the air, the "Fasten Seat Belts" warning blinked on, objects fell from the cabin's overhead compartments, and she became frightened and nauseous. After that experience, she avoided planes whenever possible and relied on buses and trains for transportation.

The woman first learned progressive relaxation. Next she developed a hierarchy of items ranging from thinking about an airplane, looking at photographs of an airplane in a magazine, and looking at an airplane passing overhead to getting ready to take a plane trip, buying tickets for the trip, and driving to the airport. After she had overcome most of her anxiety with systematic desensitization in imagery, she began in vivo exposure to the items. Whenever she experienced any anxiety, she would cue herself by silently saying "relax" and relaxing her body. She also took a tape recorder with her to describe her surroundings and to capture the background noise of the airport as, for instance, she bought her ticket. Later, she practiced relaxing to the sounds on the tape. The tape of her own voice also allowed her to hear herself becoming less fearful. In two weeks she had progressed up the hierarchy until she was able to remain in the air terminal, stand on the flight deck, and take a flight in a small plane.

Virtually all symptom-oriented sex therapy programs rely on the principle of systematic desensitization. Most of the common sexual dysfunctions, including premature ejaculation, impotence, and orgasmic difficulties, occur as a function of performance anxiety; that is, a person becomes anxious when he or she is expected to perform sexually, so that sexual contact becomes associated with anxiety rather than with pleasure. Effective treatment focuses on reducing anxiety so that the sexual response can occur naturally and spontaneously. One fundamental requirement of using this technique is a thorough physical examination by a competent physician to ensure that there are no physiological problems associated with the sexual dysfunction. A second requirement is a willing partner who will follow the therapist's instructions. For example, if one partner suffers erectile difficulties, the therapist will at first prohibit sexual intercourse, since it is apt to be a failure experience. The anxiety associated with performance is thus reduced by eliminating the expectation to perform. Instead, the couple is assigned various tasks that are lower on the anxiety hierarchy to achieve sexual rapport. These tasks, known as *sensate focus exercises,* involve mutual stroking, massage, and exploration, without genital contact. Partners give each other feedback on pleasurable sensations and erotic zones, so that they become relaxed with pleasuring each other's bodies. Once the couple is comfortable with nongenital contact, the therapist will instruct the partners to include genital pleasuring but to refrain from intercourse. The last step in the desensitization hierarchy, penetration with orgasm, is attempted only after the anxiety associated with sexual performance has been significantly diminished. (See Figure 2-2.)

A basic premise of systematic desensitization is that *no* anxiety at all be associated with a given image or experience; you move gradually up the hierarchy by focusing on the least anxiety-arousing item while in a state of relaxation and dismiss the item from your imagination the moment some anxiety appears. In practice, some anxiety can be experienced; the important point is that the anxiety be mild enough to allow relaxation to dominate. With subsequent item presentations, mild anxiety will usually dissipate. More recently, therapists have suggested that the anxiety response be used to cue the relaxation response (Goldfried, 1973; Meichenbaum, 1977). In this procedure muscle relaxation is taught as an active coping skill for *dealing* with anxiety. The client is urged to "relax away" anxiety while staying with a phobic stimulus. By using the onset of anxiety to trigger deep muscle relaxation, public-speaking phobics engaged in self-desensitization were able to cope successfully and perform competently (Goldfried & Trier, 1974). In another case, a 17-year-old girl who suffered from severe, widespread anxiety was taught to identify small sensations of tension and to relax them away (Goldfried, 1973). After about 30 seconds of exposure to a phobic scene or situation, she was able to relax and move on to the next item. After 13 treatment sessions, the girl felt much more comfortable with items listed in her hierarchy, including heights, insects, elevators, criticism from others, unfamiliar people, and being alone at night. She was also able to generalize the skill to other experiences of stress in the natural environment.

> When using desensitization in a self-therapy program, you may find it difficult to eliminate all the anxiety associated with the items in your hierarchy. In such cases, use the anxiety itself as a cue for coping rather than trying to eliminate it altogether. Relax and imagine a scene from you hierarchy. As soon as you begin to feel tension, visualize the item and relax away the anxiety while you are still in the situation. Once you have successfully relaxed yourself while still imagining the situation, go on to the next item.

Even when you have successfully negotiated your hierarchy, you may

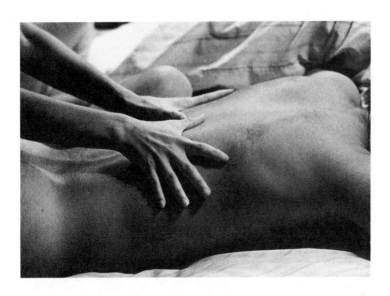

FIGURE 2-2

Sensate-focus exercises (Masters & Johnson, 1970) are frequently the first prescription in a symptomatic treatment of sexual dysfunctions. The technique is useful for enriching intimate communication between sexual partners by offsetting performance anxiety. Performance anxiety, which can create erectile or orgasmic difficulties, occurs when a person is more concerned with monitoring and evaluating his or her behavior in bed ("Will I make it?", "Am I doing all right?") than with relaxing and enjoying lovemaking. As a result, the couple must learn to pleasure each other without worrying about achieving a goal of orgasm. Typically, the first step in sensate focusing is to explore and massage one another's nude bodies, without touching the genital areas at all. The partners alternate in the giver and receiver roles. The giver strokes, and the receiver attends to the sensations aroused by the giver's caresses and comments on particular likes and dislikes. The sensate-focus technique is a desensitization procedure: the couple is instructed to stop and relax at any sign of tension or anxiety. Once the couple has comfortably completed the first stage of the exercise, they move on to include genital pleasuring. Although sensate-focus exercises are an appropriate initial intervention for almost any psychologically based sexual dysfunction, the lessening of performance anxiety is often sufficient to allow a natural sexual response to take over. For some individuals, anxiety associated with sexual stimuli may be so intense that it is better to begin with imaginal systematic desensitization on a relevant sexual theme.

experience some anxiety when you find yourself in the corresponding real-life situation. By pairing anxiety with relaxation, you can use the discomfort you experience to invoke a facilitative coping strategy.

SELF-CHANGE TECHNIQUE 4: FOCUSING

Therapeutic change has been described by clients as an internal reworking of their feelings (Gendlin, 1964). In psychoanalytic therapies, the patient is instructed to express whatever comes to mind without censoring, altering, or rearranging content. This spontaneous flow of thoughts, feelings, and fantasies is called "free association" and is the cardinal rule of psychoanalysis. When free associating, the patient makes direct reference to inwardly felt meanings, while the therapist attends to symbolic associations. When the inevitable impasses arise (usually when the patient is on the verge of experiencing painful and important clinical material), the therapist uses his or her professional skills to help the patient to "work through" the resistance. In client-centered therapy (Rogers, 1965), the therapist helps the client explore his or her internal meanings by reflecting back symbolizations of feelings and experiences. The client explores and confronts feelings that may be only half-formed while the therapist facilitates and deepens this self-appraisal.

Gendlin and his collaborators suggest that the client's ability to "focus" is centrally important to his or her progress in therapy (Gendlin, 1969; Gendlin, Beebe, Cassens, Klein, & Oberlander, 1968). Focusing ability does not involve a particular kind of emotion but considers experiencing as a *process* that begins with the attempt to "carry forward a concrete feeling process by attending to what he (the client) directly and internally feels" (Gendlin, et al., 1968). It is not a cognitive method. It does not require integrating memories, conceptualizing, or drawing inferences. The function of focusing is not to dissect a problem but to sense the problem in its entirety and to allow important elements to surface, like the cream in milk. Focusing makes use of the fact that words can arise from feelings. Some words have the effect of precisely articulating complex feelings. In focusing, words do not encapsulate the feeling experience. For example, if you are fond of someone, you may describe this feeling by saying "I love you" and by listing numerous qualities that justify your appreciation. If you stop at this point, you may have encapsulated the experience and limited your access to the total affective state. Focusing functions to generate new feelings and to make explicit formerly unassociated meanings. Gendlin calls this process a "felt shift." By focusing on your love feelings you may discover something else presently indescribable for which words will ultimately come. You may discover, for example, that the fondness is a function of feeling excited by tension and conflict, of satisfying a deep loneliness, or of eliciting feelings of childlike innocence.

The kind of therapeutic movement that occurs in psychoanalysis and client-centered therapy may be accomplished by developing your own ability to make internal meanings explicit. In a set of empirical studies, Gendlin and colleagues (1968, 1969) found that successful therapy can be reliably distinguished from unsuccessful therapy by the ability of the client to focus. He maintains that he can even predict whether therapy is or will be successful by analyzing a segment of a therapy transcript on this variable.

Gendlin has divised the following set of exercises to teach the skill of focusing. First read the exercise completely to yourself to get an idea of the focusing process. When you try to do this exercise, do not be discouraged if your first attempt to focus on your inner feelings consists of vague impressions and fleeting words. Focusing further will bring structure to your feelings. Take ten minutes of uninterrupted time and try this exercise in focusing.

> First sit down and take a few seconds to relax . . . next pay attention to a very special part of you . . . pay attention to that part where you usually feel sad, glad, or scared (5 seconds) . . . pay attention to that area in you and see how you are now . . . See what comes to you when you ask yourself, "How am I now?" "How do I feel?" "What is the main thing for me right now?" Let it come, in whatever way it comes to you, and see how it is (30 seconds). If among the things that you have just thought of there was a major personal problem which felt important, continue with it. Otherwise, select a meaningful personal problem to think about. Make sure you have chosen some personal problems of real importance in your life. Choose the thing which seems most meaningful to you . . . (10 seconds).

> Of course there are many parts to that one thing you are thinking about—too many to *think* of each one alone. But, you can *feel* all of these things together. Pay attention there where you usually feel things, and in there you can get a sense of what *all* of the problem feels like. Let yourself feel all of that (30 seconds or less).

> As you pay attention to the whole feeling of it, you may find that one special feeling comes up . . . Let yourself pay attention to

that one feeling (1 minute). Keep following one feeling. Don't let it be *just* words or pictures—wait and let words or pictures come from the feeling (1 minute). If this one feeling changes, or moves, let it do that. Whatever it does, follow the feeling and pay attention to it (1 minute). Now take what is fresh, or new, in the feel of it *now* . . . and go very easy. Just as you feel it, try to find some new words or pictures to capture what your present feeling is all about. There doesn't have to be anything that you didn't know before. New words are great, but old words might fit just as well. As long as you now find words or pictures to say what is fresh to you now (1 minute). If the words or pictures that you now have make some fresh difference, see what that is. Let the words or pictures change until they feel just right in capturing your feeling (1 minute). Now I will give you a little while to use in anyway you want to, and then we will stop. (Gendlin, 1969, pp. 5–6).

It is difficult to define focusing precisely. It is certainly a private experience in the sense that the object of focus is known only to you. You attend to a particular kind of inner event, a process that is felt and that occurs in the here and now. It is not exactly an idea or memory but rather the way your ideas and memories make you feel. The technique may be most useful for self-therapy if you either read or reread the instructions, learning them well, or record them on tape for playback. If you begin to block your feelings or to doubt your experiences, begin again or focus on the difficulty you are having in experiencing the concretely felt version of the problem. Focusing does not consist of simply attending to uncomfortable feelings. After all, staying with depressed feelings usually results in increased depression. It is not the emotions themselves but your "felt meanings" of the emotions that are central to the process.

According to Gendlin, quite soon after attending to internal feelings a shift occurs in what is felt (an "Oh!" experience), and new associations and facts spring to mind. He describes four phases of the focusing exercise. In the first phase, the feelings are vague and implicit with no verbal associations. In the second phase, vague and impressionistic felt meanings unfold and are made explicit, usually in a creative burst of insight. The third phase consists of being flooded with associations and memories reflecting past and present experiences that suddenly make sense. In the final phase, this new awareness becomes more explicit while other vague and implicit felt meanings begin to surface so that the entire process continues afresh. The end result of this process is a change in the experiential content, which creates a new way of perceiving, a newly born and realized formulation. This shift may be called insight, resolution, or closure, and it is a significant element in therapeutic change.

The following example may help illustrate the process of the focusing technique. The professor has just returned the paper that took you a month to write. You open the folder and find a low grade and few comments. Your initial feeling is anger. By focusing on the anger you contact other diffuse and vague feelings. Suddenly you recognize, and are able to make explicit, strong feelings of shame and humiliation. The accuracy of this insight leads to a flood of memories of when you were in grade school and the teacher used your essay as an example of pathetic writing. Other memories and associations also fall into place, and you begin to understand how your anger prevents you from hearing criticism or taking suggestions.

In focusing, unlike systematic desensitization, the client holds to a problem and not to a single scene or situation that is part of a hierarchy. The time limitation of desensitization does not allow a feeling to fully develop the way it can in focusing. Yet Weitzman (1967) has found that clients often report similar descriptions of the imagination experience from the two approaches. He instructed two clients to imagine a scene from their anxiety hierarchies and, when a feeling arose, to direct attention to the bodily feeling and stay with it rather than change the scene and turn off the feeling. As they waited and paid attention to the internal feeling, rather than concentrating on the hierarchy scene, their feelings increased in richness, just as Gendlin has described for the focusing technique. They experienced a flood of associations and a change in understanding their fears. The anxiety associated with the content of their fears disappeared. Most interestingly, they reported that focusing "made sense" in a way that systematic desensitization never did. Weitzman also concluded that initial training in relaxation can help bring you into contact with your internal processes and thus facilitate the subsequent impact of focusing.

In short, focusing is a generalizable, experiential tactic for generating heightened self-awareness and for moving beyond a "stuck" position to a position where we see things more clearly, more comfortably, and more completely.

SELF-CHANGE TECHNIQUE 5: AWARENESS AND FANTASY TECHNIQUES

Awareness is the ability to concentrate completely on the phenomenal world. Gestalt therapist Joel Latner (1973) suggests that, in order to be aware, the head must be empty. In many ways, meditative techniques are preparations for silencing the inner voice. However, awareness itself can become like a beam of light concentrating on the area that most captures you. In a Gestalt psychology framework, only one thing can be in true awareness at any given time. This one thing is called the "figure," and the rest of the field becomes the background, or "ground." As thoughts, feelings, images, and external stimuli fade in and out of awareness, there is a process of selecting those stimuli that become figure; that is, you direct your attention to things that are important to you, colors or voices or movements or physical tensions. As you selectively focus on some experiences, you necessarily tune out others, and consequently figure and ground are constantly shifting.

ZONES OF AWARENESS

The shift of figure and ground can occur in three zones: inner, outer, and middle. The inner zone is the area of body sensations, the outer zone is that of environmental stimulation, and the middle zone is the area of thoughts, fantasies, symbols, and images.

To get a better idea of the way in which figure and ground shift from zone to zone, try the following exercise.

> Concentrate on your external environment to the exclusion of your body state and any thoughts or fantasies that you may be having. Complete the sentence "Now I am aware of. . . . " 20 times, to let yourself know what you notice. Avoid reasoning, conceptualizing, or integrating the experience. Notice the way your attention may wander from the call of a bird or the hum of the air conditioner to competing thoughts or internal sensations. Now shift your focus of concentration to the inner zone of body sensations. These may include muscle movements, areas of tension or pressure, pangs of hunger, or sources of warmth and coldness. Again complete the sentence "Now I am aware of. . . . " about 20 times, to develop skill at concentrating your awareness. Finally, repeat the exercise a third time alternating zones, shuttling between the inner and outer zones of your awareness.

As you do this shuttling exercise, you will gradually become aware of more and more external and internal events. In Gestalt therapy, the purpose of attending to these zones is to concentrate on the here and now rather than drift from past memories to future fantasies. By becoming aware of internal bodily states, you may be able to discover ways you stop yourself from feeling or expressing your needs. Frederick Perls, the father of Gestalt therapy, believed that posture and stance, the way a person's body moved, is more revealing of his or her psychological makeup than words. Focusing on external stimuli nonjudgmentally may provide you with information on the kinds of experiences you prefer to avoid or ignore. You can also complete the sentence "I am not aware of . . . " to make this phenomenon clearer.

The third zone of awareness, the zone of thoughts and fantasies, can also be used therapeutically. Focusing is one example of the way awareness of middle-zone events can be therapeutic. However, you may experience middle-zone processes as obstacles to becoming fully aware of external events and internal sensations. With practice your attention will wander less and your thoughts and fantasies will be less intrusive.

Awareness of internal states is useful in exploring bodily tensions and psychological resistances. The following excerpt between therapist and client makes use of the withdrawal technique of Corlis and Rabe (1969). The client is a woman who complained about a lack of sensation in the genital area and about being nonorgasmic. She is asked to withdraw into herself, close her eyes, and focus her awareness on anxiety-arousing material.

> "You've talked about what you don't feel," said the therapist. "This time let's not talk, and this time, just sit with your body and let it talk to you."
> "What part?"
> "Don't talk. Just listen."
> . . .
> "It is rather difficult to concentrate on the sounds at the moment."
> "What interferes?"
> "The dominant feeling is in the belly. But that's not anything to listen to."
> "Can you stay with the belly?"

> After several minutes of attempting to concentrate on sensations from the belly came a sense of constriction and the fantasy of a belt which cinched her waist.

> "Describe the belt."

> She described physical details of the belt with growing concentration and then, "A chastity belt!" she said [pp. 71–72].

Her insight and attendant emotional reaction led to therapeutic attempts to "take off" the imagined belt and renew sexual feelings in the genitals.

> To practice this technique on yourself, begin by becoming aware of your inner zone. Attend to any body part that feels particularly

tense or excited. Stay with these sensations. Notice if they change. In the same way that the previous client's feelings in her belly generated thoughts of sexual inhibition, see if any insights or memories bubble up from your bodily sensations.

THE USE OF FANTASY

The withdrawal technique begins to overlap into the area of fantasy. Fantasy begins where awareness leaves off. With awareness you stay in the present and attend to ongoing experiences; with fantasy you imagine and intuit, remember and plan. The use of imagery and fantasy in psychotherapy has a long history, beginning at least as far back as Freud. There is no end to the number and types of fantasy situations you can explore. Shorr (1974) describes a number of "imaginative situations" that can be used to reveal significant problems or to relive significant experiences. He generally prescribes an image on the basis of his evaluation of a patient's needs. However, since most people have some awareness of their own needs or problem areas, you may be able to create your own themes or select relevant themes from the following list of imaginative situations. To do this exercise, close your eyes and try to capture the following experiences.

Imagine taking a shower with your father (mother). How would you feel? What would you say to your father (mother)? What would he (she) say to you?

Imagine yourself waking up as a baby. How do you feel? What do you do?

Imagine your mother (father) next to you. Imagine whispering something in her (his) ear. What does she (he) reply?

Imagine a large blank screen on the wall in front of you. What do you see on it? Bring someone else onto it.

Imagine looking up at a balcony. Imagine your father (mother) looking down. What does he (she) say?

Imagine unscrewing your head and looking inside it. What do you see inside? [Shorr, 1974, p. 15]

The enhancement of emotion may be the single most powerful therapeutic ingredient of guided imagery exercises. By allowing your fantasy to elaborate on a theme, you may contact feelings or memories that you would otherwise avoid. By exposing these painful experiences, you are able to explore and examine them, a much more growth-enhancing process than denial or forgetfulness.

Leuner (1969), influenced by the work of Desoille (1966), has suggested some specific standard images that he believes elicit meaningful material for diagnostic as well as therapeutic purposes. His guided affective imagery technique helps patients push through areas of resistance and fear. While the presence of a therapist is useful to cajole, instruct, and allay anxiety, the method can also be used as a self-learning experience.

Give yourself lots of time to do the following exercise slowly. Try to imagine specific scenes, locate yourself mentally in an environment, and explore it by trying to develop a series of unfolding images.

> Lie down in a dimmed room, close your eyes, relax and imagine a *meadow*. . . . Stay in touch with feelings that you have . . . describe the smells, sounds and sensations of the meadow in detail to yourself. . . . From the meadow there is a *path* . . . this path leads to a *forest* and on the other side of that forest is a *mountain* . . . As you wind your way along the path, through the forest, notice your surroundings in great detail . . . Now you approach the mountain . . . climb it and describe the landscape as you climb . . . Somewhere in the mountain there is a *brook* . . . explore the brook, tracing its origin to the source or following its course down to the ocean . . . Focus on any obstacles there may be to your progress and try to prevent them from impeding your journey [Leuner, 1969].

It is possible for consciousness to be altered to a condition similar to the meditative state in this exercise. For Leuner, the standard images have potential symbolic value. Climbing a mountain, for instance, might refer to any lofty goals you set for yourself; bathing in or drinking from the "magic fluid" of a mountain brook or an ocean may symbolize a renewal of spirit. Guided affective imagery uses other images with therapeutic potential. These include: a house, which can serve as a symbol of the self; a close relative, which facilitates investigating an emotional relationship; a lion, which helps contact aggressive feelings; and a cave or a swamp in the corner of the meadow, which are potentially frightening images, especially if a creature emerges. If the creature is hostile or frightening, Leuner suggests that you try not to extinguish the image but rather to clarify it in great detail instead. This may temporarily increase your fear to nightmarish proportions, but, according to Leuner, the best way to overcome the fear is to confront the creature-symbol. By staring the creature in the eye, you may be able to obtain a message from it. Or you could convert its destructive

This could alter the aversive potency of the symbol and create some affective change.

Another fantasy that can yield considerable information about ongoing problem areas and open the way for potential solutions is the Rosebush Identification.

Find a comfortable position, lying on your back if possible. Close your eyes and become aware of your body . . . Turn your attention away from outside events and notice what is going on inside you . . . Notice any discomfort, and see if you can find a more comfortable position . . . Notice what parts of your body emerge into your awareness . . . and which parts of your body seem vague and indistinct . . . If you become aware of a tense area of your body, see if you can let go of that tensing . . . If not, try deliberately tensing that part, to see which muscles you are tensing, and then let go again. Now focus your attention on your breathing . . . Become aware of all the details of your breathing . . . Feel the air move in through your nose and mouth . . . Feel it move down your throat . . . and feel your chest and belly move as you breathe . . . Now imagine that your breathing is like gentle waves on the shore, and that each wave slowly washes some tension out of your body, . . . and releases even more . . .

Now become aware of any thoughts or images that come into your mind . . . Just notice them . . . What are they about, and what are they like? Now imagine that you put all these thoughts and images into a glass jar and watch them . . . Examine them . . . What are these thoughts and images like, and what do they do as you watch them? As more thoughts or images come into your mind, put them into the jar too, and see what you can learn about them . . . Now take this jar and pour out the thoughts and images. Watch as they pour out and disappear, and the jar becomes empty . . .

Now I'd like you to imagine that you are a rosebush. Become a rosebush, and discover what it is like to be this rosebush . . . Just let your fantasy develop on its own and see what you can discover about being a rosebush . . . What kind of rosebush are you? Where are you growing? What are your roots like? . . . and what kind of ground are you rooted in? . . . See if you can feel your roots going down into the ground . . . What are your stems and branches like? . . . Discover all the details of being this rosebush . . . How do you feel as this rosebush? . . . What are your surroundings like? What is your life like as this rosebush?

. . . What do you experience, and what happens to you as the seasons change? . . . Continue to discover even more details about your existence as this rosebush, how you feel about your life, and what happens to you. Let your fantasy continue for awhile.[4]

This is a rather detailed fantasy experience. Your identification with the rosebush image is considered a "projection" of the ways in which you see yourself. Since you become the rose, the characteristics you associate with the rose may be considered symbolic of your perception of yourself and your life. The concept of *projection* is fundamental to the therapeutic use of fantasy techniques. In projection you ascribe to some stimulus or person outside of you those features, beliefs, or feelings that are characteristic of you. Since we are not always aware of our innermost thoughts and feelings, the use of a neutral image on which to spin our fantasies provides us with a line to the unconscious mind. The following fantasy exercise may help to illustrate the therapeutic use of projection.

Find a comfortable place to sit and close your eyes. Imagine you are on a road leading to a large mansion. . . . Stop and notice the mansion in all its detail. . . . Now enter the house, moving from room to room, paying close attention to the decor, furniture, objects, inhabitants. Explore the mansion in its entirety . . . Now you are going to leave the mansion, but before you exit select some item from the house to take with you . . . Now leave the mansion and study the object you chose—its size, shape, texture, and use. Finally, *become* that object. Say to yourself, "I am a _____." Describe yourself as the object. Describe how you feel as the object.

To what extent are the characteristics of the object really aspects of you? How do your attitudes about the object reflect attitudes you have about yourself? To more fully appreciate the projective features of the exercise, think of your visit within the mansion as a journey within yourself. What new, used, vibrant, and abused parts of yourself did you discover or confront? What are your feelings about this "mansion" and the rooms and spaces within it? The projective aspects of fantasy work help you see your hidden inner self and retrieve valuable information in a nonthreatening way.

[4]From *Awareness: Exploring, Experimenting, Experiencing*, by J. O. Stevens. Copyright 1971 by Real People Press. Reprinted by permission.

THE TOP-DOG/UNDER-DOG SPLIT

One of the most useful applications of imagery techniques is to investigate splits or conflicts within yourself. One persistent and powerful intrapsychic conflict has been labeled the "top-dog/under-dog" game (Perls, 1969). It consists of a split in the personality between a critical, parental, authoritative aspect (the "top-dog") and an apologetic, childlike, dependent, and at times rebellious role (the "under-dog"). The top-dog tells you how to live your life. It relies on rules and quotes, uses "should" and "ought" a lot, makes critical judgments regarding your behavior, and warns about horrible outcomes if you give in to your wishes and impulses. The under-dog tends to feel overwhelmed by the top-dog and apologetic for its very existence and relies on deviousness rather than confrontation to get what it wants. The clash between top-dog and under-dog is a self-torture game that is familiar to practically everybody. Try the following exercise to contact your top-dog and under-dog. It is most effective if you have an empty chair in front of you.

Sit comfortably with eyes closed, and try to form a visual image of yourself in an empty chair in front of you, as if you were looking in a mirror. Now pretend that this image of you is another person and begin to criticize that person. Tell that person what he or she should be doing. Notice how you sound and how you feel as you do it. Now change places with the image and become the criticized image. Respond to the criticisms and experience the emotions you are feeling as you do this. Now switch again and return to the role of critic. Keep switching back and forth and maintain this critical/defensive dialogue. Throughout the experiment notice how you sound in your voice and how you feel as you play the two roles.

As you finish the exercise you may recognize the critic in your head as someone in your life, most likely a parent, or a husband, wife, boss, or someone else with influence over you. Of course, there is a difference between the other person and the image that you have created. You have introjected or incorporated the image into your personality, to carry around with you, to conform to or rebel against. This image stands in the way of you becoming your own person. One of the most difficult lessons in life is learning to do what you want to do in spite of the fact that someone else wants you to do it. In other words, you cannot effectively deal with problems until you sort out how you feel about something and understand the influence of others on your behavior and feelings. The internal dialogue procedure allows you to discover the splits or conflicts within you and their

source, including messages from your distant past, and to set about integrating them into a fully functioning personality. It may be, for instance, that you are trying to decide whether to move out of your parent's house. Rather than intellectualize the disagreement, try to capture it experientially by engaging in a conversation between the disparate parts of yourself. Play the role of the part of you who wants to move away, and argue with the part of you who wants to stay at home. Then switch roles and maintain the conversation until you reach some new understanding or clarification about the issue.

OTHER POLARITIES

Each person develops his or her own polarities. The challenge in resolving the polarity is to help each part express itself to its fullest while simultaneously discovering its opposite extreme. The following Gestalt dialogue is by a woman who felt quite helpless about coping with her underlying anger. The dialogue moves from an initial incompatibility between the two sides toward a natural softening and synthesis of the conflict (Polster & Polster, 1973, pp. 62–64):

> Helpless: I am really quite helpless. I can't make any real changes in my ways of functioning. I go along keeping quiet about things, letting other people determine the course of action or whatever.
>
> Anger: I am getting fed up with your cop-outs! That's all they are. You don't like how things are but you don't do anything to change it.
>
> Helpless: The reason I don't change it is you! If I let a little of you out you will take over. There will be nothing left of me. You will go on a rampage until you destroy everything! Even now I cry when I think of it—you always make me cry. When I cry I defeat you because then you can't do anything—but I can't do anything either. So it ends up that I'm nothing—only weakness and tears.
>
> Anger: If you would only trust me I could show you that anger can be useful, not just destructive.
>
> Helpless: No!—
>
> Anger: Then go on being the weakling you are.
>
> Helpless: I don't want that either. It's an impossible dilemma—It's your fault—if you weren't there I could do things. If you hadn't kept me down for so long—if you hadn't denied me, if you hadn't tried to be such a fucking angel so everyone would like you—you wouldn't be in this fix. I know all that—but it doesn't change anything. I can't change.
>
> Anger: You act like you have to do something—all you really have to do is let me be. Get to know me—relax and let things happen if they will. Maybe if you are not always so

	much on guard—take the clamps off your jaw, make a direct route from thought to speech.
Helpless:	I know what you are saying—it's what I want. I'm thinking of the terrors of anger—and I'm crying again. I see my father standing at the foot of the stairs with a butcher knife in his hand and threatening to kill my aunt—I see him with his pale blue eyes popping and staring and him yelling—and yelling—and yelling—I can't stand it!
Anger:	Stop it—that was him—it's not the whole world.
Helpless:	His anger ruined his life for him. He is a bitter and lonely man.
Anger:	Your anger is ruining your life for you because you deny it—is that better?
Helpless:	No. I do understand all that—but like I say—it is always the tears that get in the way.
Anger:	Fuck the tears! You can go past them—or with them—or in spite of them—that's no kind of excuse.
Helpless:	How can I use your—no—be with me—maybe that's the trouble—I talk like you are some kind of weapon—It shouldn't be like that—I don't want to fight you—or use you—just be part of me.[5]

Some common intrapsychic conflicts or polarities include:

1. being fearful and intimidated by the disapproval of others versus being unrealistically strong and totally ignoring the opinions of others;
2. being hysterical and overemotional versus being glacially cool and super rational;
3. being cloyingly gentle and sentimental versus being tough and abrasive;
4. being naively trusting and gullible versus being severly circumspect and suspicious;
5. being oversexed versus being undersexed;
6. being clingingly dependent and appeasing versus being rejectingly independent and aloof.

Whenever you use the dialogue technique, be sure to move slowly enough from role to role to fully appreciate the distinctions between them and your own feelings. Sometimes it may be more helpful to conduct the dialogue in the presence of someone you trust. Keep an empty chair avail-

[5]From *Gestalt Therapy Integrated*, by E. Polster and M. Polster. Copyright 1973 by Brunner/Mazel, Inc. Reprinted by permission.

able—you will probably find the technique more effective if you change places physically as you go from role to role. (Some people, however, experience the physical switching of chairs as unnecessarily cumbersome.) Remember to make maximal use of learning from all your senses—*hear* the rate and tonal qualities of the two voices, *see* the visual features and postures of the two roles, *feel* the physiological arousal and kinesthetic changes as you spatially shift between the two positions. Before switching to a new role in the dialogue, first hear, see, and feel the image of the role you have just completed.

FANTASY DIALOGUES WITH OTHERS

Sometimes the disagreement and lack of integration is not so obviously within you. The dialogue technique has application to interpersonal dramas as well. By closing your eyes, you can call up anyone in the world, living or dead, to appear before you in debate. The dialogue technique offers you the opportunity to be completely open and honest since there can be no repercussions from a fantasy that you invent. Perhaps there is unfinished business between you and a parent.

> With eyes closed imagine having a dialogue with the parent sitting in the empty chair in front of you. Notice him or her clearly, his or her clothing, facial expressions, and posture. Notice your own feelings. Begin by saying things you wish you could say or could have said but have not or could not . . . Now shift roles and become your parent. Respond to your son or daughter. Be aware of how you feel as a parent toward your child. Tell the child openly how you feel and what you think about him or her. . . . Switch roles again. Keep the conversation going, expressing your demands to each other in this forthright and uninhibited way. You may find that your feelings about your parent, feelings of anger, sadness, closeness, or fear, become magnified. Try not to focus exclusively on negative comments in this fantasized dialogue with your parent. Find something you appreciate about your parent and share that. . . . Change roles and, as the parent, express some appreciation to your child by telling him or her in detail what you like. As you keep articulating these unspoken thoughts and paying attention to your feelings, there will be periods in which you will feel stuck. It may take several attempts with this exercise to push through and to clarify the relationship. See if you have learned something from the dialogue about your parent that can help you understand his or her real-life response

to you and perhaps enable you to cope more effectively with him or her. Ultimately, you may wish to experiment by risking to say some of these things to your real-life parent and carry the growth process beyond your own internal understanding toward resolution in the real world.

Many of us are plagued by ghosts from the past that we have not dismissed. These ghosts may be deceased parents or remnants of ruptured relationships. The pain that you continue to suffer may be the result of an unfinished dialogue, things you never said for lack of time or lack of courage. It may be time to raise and exorcise these ghosts, to call them forth and say what could not or would not be said, thus providing a sense of closure and a final goodbye.

Both interpersonal and intrapersonal work with the fantasy dialogue technique can be combined in one comprehensive exercise.

> Begin by becoming aware of an intense or uncomfortable feeling you may have about a person or situation. The feeling might be one of hurt, disappointment, anxiety, depression, anger, embarrassment, jealousy, disapproval, or helplessness. Sink into the feeling as deeply as possible. Ask yourself if you experience some other emotion as well. An apparent feeling of resentment or anger may shroud a more profound sense of hurt or sadness; a surface feeling of indignation or embarrassment may cover a sense of excitement or envy. Next have a fantasy confrontation with the other person in the drama, playing each role alternately. Express the thoughts and feelings of both parties in the dialogue more forthrightly and honestly than you would do in real life. Of course, you don't know exactly what the other person is thinking, so be sure to express all the thoughts that trouble you even if you think you are being irrational or overly suspicious. Ham it up a little and exaggerate both positions to really intensify the feelings.

> At this point see if there is any pattern in the kind of dilemma you are experiencing. Ask yourself if this situation reminds you of other incidents in the past. Try to identify someone from your past, a memory triggered by your dialogue. This new person may be a parent or family member. Now direct your comments to this person and engage him or her in a dialogue.

You may find that by reaching into the past you can clarify the present, discovering and understanding the significance of patterns of behavior or stock responses to particular external stimuli. Such awareness may provide some relief from painful emotions and help you relate to people more appropriately.

The final push for instituting more long-lasting self-change is to become aware of the interpersonal dialogue as an internal statement about two sides of yourself (Schiffman, 1971). We are more likely to behave inappropriately when we see (or refuse to see) unwanted aspects of ourselves in another person. Situational conflicts make some statement about our own hidden needs and feelings. By taking the risk and becoming aware of those aspects of yourself that are represented in interpersonal conflicts, you begin to peel away yet another layer of self, examine it, and integrate it into your being.

Proceed with the fantasy dialogue, but this time imagine that each side in the interpersonal conflict represents a part of you. Do not prematurely reject or disown any one part of the polarity. Instead, try to reduce the gap between the two sides by seeking a compromise. As you begin to recognize hidden aspects of yourself, you may discover that even the most distasteful characteristic may be softened and amended into a worthwhile quality. The final step in this exercise, as in all self-therapy exercises, is to make some small change in your behavior that reflects your new and expanded awareness of self.

Perhaps an example can best illustrate the transition from an interpersonal confrontation to an intrapersonal dialogue. Not long ago I received feedback from a student about being abrupt in ending a conversation with him in my office. By allowing myself to become aware of my abrupt dismissing gestures in that particular incident, I was also able to get in touch with other interactions in which I peremptorily terminated a pleasant conversation with friends by suddenly becoming engaged in my work. Part of my subsequent fantasy dialogue about my experience in that initial confrontation went as follows:

Me: That's all the time I have. Please go now.
Student: But we were having such a nice conversation. I don't understand what happened.
Me: It was nice, but I have other things to do.
Student: But I feel rejected and dismissed.
Me: I can't help that. I feel that you would have stayed forever.
Student: Yes, I wanted to stay so much, and now you've pushed me away.
Me: I'll be stuck here with you clinging to me forever.

At this point I began to realize that I was irrationally projecting my own fears onto the student and that he would have left without feelings of discomfort if I had ended our interaction more sensitively; that is, I became aware that my abruptness reflected my own fear of being overwhelmed by the demands of others and a distrust in my ability to gently and assertively end an interaction. At that point I continued the dialogue between two parts of myself:

Me 1: Get out! Let me work!
Me 2: No! I'm having so much fun distracting you.
Me 1: I have things to do! You're insatiable. Go!
Me 2: Let's just have fun. I'm not going to let you work. You can't resist me!

Here I had moved to a different level entirely; the internal dialogue exposed my own ambivalence about wanting to play instead of work and my abrupt way of "getting down to business" for fear of being lured by something more enjoyable. At this point I was able to acknowledge my desire for fun and give myself some more time for it without feeling guilty.

OTHER USES OF THE DIALOGUE TECHNIQUE

The dialogue technique can be used with uncomfortable situations that give you trouble either in reality or in fantasy. Nagging feelings of self-doubt, unhappiness, or loneliness and interpersonal conflicts with peers and family members are especially appropriate targets for exploration. The beauty of the technique is that you don't have to be in the middle of an emotion to work; you can decide in advance on something to explore. Have a dialogue with the neighbors with whom you argue, with the liquor bottle that has enslaved you, with the supervisor you avoid, with the stereo that never works. If you feel terrified by the idea of giving a speech for fear of what the audience will think of you, rather than dwell on the anxiety try to use the dialogue technique. First identify with the imagined audience. Address the speaker, saying "You look stupid up there. You don't know what you're talking about. . . . " Then switch roles and respond to the audience from your stronger side, the one that wants to give the speech. Part of you is afraid that you are indeed a stupid, ignorant speaker, and it is this part that scares you away from the challenge. These feelings are "projected" onto the audience, and it may or may not be that the audience will react in the way you fear. Have you ever imagined someone's response to you and been pleasantly surprised that the response was not nearly so devastating as you had anticipated? Playing the roles and identifying with each is a step toward integrating these fragmented parts of your personality.

One more use of the fantasy dialogue is in dealing with internalized symptoms (Stevens, 1971). In this context, a symptom refers to a problematic behavior, such as loss of appetite or a fear of women, or to a source of pain, such as a headache or tense stomach. Awareness of the inner zone is also important in this exercise.

> Close your eyes and identify a bothersome symptom. Choose one that you are currently experiencing so that you can thoroughly explore the discomfort of it. Note the body areas that are affected and the sensation in them. Try to bring the symptom into the foreground of your awareness by increasing it, exploring it, even exaggerating it. . . . Now, rather than becoming another person, become the symptom, and talk to the person you are disturbing (that is, yourself). Tell him or her what you are like, what you do to him or her, and how you feel about it . . . Now switch roles and respond to the symptom, telling it how you feel about it . . . After focusing on negative attributes, become the symptom once more and tell the person you are useful and helpful. Perhaps you make life easier in some way, by helping him or her avoid certain responsibilities or awkward moments . . . As the symptom, try talking to other people close to you and tell them how you affect them, negatively and positively.

An abbreviated conversation with a nagging stomach ache might go something like this:

Client:	"Why are you bothering me?"
Stomach Ache:	"I've got you and you're not going to get away."
Client:	"I'm afraid of you, go away!"
Stomach Ache:	"I won't. I'm always going to be around to plague you."
Client:	(realizing that it is her mother who is saying that): "You're not going to bother me anymore. I've had it with you!"

End of stomach ache!

It may seem strange to you that symptoms can have advantages —that, in fact, people sometimes make a decision to behave in a particular way (symptomatically) because it is the easiest course to follow. Sometimes the advantages are readily apparent—for example, the headache that enables the wife to avoid having sex with her husband or the fear of driving that allows the reluctant driver to requisition friends to take him places. Sometimes the advantages are much more subtle. By engaging in a dialogue with your symptoms you can learn about how you *use* the symptoms to get what you want and influence other people along the way: The ultimate task of therapy is to help you learn to achieve what you want without the use of symptoms and, particularly, without the disadvantages of symptoms, such as suffering, fatigue, and embittered feelings. This therapeutic step demands that you ask for what you want directly rather than symbolically. Unfortunately, we have been taught to believe that psychological symptoms exist outside of our volitional control and that, consequently, we are not accountable for them in the same way as we would be if we used direct requests or unambiguous statements.

In summary, awareness and fantasy techniques are valuable tools for reducing anxiety and fear and for learning to cope with situations, objects, or people that you might otherwise avoid. There is evidence to suggest that fantasy fosters mental health by reducing dependency on outside forces for stimulation, encouraging patience (Singer, 1974), controlling the accumulation of hostility and tension (Mischel, Ebbesen & Zeiss, 1972), and promoting an awareness of the meaning of one's inner life (Jung, 1964). The techniques can also help you to generate ideas about alternative ways to approach problem situations and a means of trying them out. Sometimes the act of bringing conflicts to life through fantasy techniques will temporarily cause an increase in anxiety. Generally speaking, people are quite adept at terminating these exercises if the resultant anxiety becomes excessive. In fact, the most common shortcoming of proceeding without a guide is not going far enough into the experience. However, if you doubt your ability to handle the anxiety that the techniques may generate in you, treat yourself kindly by going slowly or seeking reassurance from someone you trust.

SELF-CHANGE TECHNIQUE 6:
DREAM WORK

THE SENOI APPROACH TO
DREAMS

Although people have always been fascinated by their dreams, in Western cultures we typically attach little significance to them. We may view dream characters as bewildering strangers from some netherland or respect them as carriers of portentous news, but generally we are mystified by their symbolic messages. It is somewhat surprising to discover that there is a tribe of preliterate people living in the Central Range of the Malay Peninsula who use their dreams in a more sophisticated way then we tend to do. The Senoi people (Greenleaf, 1973; Stewart, 1969) live in community houses, maintain an agricultural economy, and imbue their "halaks," primitive psychologists, with considerable authority. The Senoi live according to democratic principles, value contracts and agreements among their members, and have kept violent crime and intercommunal conflict to a negligible minimum for centuries. Stewart maintains that they are able to function autonomously in this way partly because neighboring tribes sense a magic in their culture and leave them alone.

In Senoi culture, dream interpretation is an important aspect of a developing child's educational program and becomes a daily communal practice. Although Senoi theory regarding the structure and formation of dreams is highly debatable, their approach to processing dream material has implications for self-change. Essentially, their theory suggests that images of the external world that people incorporate into their minds may result in conflict intrapersonally and interpersonally. When these internalized images are experienced as dream beings, they can create havoc with the dreamer in the way the external sources did.

The Senoi believe that each individual has the power to comprehend and conquer the inhabitants of his or her dream universe. Your dream life is an extension of your waking life, and you can control and rule each universe. The Senoi conduct daily dream workshops around the breakfast table, where first the dreams of the children are analyzed by their elders and then the adults analyze one another's dreams. The child receives considerable social recognition for discussing upsetting dream material. Moreover, the child learns that the workings of his or her psyche are trustworthy and rational even during sleep and that with effort dreams can become rich sources of information and insight.

For example, the adult's response to the frightened child's anxiety dream of falling off a cliff into an unknown void is: "Wonderful dream! Where did you fall? What did you discover?" The message is clear: the dream is purposive, so relax and enjoy it. It is not long before frightening dreams of falling change to joyful dreams of flying! The dreamer is taught always to attack in the face of danger, because shrinking in fear means that unresolved hostile impulses will remain to haunt him or her some other day. (In fact, the Senoi are instructed to make restitution in real life to any persons who have been harmed or slighted in their dreams. This is a fascinating method of resolving potentially disruptive interpersonal conflicts on a community level.) Likewise, dreams of pleasure are to be explored fully and shared with the group around the breakfast table. A sexual dream is only resolved through orgasm, and the dreamer is told to request a gift from the dream lover in the form of a poem or song or dance, which he or she can share with the group as an affirmation of the lover's beauty.

The process of Senoi dream work is depicted in the following example, in which the therapist makes use of three stages in helping the client work with the dream: (1) initiation and reconstruction—reporting the dream unhurriedly in the present tense; (2) dialogue and confrontation—establishing contact with the main figure in the dream and developing a dialogue or confrontation with it; and (3) resolution—sealing an alliance between the dreamer and the central dream spirit by asking the main figure for a gift.

A fifty-five year-old woman tells of having a significant dream a month and a half ago and having had no dreams since that time.

She is told to close her eyes and tell when she is in the dream. She is asked to relate what is happening and what she experiences. The patient relates that she is in an open space surrounded by her friends. Everyone is dressed gaily and is laughing and dancing. There is a bright sun shining in the background. The woman becomes aware that she is radiating energy and she feels strong and wonderful. She is aware of a sense of power and she begins to gather momentum. She becomes like the boy in the tire ads who has wheels on his feet and hands. She begins to go faster and faster and is heading for a great wall. She becomes frightened because she knows she will run into the wall at a terrific speed. The patient does not stop and she crashes into the wall. Here the original dream ends.

Th: Look around you and tell me what you see.
Pt: I see a lake, a mountain and fields of grass.
Th: Now go back to the wall and tell me when you arrive. What do you see?
Pt: Drapes.
Th: The wall has turned into drapes?
Pt: Yes.
Th: Pull back the drapes and tell me what you see.
Pt: I see the bright sun and I see my friends dancing. I am now back on the other side of the wall and I am looking back at the drapes.
Th: Ask the drapes to take you to the source of their power. Let me know when you have arrived (pause).
Pt: I have been taken to a very bright fire.
Th: Is the fire friendly?
Pt: Yes, it feels very pleasant - very good.
Th: Ask the fire spirit why you are unable to dream. Tell me what is happening?

Pt: The fire puts me up on a box and tells me that I am at a new level. He says that now I will be able to dream again.

Th: Move into the center of the fire and tell me when you have done this. What do you experience?

Pt: It is a very pleasant feeling. There is such energy around me. I can feel it coursing in and out of my body. It hovers around me and I am aware of bright colors.

Th: Ask the fire spirit for a gift which represents the essence of his power. Tell me when you have done this.

Pt: He has given me an array of bright colors.

Th: Do you feel that this gift is the essence of power?

Pt: Yes, but it seems nebulous.

Th: Accept the gift but ask him for something more concrete—more tangible.

Pt: He has given me a torch. (Patient holds out her hands as if holding the torch.)

Th: This fire spirit seems to be especially friendly towards you. You may wish to ask him if he will be willing to serve as your guide in your dream life.

Pt: He says that he will be my guide and will come to me in many and diverse forms within my dreams.

Th: Now, finish whatever you need to take care of in your dream and when you have completed your dream adventure open your eyes.

Pt: What shall I do with my torch?

Th: Bring it with you back to this world of waking.

Pt: (slight disorientation) I feel like I have been very far away. I feel strange. (Patient still holds torch.)

Th: Can you draw the torch?

Pt: Yes, I would like that.

Th: I believe that you will now be able to dream again. You now have the torch to light your way and your drawing can serve as a symbol of your new power and of your dream ally.

Pt: Thank you.[6]

The Senoi are at the opposite end of the continuum from our Western culture, in which dreams are generally treated as alien spirits best ignored ("There, there, don't be upset; it's *only* a dream"). Freud reclaimed dreams for therapeutic use, characterizing them as the "royal road to the unconscious." Certainly, the psychoanalytic tradition continues to wrestle with

[6]From "Senoi Dream Therapy," by M. L. Murray, *Voices: The Art and Science of Psychotherapy*, 1978, 14 (1), 36–48. Copyright 1978 by the American Academy of Psychotherapists. Reprinted by permission.

the meanings inherent in fractured dream images and to attempt to integrate them into the ongoing, conscious mental activity of the dreamer. Freudian theory suggests that dream symbols protect us from unacceptable thoughts or impulses. By expressing these thoughts or impulses in the elusive language of dreams, the conscious mind is spared the harangues of the unconscious. According to Freud, dream symbols have predominantly sexual meanings. For example, a projectile-shaped object such as a tower, umbrella, tree, knife, or gun is taken to represent male genitals, and caves, tunnels, bottles, jars, churches, or rooms represent female genitals.

JUNGIAN AND FREUDIAN APPROACHES TO DREAMS

Jung, in his early years a disciple of Freud, countered that dream symbols do not refer merely to sexual content but represent mythological motifs and hidden or mysterious aspects of the self. One dream symbol in Jungian theory, for example, is the *animus,* the personification of the masculine aspect of the woman. The animus is shaped by the woman's father and represents her ideal, unattainable mate. Similarly, the *anima* is the personification of the feminine psychological aspect of the man and is influenced by his mother (Jung, 1964). Both animus and anima are also consistently represented in mythology and legend as the pagan father-image and the high priestess. Another dream symbol, the "shadow," represents unknown qualities of the self.

Freud stated that conflicts that have not been dealt with during the day or that have been provoked by barely conscious thoughts set in motion during the day persist into the sleeping state (Freud, 1953). However, Freud's dynamic model of dreaming emphasizes intrapsychic themes rooted in early childhood with which the individual is struggling. A more recent approach, the adaptive model of dreaming, suggests that dreams can reflect any current, here-and-now difficulty that has not been adequately resolved (Greenberg, 1976).

Further evidence for adopting a broader perspective toward dream work has been generated by a number of studies on the physiology of dreaming conducted in experimental dream laboratories (Dement, 1964). In the last few years, it has been possible to monitor a subject's dreams throughout the night by relying on electrophysiological measures of the stages of sleep. Rapid eye movement (REM), for example, has been shown to correlate with dream activity. All of us typically dream between five and seven times per night, a fact unknown to Freud. Although we may not remember all of these dreams, studies suggest that dreaming is a necessary ingredient for normal psychological and biological functioning.

SUGGESTIONS FOR WORKING ON YOUR DREAMS

There is considerable controversy among psychologists concerning both the value and the process of dream interpretation. However, most agree that ongoing conflicts and issues do continue into the sleeping hours and may become manifest in dream images. By considering the experience of the Senoi as well as the Freudian and Jungian traditions and adding the contributions of contemporary dream theorists, we can establish guidelines for doing dream work for self-therapy purposes. It is possible to do a majority of your dream work on your own, although the best strategy might be to cultivate a "dream friend," someone with whom you feel comfortable sharing and exploring your dreams. As with most experiential techniques, the greatest disadvantage of working without the aid of a caring other is the likelihood that you will not explore as deeply as you might.

The first requirement in dream work may appear obvious.

> Pay attention to your dreams. Consider the content of your dreams as an important part of your intrapsychic life rather than as something alien. We have within us great resources, wells of excitement, creativity, and healing. Our dreams may be seen as the key to these psychic treasures (Mittermaier, 1978). Try to form a friendship with your dreams rather than becoming prematurely intimidated or repelled by these unconscious communications. Greet your dreams with openness and curiosity.

Although you may find that you soon forget the details of specific dreams, remembering them is a learnable skill. As you systematically record them, you will be surprised to discover how many dreams you actually have.

> Keep a note pad and a pencil by your bedside to record your dreams, or, as an alternative, use a tape recorder. You may be able to capture more of the tones and nuances of the dream on a tape than in writing. Whichever method you choose, record your dreams as quickly as possible after they occur. Don't trust your dreams to memory. The dream that you're sure you'll remember in the morning will fade away if you procrastinate. Report any and all details of the dream, no matter how ridiculous or irrelevant they appear to be. Note your feelings during the dream and upon awakening. With a little practice you can learn to wake up after a dream and record it without losing a significant amount of sleep.

Avoid judging your dreams. No one dream is better than another for working on, regardless of how meaningless or insignificant it may appear to be. Dreams that seem frightening at first may not be so scary after a little exploration. It may be that, in order to get your attention, your unconscious self needs to do something dramatic. Any part of a dream, including a single dream image, is useful to work on. Don't worry if you forget many of the details of a dream; if the message is sufficiently important, these images will occur at another time. You may find that you are drawn to certain dreams or images. Recurrent dreams, for example, are particularly interesting to work with since they reflect important ongoing concerns. Or you may focus on a dream that generates strong feelings because of a sense of urgency and need to explore it. Old dreams that still have some energy or interest for you are also quite appropriate, although more recent ones may be more concrete and vivid. Nonetheless, it is important that you not judge a dream by its exotic qualities or by its banality. A dream is a personal letter to you; you have to open it to discover its contents (Mittermaier, 1978).

Once you have selected a dream or dream image, try to recapture the dream in as much visual and emotional detail as possible.

> Close your eyes and reenter the dream. Try to retrieve as much information as you can. Notice shapes, forms, and colors, sounds and smells, your bodily sensations. Try not to intellectualize or interpret but to approach the dream with curiosity and gentle interest. If you feel that you haven't a lot of time to work with the dream, say to it "Don't give me too much information now; just give me a little bit." If you find yourself terrified by the dream, take active control to change the spatial arrangement of dream characters or images by saying "Don't come too close. Stay where I can see you but where you won't scare me too much." As you relive the dream, try to remember or clarify some of the feelings or details that were not clear originally. In this way you can extend a dream, or even finish an incomplete dream, in a waking-state fantasy (Garfield, 1974). For example, close your eyes and ask a dream image "How may I help you?" Listen introspectively for a response and continue the fantasy.

Most dream theorists agree that daily events trigger or precipitate particular dream images or symbols. Freud called this the "daily residue." It may be helpful to try to link your dream with these life events.

> As you relive the dream, either by yourself or with your dream friend, shuttle back and forth between the events in the dream and events in your recent past, particularly the day and evening preceding the dream. Ask yourself when, during the last few

days, you saw, thought about, fantasized, imagined, or attended to a particular element from the dream. Your dream images may be direct transpositions of recent events or objects such as the beach ball you saw in the department store window yesterday. In some instances, ideas or other nonphysical stimuli may be represented in the dream, such as the recent thought that your brother has been gaining weight. Dream images are frequently so arcane and unfamiliar that they may not be easy to relate to familiar events. Try to free associate your dream images in your waking experiences without being critical or rejecting. Some of the elements in your dream may be a combination of diverse fragments from waking life. You may have to examine closely the dream image of the strange creature with wooden shoes in order to dissect it into discretely observable units of hair, facial expression, and shoes, and relate each of these elements to daily events.

The exploration of dream images is only one way to work on a dream. Another approach is to recapture strong feelings from the dream. One way to reexperience the full impact of the dream is to narrate it in the present tense. Instead of recalling that in the dream you were alone on a desert island, you reach a closer approximation of the dream experience by saying "Here I am, all alone on a desert island. I am sitting on a rock looking out to sea. I'm looking for a boat, but there is nothing out there."

Another way to work on the dream as a whole is to spontaneously give it a title. In a dream that I experienced recently I was at a race track betting on a horse. I impulsively entitled this dream "Gambling Never Pays," and subsequently I examined my willingness to take risks in life.

Faraday (1972) suggests trying to identify the theme of the dream. If you fail to get the message intended in one dream, the same theme will recur in a later one. When looking for a theme, consider symbols and metaphors as well as concrete objects or events. The following are some examples of themes illustrated by dreams:

1. A dream of flying may suggest feelings of being high or on top of the world.
2. A dream of exploring an old house and finding unexpected things may reflect possibilities you are now exploring inside yourself and in the real world.
3. A dream of a tidal wave threatening to overwhelm you may relate to feelings of being overwhelmed rather than to the ocean per se.
4. A dream of a burglar climbing in your window may suggest trying to keep someone or something out of your life.

5. A dream of war and battles may reflect your feeling that your life is a battleground on which you are caught.[7]

AN EXPERIENTIAL APPROACH TO DREAMS

Dreams may be assumed to express important needs, drives, or goals that are not totally realized in waking life. To work on these issues, it is important to explore that moment in your dream when you experienced the most intense feelings. At that moment, when your feelings are at their peak, your motivation or need is closest to breaking through to conscious expression (Mahrer, 1971).

> Focus your attention on the dream images that occur at the moment of the peak feeling. As you do this, the images may become clearer. Notice the bodily feelings elicited by these images. Try to reexperience these feelings—grief, terror, embarrassment, or ecstasy. You may want to try to surrender completely to the feeling. Allow the feeling to take over by asking yourself "What am I fighting against?" "What am I holding back or blocking?" "What can intensify this feeling?" Don't push yourself. Go as slowly as you need to feel in control of your own dream work.

This exercise is complete when you can pinpoint details and actually reexperience the entire event. As in Gendlin's focusing technique, a dramatic, unmistakable experiential shift will occur as the feeling becomes vivid and words arise within you to describe it (Mahrer, 1971). The general strategy is to reenter the critical moment of the dream, identify the peak feeling, and identify with the dream character who is experiencing that feeling. As you focus on the character's behavior in minute detail, the accompanying feelings surface and begin to fully express themselves. Your experience at this step may be tremendously expressive and volatile (Mahrer, 1971). This part of your dream is complete when bodily feelings are welcomed rather than denied, have become positive rather than negative, and have become integrated rather than splintered.

Once the dream has been thoroughly reexperienced, it is important to

---

[7]From *Dream Power*, by A. Faraday. Copyright 1972 by Coward, McCann, & Geogheagan, Inc. This and all other quotations from this source are reprinted by permission of the publisher and Wallace & Sheil Agency, Inc., as agents for the author.

try to identify any situational context containing similar feelings and motivations. The dream can then provide a means for clarifying that life event.

> Try to get in touch with some recent life event that evoked a
> feeling similar to the one in your dream. This is the critical
> moment. Recreate that life situation in your mind. Reexperience
> your motivations and feelings. Try to allow the feelings you
> discovered in your dream work to grow and become intense. Try
> to accept the feelings without resistance or interpretation. As you
> reexperience your desire to behave in a particular way and sink
> into the fear, anger, or anxiety of the moment, negative feelings
> are replaced by a greater sense of control and acceptance.

You can also trace the motivations and feelings from recent critical events to historically remote critical events. Explore the nature of the feeling in each recent critical moment, and ask if there are precursors for these feelings earlier in your life. As you reach back, recall similar scenes when that particular feeling was strong. The puzzle pieces from the recent past may converge on a distant memory that elicited similar emotions. This historical scene is unfinished business and needs to be similarly experienced to completion. Finally, the closure and integration derived from working through each unfinished goal-directed experience in the mind points the way to making behavior changes in your current life.

THE USE OF DREAM IMAGES

The characters in your dream provide information on two levels. On an obvious level, the dream may provide some commentary on a real-life interpersonal relationship. When an interpersonal issue is reflected in a dream, it is generally a good time to work on it. Dreams can foretell a crumbling relationship or presage the mood you will carry for the rest of the day because they tend to be more sensitive to and more affected by your feelings and the feelings of others than you might admit in your waking state.

On another level, dream characters can be considered different aspects of the self and, consequently, reflect intrapsychic processes, your relationship with yourself. Dream work provides a valuable and exciting route to your intrapersonal life. Begin by examining the similarities and differences between you and each dream figure. The "shadow" figure in your dream will share some of your features. Exploring the shadow may provide some feedback on life events and the way they are affecting you. By identifying with the shadow in your dream, you can discover something about your less obvious characteristics, feelings, or needs. A positive relationship between the dreamer (you) and the shadow indicates that the shadow gives you solid support. If the shadow has mostly negative features or if there is a negative relationship between the dreamer and the shadow, you may be more reluctant to accept and integrate some of his or her aspects as your own. Female figures in male dreams (anima) and male figures in female dreams (animus) also provide information about hidden aspects of ourselves. It is important to bear in mind that our waking, rational (ego) model of ourselves is apt to be narrow and limited, whereas our unconscious has a much broader, richer view. By exploring the shadow or animus/anima figures, we enter the mysterious and often frightening realm of the deeper self.

The best way to sort out these two levels, the external or interpersonal and the internal or intrapersonal, is to identify with your dream images.

> Begin by listing all the relevant images in the dream, whether animate or inanimate. The list may include, for example, the image of an old man, a young woman, a cat, a big room, and a brightly colored flower, as well as yourself. Now try to reexperience the dream by narrating it in the present tense from the ego state of each of these images. For example, from the ego state of the old man, the dream might be told as follows: "I am an old man with white hair and old clothes. I hold a cane. I am sitting in a corner of this very large room. I watch. No one talks to me or even sees me. I feel forgotten and lonely." Go slowly and work through the entire dream, experiencing each dream image from this new perspective. Be aware of any new feelings or information that come to you as you do this exercise. Try to identify any real-life linkages from these new perspectives. It is not important to remain loyal to all the details of your dream. It is better to go where your waking fantasy takes you.

The basic premise of this exercise is that different parts of you may be mirrored in or projected onto dream images. By identifying with several different ego states, particularly those of shadows and anima/animus figures, you may contact unknown resources or feelings. Become receptive to these many characteristics within you. By playing the role of the insect that you find so repellent in your dreams, you may contact some hidden strength such as assertiveness or independence or some hidden motive such as intimidation or punishment. For example, a restless, domineering woman dreamed of walking down a crooked path in a forest of tall straight trees. When she was asked by her therapist to become one of the trees, she began to feel more stable and more "deeply rooted" and to recover those feelings in her current life. When she played the role of the crooked path, she experienced first-hand the manipulative, "crooked" parts of her life. Clarification of these aspects of her life helped her select issues she wanted to change and areas in which she wanted to do therapeutic work (Enright, 1970).

THE GESTALT APPROACH TO DREAMS

Identifying with dream images is used also in Gestalt therapy. Unlike the Freudian approach, the Gestalt method is nonintellectual and noninterpretive. The Gestalt approach assumes that the shape and texture of the characters and objects that populate our dreams reflect disparate parts of our personalities and conflicts between them. Dream work functions to integrate these fragmented aspects of our experience and personality into a whole, unified self. Every dream image, animate or inanimate, is considered to be a portion of the self that is alienated and requires reclaiming. Instructions for this kind of dream work are like most of the other exercises in this section. Try to relive the dream as if it were occurring in the here and now by narrating it in the present tense. Then "become" each image, one at a time. Dream work can begin at any point in the dream, although most profitably at a moment of key emotion. The following short example of a patient working with Fritz Perls may help you in your own work (Perls, 1969, pp. 85–87). The patient recalls a complicated dream and is asked to begin with one small part of it, describing the action in the present tense as if she were dreaming it now:

Linda: "I dreamed that I watch . . . a lake . . . drying up, and there is a small island in the middle of the lake, and a circle of . . . porpoises—they're like porpoises except that they can stand up, so they're like porpoises that are like people, and they're in a circle, sort of like a religious ceremony, and it's very sad—I feel very sad because they can breathe, they are sort of dancing around the circle, but the water, their element, is drying up. So it's like a dying—like watching a race of people, or a race of creatures, dying. And they are mostly females, but a few of them have a small male organ, so there are a few males there, but they won't live long enough to reproduce, and their element is drying up. And there is one that is sitting over there near me and I'm talking to this porpoise and he has prickles on his tummy, sort of like a porcupine, and they don't seem to be a part of him. And I think that there's one good point about the water drying up, I think—well, at least at the bottom, when all the water dries up, there will probably be some sort of treasure there, be- cause at the bottom of the lake there should be things that have fallen in, like coins or something but I look carefully and all I can find is an old license plate . . . That's the dream.

Fritz: Will You please play the license plate.

L: I am an old license plate, thrown in the bottom of a lake. I have no use because I'm no value—although I'm not rusted—I'm outdated, so I can't be used as a license plate . . . and I'm just thrown on the rubbish heap. That's what I did with a license plate, I threw it on a rubbish heap.

F: Well, how do you feel about this?

L: (quietly) I don't like it. I don't like being a license plate— useless.

F: Could you talk about this. That was such a long dream until you come to find the license plate, I'm sure this must be of great importance.

L: (sighs) Useless. Outdated . . . The use of a license plate is to allow . . . give a car permission to go . . . and I can't give anyone permission to do anything because I'm outdated. In California, they just paste a little—you buy a sticker—and stick it on the car, on the old license plate (faint attempt at humor) So maybe someone could put me on their car and stick this sticker on me, I don't know . . .

F: OK eh, now play the lake.

L: I'm a lake . . . I'm drying up, and disappearing, soaking into the earth . . . (with a touch of surprise) *dying* . . . But when I soak into the earth, I become a part of the earth—so maybe I water the surrounding area, so . . . even in the lake, even in my bed, flowers can grow (sighs) . . . New life can grow . . . from me (cries) . . .

F: You get the existential message?

L: Yes. (sadly but with conviction) I can paint—I can create—I can create beauty. I can no longer reproduce, I'm like the porpoise . . . but I . . . I'm . . . I . . . keep wanting to say I'm *food* . . . I . . . as water becomes . . . I water the earth, and give life-growing things, the water—they need both the earth and water, and the . . . and the air and the sun, but as the water from the lake, I can play a part in something, and producing—feeding.

F: You see the contrast: On the surface, you find something, some artifact—the license plate, the artificial you—but then when you go deeper, you find the apparent death of the lake is actually fertility . . .

L: And I don't need a license plate, or a permission, a license in
    order to . . .

F: (gently) Nature doesn't need a license plate to grow. You
    don't have to be useless, if you are organismically creative,
    which means if you are involved.

L: And I don't need permission to be creative . . . Thank you.[8]

In another case, a self-important businessman in a therapy group
recollected a dream fragment about urinating on the carpet (Faraday, 1972).
He was asked to engage in a dialogue with the carpet and to move from one
chair to the other, playing both roles.

Carpet: Why are you pissing on me like that?

Man: Good heavens, I didn't even notice you. Now I come to
         take a good look at you, you're pretty old and worn out
         anyway—dirty as well—not good for much else than pis-
         sing on, I'd say.

Carpet: Well, it's not fair, I protest . . .

The man was now asked to protest with conviction to the other group
members and demand that they stop pissing on him. Afterward he returned
to the role of the carpet and remarked:

I may be old and a bit worn, but I won't have people pissing on
    me.

I'm made of good stuff and I'm hardy. I'm useful and I'm really
    quite warm. In fact, I'm a pretty good carpet really [Fara-
    day, 1972, p. 153].

The man's top-dog, under-dog conflict revolved around his low
self-esteem on the one hand and his pompous, self-righteous attitude on the
other. A Gestalt exploration of the dream fragment encouraged him to
reclaim his lack of self-confidence and feel better about himself.

It may also be helpful to engage in a dialogue with the various ego
states in your dreams or to allow these ego states to have a dialogue with one
another.

Close your eyes and visualize a single dream image. The image
might be of a family member or a monster or part of nature. From
your own ego state complete the statement "I want . . . " or "I

---

[8]From *Gestalt Therapy Verbatim*, by F. S. Perls. Copyright 1969 by Real People
Press. Reprinted by permission.

feel . . . ," directing it to the image. You might find that this spontaneous statement reflects a hidden feeling or need that you have denied conscious expression. Now become the dream image and respond to your statement. From this ego state, select another dream image and weave a dialogue.

As you develop communication between dream images, you will be using the fantasy dialogue technique discussed in the previous section. The Gestalt approach to working with dreams is especially good for working through long-standing conflicts that may be reflected in recurring dreams, especially if interpretations and free associations are not easily forthcoming. Again, since dreams contain so much potential information, they should be explored in whatever way you find most useful to obtain insight into personal problems and conflicts.

There are a number of different approaches to working with dreams. Some of them are light and relatively easy; others may be more difficult to pursue alone because of the amount of anxiety involved. Nineteen approaches have been collected by Alex Redmountain (1978) and are listed in Table 2-1. The most important thing to remember is that there is no single correct analysis of a dream. Nor is there a "right" or "wrong" technique for tackling dream material. Accept your dream at many different levels, and use any approach with which you are comfortable. The most basic instruction is to relax and enjoy your dreams.

SELF-CHANGE TECHNIQUE 7:
FLOODING

People seem to be naturally inclined to deny, avoid, and minimize the impact of unwanted feelings. As children we learn to endure all kinds of pain and not to express it (for example, "Big boys don't cry"). Affective or experiential approaches to self-therapy rest on the assumption that such noxious feelings, feelings of rage, fear, or pain, need to be reexperienced and expressed. Rather than ignored they need to be elucidated, understood, and integrated comfortably into the personality. One might even say that the moment you are out of touch with your own painful feelings you become insensitive to the pain of others, since those feelings do not even register anymore (Satir, 1972).

In focusing and in dream work you stay with a painful (or pleasant) feeling, exploring it, delving into it, allowing it to come alive before you reach a new level of awareness and understanding where the intensity of the affect fades away. The flooding technique functions in much the same way.

TABLE 2-1
Nineteen Things to Do with a Dream in the Post-Freudian Era

Take it at face value: Ignore all symbols. Stop playing an Agatha Christie detective.

Try to find some funny things in the dream, especially if it's a grim one.

Rather than just telling the dream, deliver it like an oration. Or a prophecy. Or an epic poem.

Pretend that someone else you know (your mother, your mate) had the dream. Interpret it from that perspective.

Make up several different beginnings and endings for the same dream, and see what that feels like for you.

If you were not in the dream, put yourself in it and see how that changes things.

Put other people into it, like your mother or father or Uncle Dewey, the asbestos tycoon.

Mix and match characters, settings, and plots in three or four recent dreams.

Add to the end of the dream every day for a week, and finish it on the last day.

Gestalt the dream, using Jungian archetypes as protagonists.

Interpret the dream as instructions from one of your ancestors.

If the dream is an answer, figure out what the question would have been.

Consider the dream a complete description of your character structure; figure out what it is.

If you were making a movie from the dream, who would you star in the various roles, and why?

Relate to the dream as a warning. What is it saying to you?

Take a scary nightmare and interpret it as a happy dream. Do the same in reverse

Pick a childhood age. Imagine having had this dream then; what would it have meant to you?

Arbitrarily assign the roles in any dream to members of your family. Tell it again this way and see how it feels.

If the dream were choreographed, what would the movement look like? Demonstrate.

From "Nineteen Things to Do with a Dream in the Post-Freudian Era," by A. Redmountain, *Voices: The Art and Science of Psychotherapy*, 1978, 14(1), 63. Copyright 1978 by the American Academy of Psychotherapists. Reprinted by permission.

Flooding refers to the therapeutic operation of eliciting intense anxiety in a person through prolonged exposure to threatening situations. The therapist who uses this technique works to induce and sustain high levels of anxiety in the client until the anxiety reaction dissipates. Basically, the client is prevented from avoiding anxious thoughts or behaviors in his or her customary, well-learned ways. The usual explanation for the effectiveness of the technique is that the anxiety "extinguishes" as the client is forced to dwell on upsetting thoughts or images over time (Solomon, 1964).[9]

Flooding was probably used in a psychotherapy context for the first time by Malleson (1959). Since that time it has been used to treat a variety of anxiety conditions. Flooding, as well as desensitization, can be used with specific fears and phobias that have been traumatically induced, and the evidence is divided as to which technique is the more effective. Systematic desensitization may have the edge in coping with these problems based on the sheer volume of outcome studies supporting its effectiveness (Morganstern, 1973). In addition to specific phobias, flooding has been found to be effective with multiple shifting fears and general unfocused feelings of anxiety (Marks, 1975). This kind of anxiety is sometimes called *agoraphobia*, literally "fear of the marketplace." In general, agoraphobia refers to a chronically anxious state that may lead to reclusive, stay-at-home behavior. Most agoraphobics are sensitive to any feelings bordering on anxiety, since they fear that the anxiety will escalate out of control. Treatment often focuses on determining the source of the anxiety and increasing their ability to handle it. Fears centering on thoughts and feelings, such as a fear of going crazy or obsessive thoughts of disaster, are examples of other kinds of problems that can be approached using flooding.

In the flooding technique, the client is usually exposed to anxiety-inducing situations in fantasy or imagery. The therapist may describe a scene in vivid detail, stressing those aspects that are most likely to make the client anxious and uncomfortable. The scene is repeated over and over until the anxiety it elicits diminishes. This process may take quite some time, so that sessions lasting longer than an hour are not uncommon. The presence of a therapist, of course, can help encourage the client to stay with the scene. Stopping prematurely may entail the risk of actually increasing a fear (McCutcheon & Adams, 1975). Such results are not common, but the relative unpleasantness of the procedure makes its use undesirable in cases where desensitization is effective.

[9]Flooding is sometimes used synonymously with another psychotherapy technique called implosive therapy (Stampfl & Levis, 1967). Technically, there are differences: In implosive therapy assumptions are made concerning the early psychodynamic history of the client, and the therapist uses these assumptions to theatrically elaborate anxiety-arousing situations rather than merely to present them for an extended period of time as is done in flooding.

TABLE 2-2
Some Common Applications of Affective
Methods of Self-Change

	Flooding	Dream Work	Awareness and Fantasy	Focusing	Systematic Desensitization	Meditation	Relaxation Training
Addictions						X	
Anger	X		X	X		X	X
Anxiety	X				X	X	X
Awareness of feelings			X	X			
Depression						X	
Hypertension						X	X
Insight and self-awareness		X	X	X		X	
Insomnia		X			X	X	X
Interpersonal conflicts		X	X				
Intrapersonal conflicts		X	X				
Obsessive-compulsive disorders	X						
Overcoming resistance		X	X	X			
Phobias	X				X		
Sexual difficulties					X		
Somatic complaints						X	X
Stress						X	X

Use flooding as a self-change intervention by identifying thoughts or situations that make you anxious. Sit down, close your eyes, and visualize one such situation or thought. If you have a fear of heights, an example is standing on the balcony of a high-rise apartment building. Recording the scene on tape and playing the tape back is an even better form of stimulus presentation. As you experience anxiety, do not fight it; continue holding the image until the anxiety dissipates. Allow yourself to endure as much anxiety as you can handle. Keep repeating the imagery until its emotional impact on you is negligible. The more clearly you can visualize the scene, the better. If you cannot imagine the phobic situation, describe it aloud as a fantasy. When the treatment is effective, the image will become less frightening over time, in the same way that repeated exposure or practice makes most initially terrifying experiences tolerable. Do not push yourself beyond a reasonable limit. Use flooding in a safe environment where you could conceivably call on a friend for support.

In one study (Emmelkamp & Wessels, 1975), 26 agoraphobics who were afraid to go outside their homes and walk down the street were treated with flooding in imagery. They were encouraged to sit relaxed with their eyes closed and to imagine frightening scenes as vividly as possible. Relevant scenes included images of walking down the street alone, sitting in a crowded room, and traveling by bus, train, or car. They had four sessions, each 45 minutes long. In order for the treatment to be truly effective, however, the subjects had to actually go out in the street afterward. They were instructed to walk out on the street without any "props" to help relieve anxiety (such as sunglasses or handbags) and to return home whenever they experienced undue anxiety. When they got home, they were to turn around and try it again until they were able to spend 90 minutes outside. Strictly speaking, this was not a flooding treatment since the clients were allowed to return home when they felt tense. However, the combined treatment of flooding in imagination and this desensitization procedure did prove effective.

As with desensitization, flooding can be practiced independently of imaginal exposure, by actually entering the feared situation for an extended period of time. *In vivo flooding* is probably more useful as a self-therapy technique than flooding with imagery and is more effective as well (Marks, 1975). In the previous example, flooding in vivo was just as potent as the combination of flooding in imagination and in vivo desensitization (Emmelkamp, 1974). In this condition, agoraphobic subjects were instructed to spend 90 minutes walking around the streets along a predetermined route and enduring the experience no matter how anxious they became.

When you use in vivo flooding, you face your fears directly by remaining in the phobic situation until your anxiety extinguishes. There is no graduated hierarchy. In everyday life you typically avoid feared stimuli completely or escape them rapidly, thereby ensuring that your fear is preserved. In flooding you must repeat the approach to the stimulus over and over or remain in the situation for a concentrated period of time. The longer you can remain in the feared situation, the better your chances for success.

For example, one 24-year-old woman had developed an intense fear of and aversion to escalators (Nesbitt, 1973). When she was 17, she had been forced onto an escalator and developed a fear of tumbling down. Since that time her pulse quickened whenever she approached an escalator, and she always looked for an elevator or staircase instead. In this case, the therapist took the woman, despite her anxiety, out to ride escalators with him. The first trip down was frightening to her, but she screwed up her courage and spent 27 minutes riding up and down. Thereafter, the therapist withdrew, and she went riding escalators on her own. A one-session cure by in vivo flooding!

REFERENCES

Barber, T. X. *LSD, marihuana, yoga and hypnosis.* Chicago: Aldine, 1970.

Barlow, D. H., Leitenberg, H., Agras, S. W., & Wincze, J. P. The transfer gap in systematic desensitization: An analogue study. *Behavior Research and Therapy,* 1969, *7,* 191–196.

Benson, H. *The relaxation response.* New York: Morrow, 1975.

Blanchard, E. B., & Young, L. E. Clinical application of biofeedback training: A review of evidence. *Archives of General Psychiatry,* 1974, *30,* 573–589.

Bloomfield, H. H. Applications of the transcendental meditation program to psychiatry. In V. Binder & B. Rimland (Eds.), *Modern therapies.* Englewood Cliffs, N.J.: Prentice-Hall, 1976.

Budzynski, T. H., & Stoyva, J. M. An instrument for producing deep muscle relaxation by means of analog information feedback. *Journal of Applied Behavior Analysis,* 1969, *2,* 231–237.

Cautela, J. R., & Groden, J. Relaxation. Champaign, Ill.: Research Press, 1978.

Chandhuri, H. Yoga psychology. In C. T. Tart (Ed.), *Transpersonal psychologies.* New York: Harper & Row, 1975.

Cohen, W., & Cadwallader, T. C. Cessation of visual experience under prolonged uniform visual stimulation. *American Psychologist,* 1958, *13,* 410. (Abstract)

Corlis, R. D., & Rabe, P. *Psychotherapy from the center: A humanistic view of change and of growth*. Scranton, Pa.: International Textbook Co., 1969.

Deikman, A. Implications of experimentally induced contemplative meditation. *Journal of Nervous and Mental Diseases*, 1966, *142*, 101–116.

Dement, W. Experimental dream studies. In J. Masserman (Ed.), *Science and psychoanalysis: Scientific proceedings of the Academy of Psychoanalysis* (Vol. 7). New York: Grune & Stratton, 1964. Pp. 129–162.

Desoille, R. *The directed daydream*. New York: Psychosynthesis Research Foundation, 1966.

Emmelkamp, P.M.G. Self-observation versus flooding in the treatment of agoraphobia. *Behavior Research and Therapy*, 1974, *12*, 229–237.

Emmelkamp, P.M.G., & Wessels, H. Flooding in imagery vs. flooding *in vivo*: A comparison with agoraphobics. *Behavior Research and Therapy*, 1975, *13*, 7–15.

Enright, J. B. An introduction to Gestalt techniques. In J. Fagan & I. L. Shepherd (Eds.), *Gestalt therapy now*. Palo Alto: Science and Behavior Books, Inc., 1970.

Faraday, A. *Dream power*. New York: Coward, McCann, & Geogheagan, Inc., 1972.

Feather, B. W., & Rhoads, J. M. Psychodynamic behavior therapy: II. Clinical aspects. *Archives of General Psychiatry*, 1972, *26*, 503–511.

Feldenkrais, M. *Awareness through movement: Health exercises for personal growth*. New York: Harper & Row, 1972.

Frankel, V. E. Paradoxical intention and dereflection. *Psychotherapy: Theory, Research and Practice*, 1975, *12*, 226–237.

Freud, S. *The interpretation of dreams* (1900). Standard edition. Vol. IV. London: Hogarth Press, 1953.

Gallway, W. T. *The inner game of tennis*. New York: Random House, 1974.

Garfield, P. L. *Creative dreaming*. New York: Ballantine Books, 1974.

Gendlin, E. T. A theory of personality change. In P. Worchel & D. Byrne (Eds.), *Personality change*. New York: Wiley, 1964.

Gendlin, E. T. Focusing. *Psychotherapy: Theory, Research and Practice*, 1969, *6*, 4–15.

Gendlin, E. T., Beebe, J., III, Cassens, J., Klein, M., & Oberlander, M. F. Focusing ability in psychotherapy, personality, and creativity. In Shlien, J. M. (Ed.), *Research in psychotherapy* (Vol. III). Washington, D.C.: American Psychological Association, 1968.

Girodo, M. Yoga meditation and flooding in the treatment of anxiety neurosis. *Journal of Behavior Therapy and Experimental Psychiatry*, 1974, *5*, 157–160.

Goldfried, M. R. Systematic desensitization as training in self-control. In M. R. Goldfried & M. Merbaum (Eds.), *Behavior change through self-control*. New York: Holt, Rinehart & Winston, 1973.

Goldfried, M. R., & Trier, C. Effectiveness of relaxation as an active coping skill. *Journal of Abnormal Psychology*, 1974, *83*, 348–355.

Goldfried, M. R., & Davison, G. C. *Clinical behavior therapy*. New York: Holt, Rinehart & Winston, 1976.

Goleman, D. The Buddha on meditation and states of consciousness. In C. T. Tart (Ed.), *Transpersonal psychologies*. New York: Harper & Row, 1975.

Greenberg, R. Dreams and REM sleep—An integrative approach. *Advances in Sleep Research*, Vol. 4, 1976.

Greenleaf, E. "Senoi" dream groups. *Psychotherapy: Theory, Research and Practice*, 1973, *10*, 218–222.

Jacobson, E. *Progressive relaxation* (2nd ed.). Chicago: University of Chicago Press, 1938.

Jung, C. G. *Man and his symbols.* New York: Dell, 1964.

Karoly, P. Multicomponent behavioral treatment of fear of flying: A case report. *Behavior Therapy,* 1974, *5,* 265–270.

Kondas, O., & Scetnicka, B. Systematic desensitization as a method of preparation for childbirth. *Journal of Behavior Therapy and Experimental Psychiatry,* 1972, *3,* 51–54.

Latner, J. *The Gestalt therapy book.* New York: Bantam, 1973.

Lazarus, A. *Behavior theory and beyond.* New York: McGraw-Hill, 1971.

Leuner, H. Guided affective imagery. *American Journal of Psychotherapy,* 1969, *23,* 4–22.

Lowen, A. *The betrayal of the body.* New York: Collier Books, 1967.

Mahrer, A. R. Personal life change through systematic use of dreams. *Psychotherapy: Theory, Research, and Practice,* 1971, *8,* 328–332.

Malleson, N. Panic and phobia. *Lancet,* 1959, *1,* 225–227.

Marks, I. Behavioral treatment of phobic and obessive-compulsive disorders. A critical appraisal. In M. Hersen, R. M. Eisler, & P. M. Miller (Eds.), *Progress in behavior modification* (Vol. 1). New York: Academic Press, 1975.

Marquis, J. N., & Morgan, W. G. *A guidebook for systematic desensitization.* Palo Alto, Calif.: Veterans Workshop, Veterans Administration Hospital, 1968.

McCutcheon, B. A. & Adams, H. E. The physiological basis of implosive therapy. *Behavior Research and Therapy,* 1975, *13,* 93–100.

Meichenbaum, D. *Cognitive-behavior modification.* New York: Plenum Press, 1977.

Mischel, W., Ebbesen, E. B., & Zeiss, A. R. Cognitive and attention mechanisms in delay of gratification. *Journal of Personality and Social Psychology,* 1972, *21,* 204–218.

Mittermaier, M. Personal communication, April, 1978.

Morganstern, K. P. Implosive therapy and flooding procedures: A critical review. *Psychological Bulletin,* 1973, *79,* 318–334.

Murray, M. L. Senoi dream therapy. *Voices,* 1978, *14,* 36–48.

Naranjo, C., & Ornstein, R. E. *On the psychology of meditation.* New York: Viking Press, 1971.

Nawas, M. M., Mealiea, W. L., & Fishman, S. T. Systematic desensitization as counter-conditioning: A retest with adequate controls. *Behavior Therapy,* 1971, *2,* 345–356.

Nesbitt, E. B. An escalator phobia overcome in one session of flooding *in vivo. Journal of Behavior Therapy and Experimental Psychiatry,* 1973, *4,* 405–406.

Paul, G. L. Outcome of systematic desensitization. I: Background and procedures and uncontrolled reports of individual treatments. In C. M. Franks (Ed.), *Behavior therapy: Appraisal and status.* New York: McGraw-Hill, 1969. (a)

Paul, G. L. Outcome of systematic desensitization. II: Controlled investigation of individual treatment, technique variations, and current status. In C. M. Franks (Ed.), *Behavior therapy: Appraisal and status.* New York: McGraw-Hill, 1969. (b)

Perls, F. S. *Gestalt therapy verbatim.* Lafayette, Calif.: Real People Press, 1969.

Polster, E., & Polster, M. *Gestalt therapy integrated.* New York: Brunner/Mazel, 1973.

Rajneesh, B. S. *Meditation: The art of ecstasy.* New York: Harper & Row, 1976.

Ram Dass. *The only dance there is.* New York: Anchor Books, 1974.

Redmountain, A. Nineteen things to do with a dream in the post-Freudian era. *Voices,* 1978, *14*(1), 63.

Reich, W. *Character-analysis.* New York: Farrar, Straus and Giroux, 1949.

Richardson, I. C., & Suinn, R. M. A comparison of traditional systematic desensitization and anxiety management training in the treatment of mathematics anxiety. *Behavior Therapy,* 1973, *4*(2), 212–218.

Rogers, C. R. *Client-centered therapy.* Boston: Houghton Mifflin, 1965.

Rosen, G. *Relaxation book: An illustrated self-help program.* Englewood Cliffs, N.J.: Prentice-Hall, 1977.

Sargent, J. D., Green, F. E., & Walters, E. D. Preliminary report on the eve of autogenic feedback in the treatment of migraine and tension headache. *Psychosomatic Medicine,* 1973, *35*, 129–135.

Satir, V. *Peoplemaking.* Palo Alto, Calif.: Science and Behavior Books, Inc., 1972.

Schiffman, M. *Gestalt self-therapy.* Menlo Park, Calif.: Self-therapy Press, 1971.

Schultz, J. H., & Luthe, W. *Autogenic training.* New York: Grune & Stratton, 1959.

Shapiro, D. H., Jr., & Zifferblatt, S. M. Zen meditation and behavioral self-control: Similarities, differences, and clinical applications. *American Psychologist,* 1976, *31*, 519–532.

Sherman, A. R. Real-life exposure as a primary therapeutic factor in the desensitization treatment of fear. *Journal of Abnormal Psychology,* 1972, *79*, 19–28.

Sherman, A. R. Two-year follow-up of training in relaxation as a behavioral self-management skill. *Behavior Therapy,* 1975, *6*, 419–420.

Sherman, A. R., & Plummer, I. L. Training in relaxation as a behavioral self-management skill: An exploratory investigation. *Behavior Therapy,* 1973, *4*, 543–550.

Shorr, J. E. *Psychotherapy through imagery.* New York: Intercontinental Medical Book Corp., 1974.

Singer, J. L. *Imagery and daydream methods in psychotherapy and behavior modification.* New York: Academic Press, 1974.

Solomon, R. L. Punishment. *American Psychologist,* 1964, *19*, 239–253.

Stampfl, T. G., & Levis, D. J. Essentials of implosive therapy: A learning-theory-based psychodynamic behavioral therapy. *Journal of Abnormal Psychology,* 1967, *72*, 496–503.

Stevens, J. O. *Awareness: Exploring, experimenting, experiencing.* Lafayette, Calif.: Real People Press, 1971.

Stewart, K. Dream theory in Malaya. In C. T. Tart (Ed.), *Altered states of consciousness.* New York: Doubleday, 1969.

Tasto, D. L., & Hinkle, J. E. Muscle relaxation treatment for tension headaches. *Behavior Research and Therapy,* 1973, *11*, 347–349.

Wallace, R. K., & Benson, H. The physiology of meditation. *Scientific American,* 1972, *266*(2), 84–90.

Watts, A. The sound of rain. *Playboy,* April 1972, p. 220.

Weitzman, B. Behavior therapy and psychotherapy. *Psychological Review,* 1967, *74*, 300–317.

Wolpe, J. *Psychotherapy by reciprocal inhibition:* Stanford: Stanford University Press, 1958.

Wolpe, J., & Lazarus, A. *Behavior therapy techniques.* New York: Pergamon Press, 1966.

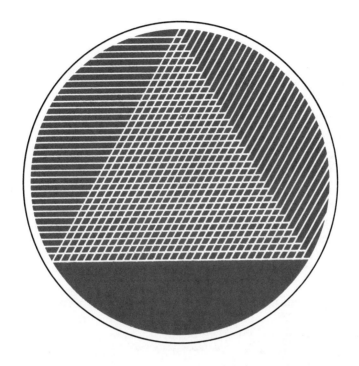

3

BEHAVIORAL METHODS OF SELF-CHANGE

SELF-CHANGE TECHNIQUE 8: SELF-MONITORING
SELF-CHANGE TECHNIQUE 9: STIMULUS CONTROL
SELF-CHANGE TECHNIQUE 10: SELF-REINFORCEMENT
SELF-CHANGE TECHNIQUE 11: SELF-PUNISHMENT
SELF-CHANGE TECHNIQUE 12: ALTERNATE RESPONSES
SELF-CHANGE TECHNIQUE 13: PARADOXICAL TECHNIQUES

In the first chapter we discussed the importance of thinking of psychological problems along a continuum from more to less severe. We also suggested that behaviors are problematic as a function of their frequency (or intensity or duration) and the context in which they occur. Behavioral approaches to self-change require the translation of psychological complaints into unambiguous language and the clarification and crystallization of target goals. Behavioral techniques are especially useful for modifying problem behaviors that are overt and readily observable, as opposed to cognitions and feelings, which are private events. However, behavioral interventions can be used with symptomatic thoughts or feelings if those thoughts or feelings can be related to overt behavioral referents or stimulus situations. As an initial step, it is important to determine whether symptoms, or problem behaviors, can be identified as problems of *excess* or of *deficit*. Thereafter, behavioral self-change strategies deliberately approach the symptom in its environmental context, assuming that the probability that a particular behavior will be repeated is a direct function of the consequences that the behavior produces.

Behavioral therapy techniques have appeared in the psychological literature from at least as far back as 1924, when a young graduate student at Columbia University named Mary Cover Jones treated a 34-month-old boy who had an intense fear of rabbits and other furry objects. Rather than probe deeply into the child's unconscious mind, as Freudian theory might suggest, Jones focused on the behavioral manifestations of the problem by gradually and systematically bringing the child into contact with the rabbit while he experienced being in a safe and comfortable situation. Since that time, behaviorists have been prolific and meticulous in describing and documenting their treatment methods. (Some of the most common applications of behavioral self-change methods are shown on p. 142.) They have also extended their principles and their technology in the direction of self-initiated change.

One behaviorist has divided self-change techniques into conditions of *endurance* and *restraint* (Kanfer, 1977). Endurance techniques encourage one to endure a negative experience even in the absence of an external influence. The jogger who rises at 5 A.M. to run several miles in order to fulfill his contract for physical fitness is enduring pain in the present to prevent some unpleasant consequence, such as a heart attack, in the future. Restraint involves a denial of immediate reward in order to achieve more sizable positive consequences in the future. This condition, known as "delay of gratification," tends to be difficult for all of us, especially for impulsive, present-oriented children and adults. The following story illustrates this concept of restraint. When Odysseus and his men were being lured by the Sirens, whose song led ships to destruction on the coastal rocks, he commanded his oarsmen to plug their ears with beeswax so that they would not hear the song. He then implored his men to tie him to the mast and not release him under any circumstances. Odysseus was able to circumvent the power of the Sirens by recognizing his own lack of willpower and—to describe it in terms of our discussion—by remaining cognizant of the relationship between environmental factors and behavior change. Contemporary behavioral self-change techniques are variations on this theme.

SELF-CHANGE TECHNIQUE 8: SELF-MONITORING

The fundamental prerequisite of behavioral self-change techniques is the ability to observe and record your own behavior with the utmost accuracy. Virtually every therapeutic school or orientation maintains that change occurs as a function of awareness or insight. Behavioral techniques are no exception. However, awareness is focused on concrete and observable behaviors rather than on historical events or affective experiences.

SELECTING A BEHAVIOR TO MONITOR

The first step is to identify which behavior to place under observation. This behavior may be apparent, especially if you have already identified your problem as a behavioral excess or a behavioral deficit. However, at first you may find it more difficult to translate some of your negative feelings into categories of behavioral excess or deficit. Your feelings are associated with behaviors. By applying behavioral self-therapy techniques to the behavior, a concomitant change may occur in your feelings as well.

Some situations are better than others for discovering the behavioral correlates of your emotions. Kanfer (1973) suggests the following situations as optimal opportunities for making this kind of discovery:

1. whenever you are operating at a highly charged emotional level—for example, when you are feeling particularly depressed, joyful, angry, afraid, or embarrassed;
2. whenever you have predicted that your behavior would result in certain consequences and your predictions have proven unexpectedly to be inaccurate;
3. whenever other people in your environment praise, criticize, support, or contradict you; or
4. whenever you must choose between two compelling, equally attractive or unattractive alternatives.

Use the opportunity that these situations provide to monitor your behavior and the environmental events that precede and follow.

OBSERVING AND COUNTING BEHAVIORS

The second step is to learn to observe and keep count of the behavior problem you have chosen to work on. Generally speaking, people are not very precise observers of themselves (or others). Ask a nail biter how often he bit his nails yesterday. Or ask a smoker precisely how many cigarettes she smoked in the last three hours. On the one hand, people usually tend to underestimate the frequency of occurrence of their problem behaviors in order to minimize the significance of their difficulties. At other times, they overestimate or exaggerate the count and are later surprised to learn that they have needlessly catastrophized their behavior. Depressed people are particularly prone to overestimating rejections and failures. On the other hand, problem behavior becomes habitual over time, and then it can escape conscious awareness. By registering the frequency of occurrence of your target behavior, you begin to interfere therapeutically with this automatic process. In short, observing and recording behavior helps to overcome the distortions inherent in human judgments.

Learning to count behaviors serves at least two useful functions. First, you discover that the negative and disruptive feelings you experience do indeed have observable concomitants in your behavior. This correlation enables you to acquire a different, more useful perspective on the goals you wish to reach. Second, counting behaviors provides you with a "baseline" —a reference point for evaluating progress, change, and the success or failure of a self-change program. For example, if you wish to exercise more consistently, the baseline refers to how much you currently exercise, perhaps

on the average of one hour per week. The effectiveness of your program could be judged by the number of hours of exercise per week you attain beyond your baseline.

There is also evidence to suggest that, at times, the process of observing behavior can by itself produce change in a positive direction (McFall, 1970). Hallucinations (Rutner & Bugle, 1969) and repetitive motor behaviors (Maletzky, 1974), for instance, have been altered merely by the act of self-monitoring. In one case, a 20-year-old habitual nail biter wore a cumulative wrist counter and pushed the counter each time the behavior occurred (Maletzky, 1974). Over an eight-week period, her nail biting declined as a result of her monitoring the response. In order to maintain the cure, however, she had to periodically wear the wrist counter and gradually taper off the counting process.

There is a certain rudimentary technology available to aid in developing your observational skills. These tools include the use of index cards, wrist counters, pocket counters, and graphs.

> For discrete behaviors that occur infrequently, such as headaches or anxiety attacks, it may be sufficient to carry around a packet of 3 × 5 index cards to record each occurrence and a brief description of the situation. For more frequent, observable behaviors, such as smoking, snacking, yelling at the kids, nail biting, or apologizing (excesses) or studying, dating, swimming, room cleaning, or using praise (deficits), you might want to invest in a pocket calculator. Small wrist counters, readily available at most sporting-goods stores, are also very useful. Simply add to the count each time the behavior occurs.

The accuracy of self-monitoring is increased when you stop relying on your memory and record your target behaviors as they occur. One approach to recording smoking behavior, for instance, may be to attach a note pad directly to your cigarette pack. To record snacking, place a chart on the refrigerator door. The optimal way to monitor your behavior is to observe and record each occasion of the target response throughout the day. For best results, actively record the response rather than keep the data in your head. Do not wait until the end of the day because your count will not be as accurate. Table 3-1 shows the data collected by a man who recorded his stomach aches for a week. This client was able to track the number of stomach aches he suffered on a given day and in a given week. He did not rely on memory. In this way he could assess the effectiveness of his self-therapy program. By noting when he suffered each stomach ache, he was able to gain some understanding of the circumstances that related to his symptom as well as the times during the week that were particularly stressful to him. He discovered, for instance, that his stomach aches were especially likely to occur whenever he arrived at work, had an argument with his son or a neighbor, paid the bills, saw his mother-in-law, or had sex with his wife!

Self-monitoring will increase your understanding of the relationship between a given behavior and the situations in which it takes place. It is possible to include the circumstances in the recording process by indicating

TABLE 3-1
Recording Stomach Aches

	S	M	T	W	Th	F	S
9 A.M.		✓	✓		✓✓		
10					✓		
11			✓			✓	✓
12 noon		✓					
1 P.M.				✓	✓		
2	✓	✓					
3							
4							
5		✓	✓	✓	✓		
6						✓	
7							
8			✓		✓		
9							
10					✓		
11	✓			✓		✓	
12							
Total stomach aches	2	4	4	3	6	3	1

the situational context of each occurrence of the target behavior. A day in the life of a caffeine addict might look like this:

Coffee Drinking

Monday:	
at breakfast:	2
while working:	4
at lunch:	2
in meeting:	3
while working:	1
after dinner:	2
while watching TV:	1
Number of cups:	15

THE USE OF SAMPLING

If such assiduous monitoring is too inconvenient, you may have to rely on a sampling schedule. When you use a sampling schedule, you select a block of time and record your target behavior each time it occurs within that period. This approach is called *event recording*. For example, you might record the number of times you swear during a particular two-hour time period each day. Or you may want to count the number of times you bite your nails during several ten-minute periods in the same day. It is extremely important that you devote sufficient time to recording your behavior in order to generate data that are representative of your performance throughout the week. If a response is stable—that is, relatively uniform—throughout the day, one short period of observation each day during a one-week period is enough; if a response is more predictable at certain times during the day or week, you will need to monitor your behavior consistently at those times. The general rule to bear in mind is to decrease the length of the recording interval with more frequent behaviors.

There are other ways to monitor your target behavior. Counting is especially appropriate for behaviors that occur as discrete events with discernible beginnings and ends, such as tics or cigarette smoking. With behaviors that are very frequent but difficult to count because they are so habitual, such as nose picking, teeth grinding, or worrying, simple counting may be inadequate. An alternative strategy is to determine if the behavior is present or absent during short time intervals. This is called *interval recording*. For instance, you might add a count if the behavior has occurred at least once during a five-minute interval in a two-hour sampling period. Another option is to add to your tally if you are engaging in the behavior at specific monitoring times. You might want to use a kitchen timer or alarm clock set to go off at regular intervals. If you are grinding your teeth when the alarm rings, add a count to your total. The interval method is advised when it is difficult to determine the beginning and end of a particular behavior. The length of an interval is chosen to minimize the loss of information. In other words, you would choose a short interval such as 15 or 30 seconds if the behavior occurs very frequently or for a long period of time. With a larger interval, such as 15 minutes, you would never know how many times or for how long you actually clenched your jaw since you would only record "no" during the interval. With less frequent behaviors, longer intervals are more appropriate.

If your target behavior does not fall into a discrete category, it may be more appropriate to time the response. This is called *duration recording*. If you want to increase the amount of time you spend interacting with your children, for example, you record the length of time you spend with them each day. You would probably want to measure time durations if you are a student who wants to increase study time, a claustrophobic who wants to increase time spent in a small room, or a consistently tardy individual who wants to increase his or her punctuality. A stopwatch is the best device for recording this kind of information.

When the intensity of a symptom is a relevant consideration, you may wish to record its occurrence using a rating scale. Depression, for instance, is not an all-or-nothing event. You can rate the degree of joy or depression you experience on a 5-, 7-, or 9-point scale and record the rating. For example, the values on one 7-point scale might have the following meaning:

+3 very happy
+2 happy
+1 somewhat happy
  0 neutral
−1 somewhat depressed
−2 depressed
−3 very depressed

Your choice of recording procedure should depend on how much information it conveys and how accurately the information can be obtained. It is desirable and important to collect enough data to establish a clear baseline prior to instituting any behavioral intervention program. A reasonable period for collecting this kind of data is, at the very least, three or four days. You need to observe your behavior on a minimum of three separate occasions to be reasonably confident about the accuracy of your baseline. The greater the variation in the behavior from day to day, the more time you will need to obtain a stable baseline. If you have difficulty in establishing a meaningful baseline, be sure you have defined the behavior you are observing carefully and specifically enough. It is only when you have a quantifiable index of your present ongoing behavior that you will be in a position to evaluate the success of your interventions.

CHARTING AND GRAPHING BEHAVIORS

Your total counts should be transferred at the end of each day to a chart, preferably on graph paper, to provide you with a visual illustration of the number of times the target behavior occurred during the interval that you self-recorded. A graph illustrates data in relation to time by showing behavior on the vertical axis and time on the horizontal axis. Bear in mind that the more precisely you transfer your counts to your graph, the more information your tallies will provide. Post the graph where it will be readily accessible to you. In this way, you can get an overall indication of your behavior at any given point in time. One of the most plaguing problems with self-therapy programs is impatience; we want to experience change quickly and dramatically. By maintaining a chart on which your behavior is regularly recorded, you receive instant feedback on how you are progressing, even though progress may be painstakingly slow. By maintaining the graph throughout the entire self-therapy program, you will have the evidence you need to determine if your strategy is having the desired effect (Watson & Tharp, 1977). The graphs in Figures 3-1 and 3-2 show the progress made by individuals in two different self-change procedures.

· Charting and graphing are not used only by psychotherapists and their clients. Ernest Hemingway used to record the number of words he wrote each day and tally them on a large chart pinned to a wall under the nose of a mounted gazelle head! Novelist Irving Wallace graphs the date he starts each chapter of a new book, the date he finishes it, and the number of pages he writes per day (Wallace, 1977).

ADDITIONAL HINTS FOR
SELF-MONITORING

There are a few additional hints that will help you maximize the effectiveness of the self-monitoring procedure. For example, it is usually preferable to observe and count positive behaviors, those behaviors that you

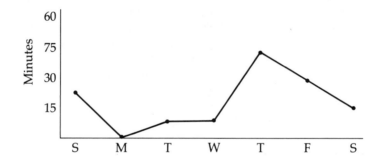

FIGURE 3-1
Time spent interacting with children.

FIGURE 3-2
Cigarettes smoked in the course of a week.

are interested in increasing. This removes you from the role of constant critic so that you can appreciate your better points. If your target behavior is your uncontrollable anger, for instance, you may be better advised to attend to thoughts and behaviors that are kind, tender, and helpful. The rationale for this approach is that there is usually some deficit behavior that is incompatible with the excess behavior that you are attempting to eliminate. Here are some examples of possible translations for converting negative behaviors into positive ones.

Negative	Positive
Too critical	More complimentary
Too dirty	More bathing and washing
Too late	More punctual
Too much TV watching	More reading and pursuing of hobbies
Too much talking	More listening
Too much staying home alone	More going out

A second point is that it is often to your advantage to ask someone else to monitor your behavior since he or she may be in a better position to observe it. However, be sure you enlist the aid of someone who is genuinely interested in your therapeutic plan—not someone who is eagerly awaiting the opportunity to punish you for past sins! In order to put this plan into effect, you must, of course, clearly describe to this other person *exactly* which behaviors to note.

A third hint is that the earlier you intervene in the behavioral chain, the better the prognosis for change. Most symptoms involve a series of actions and responses that evolve over a period of time. For example, you may find out that frustration builds, you attempt to cope, your strength and resources diminish, and eventually you lose control and explode with rage. Rather than counting those instances where you lost control, try to attend to the initial steps in the behavioral chain by charting the first moments of frustration. For example, a 49-year-old woman who was a heavy smoker for 25 years recorded the time and place of each cigarette *after* she smoked it (Rozensky, 1974). This monitoring helped very little to reduce her habit. When she recorded the same information *before* smoking a cigarette, however, her rate dropped off to zero in a few weeks. Unfortunately, there is no foolproof method for stopping smoking and staying abstinent, although self-monitoring can be helpful to some people.

Feelings of dissatisfaction and disappointment often accompany unachieved goals. If you have been wishing, without success, to achieve a particular goal, such as dating someone you find very attractive, try to observe the *chain* of behaviors that are necessary in order to attain the desired goal. It would be difficult, for instance, to meet a potential date by hanging out in a place where eligible people rarely or never congregate. Try to self-monitor those times when you go to places where other singles are in attendance. If you are ineffective in achieving a desired goal, you can generally assume that you have neglected some instrumental behavior earlier in the chain.

As we mentioned earlier, although self-monitoring is an initial step toward behavior change, there is some evidence that the simple act of recording a behavior has an ameliorative influence on it. This effect occurs whether we are noting our own behavior or the behavior of someone close to us. Sometimes it's helpful just to take notice of good behavior. In one study parents tracked their problem children's good behavior using golfer's wrist counters (Herbert & Baer, 1972). As they recorded desirable behaviors, they actually became more positive in their interactions with their children; the children, in turn, became more cooperative and less aggressive. Patterson (1971) has also found that the parent who records his or her child's maladaptive behavior may actually begin to see less of it. One explanation of this effect is that the behavior begins to be seen as a function of a particular situational context rather than as a random or habitual event. The observer also sees and evaluates his or her role in the interaction more clearly and so may subtly change the cues he or she gives that help maintain the behavior.

The potential effects of self-monitoring and charting are nicely illustrated by the case of a 25-year-old obsessive thinker (Frederiksen, 1975). This bright and basically stable woman had a well-developed habit of ruminating several times a day about having breast or stomach cancer. She was in perfect physical health, but these thoughts were very upsetting to her and had been occurring for six years before she began a self-monitoring technique. First she tallied and graphed each episode on a visual chart. Very soon her ruminations declined from about ten episodes per day to two episodes per day. Then she monitored in a more detailed fashion, recording not only occurrences of ruminating but also the date, the time, the activity she was engaged in, the thoughts that preceded the behavior, the actual content of the ruminations, events that occurred immediately afterward, and a rating of severity on a ten-point scale. This intensive self-monitoring totally eliminated the problem. During the final 25 days of recording, she experienced only five such episodes. When questioned six months after the treatment, the woman reported that the problem had not returned. This woman's graph can be found in Figure 3-3.

By faithfully recording instances of your own problem behaviors, you will find it difficult to deny their existence. It is analogous to visiting the doctor who shows you X-rays of your clouded lungs, the result of your habitual smoking. We may lie to ourselves about our weaknesses, but it is not so easy to deny objective evidence.

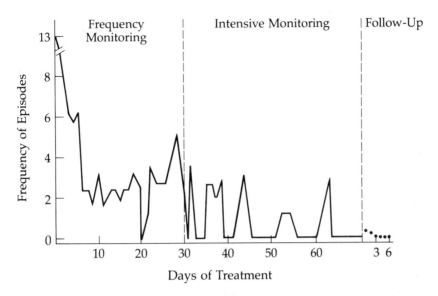

FIGURE 3-3

Frequency of ruminative episodes during treatment and follow-up. From "Treatment of Ruminative Thinking by Self-Monitoring," by L. W. Frederiksen, Journal of Behavior Therapy and Experimental Psychiatry, 1975, 6, 258–259. *Reprinted by permission of the author and the publisher, Pergamon Press, Ltd.*

SELF-CHANGE TECHNIQUE 9:
STIMULUS CONTROL

THE INFLUENCE OF THE
ENVIRONMENT ON BEHAVIOR

A major assumption of behavioral self-therapy is that behavior varies dramatically with the events that precede it. These antecedent events are known as *stimulus conditions* or *stimuli*. It follows from this assumption that one way to alter the likelihood that a given response will occur is to change the environmental cues that precede and maintain it. It is well known that a couple with a long history of poor communication may be able to revive their marriage, including a dormant sexual relationship, by leaving home and taking a vacation. One reason for this is that the stimulus cues that maintain such responses as arguing, anxiety, and impotence are replaced by the excitement of such novel stimuli as an unfamiliar hotel room and recreational surroundings. This may partly account for the success of behavioral sex-therapy clinics in reviving dying relationships: they provide a new setting for building fresh responses.

Everyone relies on environmental aids as cues to control his or her behavior. However, you probably haven't given yourself credit for setting up the technique! For instance, some people are quite capable of waking up every morning at the right time without an alarm. Why, then, use an alarm clock? Precisely because most of us can admit to a certain lack of internal control or will power as a reasonable human limitation. The clock serves to compensate for this confessed "weakness." Why keep a written record of dates and appointments on a conspicuous calendar? Again, precisely because you realize that multiple demands are being placed on a fragile memory system that has better things to do than store your appointments for future recall. The calendar serves as insurance to help you regulate your life.

"Environmental planning" (Thoresen & Mahoney, 1974) or "stimulus control" methods (Goldiamond, 1965) are self-change procedures that focus on the relationship between responses and the environmental cues that increase or decrease the likelihood of their occurrence. With stimulus control methods you engineer your environment to alter your behavior in desired ways. B. F. Skinner (1953) expresses the following rationale for techniques in which the environment is directly manipulated: "When all relevant variables have been arranged, an organism will or will not respond. If it does not, it cannot. If it can, it will." Accordingly, as mobility and awareness increase it is easier for people to select their environments rather than adapt to the environment in which they are cast.

Stimulus control methods have been successfully applied with a wide range of problem behaviors, including smoking, overeating, poor study habits, and marital discord.

> The first step is to isolate the target behavior and its unique controlling stimuli. This is not as easy as it might appear. You might imagine, for example, that the most likely stimulus for eating is hunger. Yet the problem overeater does not isolate his or her eating behavior to mealtimes at the dining table (Ferster, Nurnberger, & Levitt, 1962). Instead there are a host of cues in our culture that easily potentiate the likelihood of eating. For many people it would be inconceivable to go to a movie without the companionship of a bag of popcorn. For others the stimulus of turning on a television set leads to the response of going to the

refrigerator for a beer. Consequently, eating is confounded with the pleasure derived from watching a movie or television program. In order to isolate the controlling stimuli of your target behavior, monitor the objects, people, and events in your environment that are present when the target behavior occurs. Note the time, place, setting, and personal contacts that exist simultaneously with the unwanted behavior. Do not become too discouraged if you cannot identify specific stimuli that correlate with your problem. They are sometimes very difficult to determine.

The second step in your stimulus control program is to select strategies that will most effectively restrict the target behavior.

Examine the present stimulus conditions of your target behavior and determine which are the most appropriate conditions. If you are concerned with working creatively, you may decide that the most advantageous conditions for creative work are in your office with music turned on but out of earshot of screaming kids. Once you have selected the most appropriate stimulus condition for your target behavior, ensure that it occurs only in that environment. The more an environment limits a class of behaviors, the better it is for achieving stimulus control.

EXAMPLES OF THE USE OF STIMULUS CONTROL

The first strategy in learning to control overeating is to restrict the behavior to those few stimulus conditions that are most appropriately related to eating, most often sitting at the dining room table. Do not combine eating with such rewarding and enjoyable events as movies or television. Try to eat whenever you want, but make sure that you eat only at the dining room table with your attention focused exclusively on the eating process. Other suggestions for reducing the stimulus control of eating are shown in Table 3-2.

This strategy is equally applicable to many other problem behaviors. Goldiamond (1965) cleverly used stimulus control procedures to improve a student's study habits. He engineered her environment by setting up a desk to control her study behavior. When she sat at the desk, she had to study; if she wished to engage in some other, competing response, such as letter writing, daydreaming, or eating, she was to vacate the desk and engage in that behavior elsewhere. By recognizing her motivational difficulty in studying, the student was able to engineer her environment to help her capitalize

on the naturally existing links between the cues for studying, the desk, and study behavior itself.

Some people have a shorter fuse than others. They have difficulty curbing their tempers. They find that they tend to respond to frustrating situations with aggression and anger, culminating in unfortunate consequences. For example, a man who comes home from work tied up in knots

TABLE 3-2
Procedures to Reduce Stimulus Control
of Eating

Modification of Meal Quantity

1. Eat slowly; gradually increase minimal time allowed for each meal.
2. Take small bites.
3. Put eating utensil (or food item) down while chewing.
4. Take one helping at a time.
5. Leave table for a brief period between helpings.
6. Eat one food item at a time (e.g., finish meat, before taking vegetable).
7. Serve food from kitchen rather than placing platter on table.
8. Use small cups and plates.
9. Leave some food on plate at end of meal.

Modification of Meal Frequency

1. Do nothing else while eating.
2. Eat in only one place, sitting down (preferably not in kitchen and not where you engage in other activities).
3. Eat only at specified times.
4. Set the table with a complete place setting whenever eating.
5. Wait a fixed period after urge to eat before actually eating.
6. Engage in an activity incompatible with eating when urge to eat appears.
7. Plan a highly liked activity for periods when the urge to eat can be anticipated (e.g., read evening newspaper before bedtime).

Modification of Types of Food Eaten

1. Do not buy prepared foods or snack foods.
2. Prepare lunch after eating breakfast and dinner after lunch (to avoid nibbling).
3. Do grocery shopping soon after eating.
4. Shop from a list.
5. Eat a low calorie meal before leaving for a party.
6. Do not eat while drinking coffee or alcohol.

From "Behavior Therapy for Weight Reduction: An Evaluative Review," by A. S. Bellack, *Addictive Behaviors*, 1975, *1*, 73–82. Reprinted by permission of the author and the publisher, Pergamon Press, Ltd.

after an unpleasant day is preset like a time bomb, ready to explode and deliver pain to members of his family. This person may need a "sanctuary" in which to cool off. Rather than inviting the inevitable onslaught of hostility, the aggression-prone person can use stimulus control by arranging to have a neutral corner, such as a study, bedroom, or basement, where he or she can unwind or let out anger.

Many clients have found stimulus control procedures helpful in their attempts to cut down on smoking cigarettes. One woman noted that much of her smoking occurred when other people were around, when she watched television, when she read, and when she lay down to relax (Nolan, 1968). An obvious strategy was to eliminate the impact of other activities and circumstances by restricting her smoking to a prescribed place. A chair was selected as her smoking chair. It was positioned so that she could not watch television or easily carry on a conversation while seated in the chair. During the self-change program she limited her smoking to that chair while not allowing herself to engage in other reinforcing activities such as reading. Other members of her family were requested not to approach her or talk to her while she was in her smoking chair.

Based on the woman's daily record of her cigarette smoking, her smoking rate decreased rather rapidly. These data are reproduced in Figure 3-4. Her base rate of smoking was about 30 cigarettes per day. The smoking chair brought the rate down to about 12 cigarettes per day as she followed

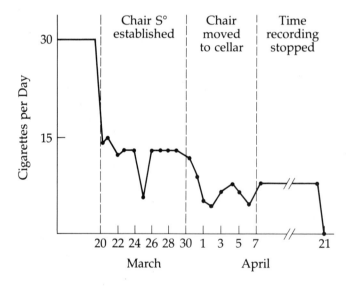

FIGURE 3-4

Reduction in rate of cigarette smoking. From "Self-Control Procedures in the Modification of Smoking Behavior," by J. D. Nolan, Journal of Consulting and Clinical Psychology, 1968, 32, 92–93. Copyright 1968 by the American Psychological Association. Reprinted by permission.

the procedure faithfully. Nine days after the program began, she attempted to lessen her smoking even more by moving the chair to the basement and making it less accessible. As shown in the graph, her smoking rate now decreased to five cigarettes per day. Finally, a month after the smoking chair was set up, the woman became so disgusted with her residual smoking that she quit altogether. The smoking chair was returned to the living room, and her abstinence pattern continued.

Using stimulus control procedures in marital therapy, Goldiamond (1965) treated a man who tended to sulk during interactions with his wife. This behavior was extremely disturbing to the wife and was not particularly appealing to the husband either. The man was not told to try to stop sulking. Instead, he was encouraged to restrict his sulking behavior to a special "sulking stool," located in the garage. He was instructed to go there as often as he wished, to mutter to himself about his misfortunes, and to leave when he was through sulking. By allowing the stool to control his behavior, the husband became increasingly aware of his sulking and *his own ability to change it.*

This example illustrates an important point. Although it may appear that the environment controls the person, these self-therapy techniques enable a person to *select* the environment that controls him or her. Environmental stimuli have a powerful effect on human behavior. However, given the basic strategies of stimulus control, the individual is able to structure his or her environment, within limits, to reduce the potential of engaging in symptomatic behavior. Goldiamond's use of stimulus control in marital therapy also provides some indication of the potency of the procedure in an ongoing relationship between two or more persons.

CHANGING THE BEHAVIOR OF OTHERS

Stimulus control techniques can be used not only for altering your own problematic behaviors but also for influencing the behavior of others. You can strengthen desirable behaviors and eliminate problem behaviors in others by altering their social environment. Remember that you constitute an integral part of the social environment of those close to you. By analyzing the stimulus value that you have for others, you are better able to understand their disturbing behavior and to influence it by altering your own. In marital relationships, for example, a predictable sequence of events usually precedes the onset of tears, assault, escape, or tension. When the husband grabs a newspaper and ignores his wife, his actions can easily lead to a fight and mutual avoidance. However, the husband's newspaper-reading behavior may have been precipitated earlier when the wife complained about family finances. In other words, the chain of events leading up to their argument may begin with the stimulus condition of the wife's discourse on money matters. Or it may have originated earlier with a tactless comment by the husband about his wife's clothing. It is important to ascertain your own contribution to the vicious cycle. Stimulus control techniques do not recommend that the wife avoid dealing with financial issues; rather, she should experiment with discussing money in a different way or at different times that do not cue her husband's newspaper-reading behavior.

> It is quite possible for you to create novel cycles of positive behavior exchange between you and others by assessing and modifying the stimulus value you have in the social environment. Try not to focus on your criticisms of the other person's behavior. Instead try to examine the chain of events that precedes his or her undesirable behavior, particularly where it covaries with your own. Experiment by changing your own behavior in an attempt to "short out" the potentially destructive behavioral circuit. If your new behavior does not effectively produce change in the other person, you may not have intervened early enough in the chain or you may need to experiment with some other behaviors.

One client found it difficult to tolerate conversation with his wife because she constantly complained of headaches and depression and acted helpless (Liberman, 1970). His response was to escape from the house as often as possible, burying himself in his work and interacting with his wife only when her complaints became too difficult to ignore comfortably. Since symptoms in one partner are usually a function of interactions within the marital system, Liberman's therapeutic approach was to have the husband focus on the impact of *his* behavior in maintaining his wife's headaches and depressive style. Since the husband was a very active man, his wife got his undivided attention only when she developed physical symptoms, stopped functioning as a wife and mother, and stayed in bed. At these times he was quite tender and solicitous. The husband experimented by altering his responses, attending to his wife when she manifested adaptive strivings such as independent functioning and efforts at adequate housekeeping and competent child rearing. When he came home from work, he began to inquire about the day's activities rather than flee to his newspaper. He occasionally suggested movies or dinner out to acknowledge her homemaking efforts. As a result, he began to see his wife as a competent, independent person rather than as an unhappy and depressed patient. The husband was instructed not to offer sympathy or reassurance to attempt to terminate her complaints. He was told to stop bringing her medication, calling her doctor for her, or catering to her every need while she was bedridden. He learned instead to acknowledge her distress only briefly and then resume his own activities. Within a few weeks the relationship improved and became more satisfactory to both of them. In summary, the typical chain of behavior that Liberman discovered in this couple was that the wife demanded attention, the husband buried his head in the newspaper, and the wife became afflicted with symptoms. The husband was encouraged to alter the stimulus conditions of his wife's behavior. By altering the response that appears to maintain the symptoms, one partner can effect change in the marital relationship. Liberman's suggestion that the husband attend to and praise adaptive or positive behaviors stems from the notion of positive reinforcement, an operant behavioral technique that will be discussed in the next section.

In order to achieve stimulus control, you may want to avoid situations that trigger the behaviors you are trying to eliminate. Avoidance is usually a temporary solution; it provides a moratorium from stress or temptation while you systematically work the problem through. If the gang can reduce you to putty when they suggest committing some outrageous act, you may want to stop seeing them while you develop more assertive ways of saying no. In other cases avoidance can be a shrewdly maneuvered permanent solution. Since you cannot eat food that is not available, if you are an overeater, you could benefit by not keeping food around the house. One client set a time lock on her refrigerator that allowed her access to her food only at prescribed meal times (Ferster et al., 1962). Obviously, the strategy of avoidance can be carried to an extreme, as in "invalidism," a condition in which the person spends most of his or her time in bed complaining about imagined ailments. Adler (1927) has noted that even this life-style can exert impressive stimulus control over solicitous friends and family who conscientiously care for the invalid.

SELF-CHANGE TECHNIQUE 10:
SELF-REINFORCEMENT

A reinforcer is an event or object that has the effect, when presented or withdrawn, of increasing the probability of the response that precedes it. Reinforcers are present in all ongoing patterns of behavior, although they are best known for their role in behavior modification. For example, the therapist who painstakingly provides the regressed, nonverbal boy with

M & M's whenever he gives the slightest vocal response is using positive reinforcers to reward the child and urge him on toward more and more complex speech. This is known as the intentional application of operant conditioning principles to human behavior.[1] However, reinforcers are not restricted to the therapeutic situation; they are also used in daily life to increase the frequency of desired behaviors. How many people, for instance, would continue to show up at work at 8 A.M. sharp if their employer arbitrarily decided to withhold their paychecks? At a more subtle level, notice the smiles, the appreciative glances, the hugs that encourage a particular kind of response and increase the likelihood that that behavior will be repeated in the future. The therapeutic use of reinforcers is not a question of whether or not to use rewards, since they are unavoidable, but how to use them appropriately and effectively to change behavior.

The use of reinforcing stimuli to change the behavior of others is one of the cornerstones of modern behavior therapy. However, the task here is to examine the use of self-reinforcement, the control and application of rewards to encourage the kinds of changes you seek for yourself.

CHOOSING APPROPRIATE REINFORCERS

One requirement of a functional analysis of behavior is that you define your set of potential positive reinforcers. List the kinds of objects and events that are rewarding to you. For example, some of the reinforcers that motivate people include:

> taking a drive in the country
> attending a sports event
> attending a rock concert
> going to the beach
> painting
> camping
> doing a mechanical problem
> playing cards
> solving a puzzle
> buying new clothes
> taking a shower or bath

[1]Operant conditioning refers to procedures for instituting behavior change based on B. F. Skinner's use of principles of reinforcement. As a science, operant conditioning examines the way that free behavior becomes attached to a specific stimulus through regulation of the consequences that follow the behavior.

playing with a dog
singing
throwing a party
attending a convention
eating dessert
taking a nap
dancing
sitting in the sun
getting a massage
taking photographs
window shopping
helping counsel someone
learning a new skill
daydreaming
going to a movie
making love
reading a book
skiing
making a new friend
earning money
seeing old friends
pleasing a friend
going on a vacation
being alone
watching television
going to a restaurant
listening to the radio

To generate your own list of reinforcers, ask yourself what you enjoy doing. A useful reinforcer in a self-therapy program should be both appealing and accessible. A three-month trip to Australia might not be realistic given your financial resources and a date with Miss America has little hope of being realized. According to Watson and Tharp (1977), a key question to ask yourself is "Do I really think I will stop performing the undesirable behavior or start performing the desirable one—just because I will gain such and such a reward?"

Premack (1965) showed that there is nothing inherently magical about a reinforcer. It is potent only because it is a behavior or activity that is preferred over some alternative. In effect, any behavior that is already in your repertoire and that you would select in a free-choice situation can be used effectively to reinforce the low-frequency behavior that is your target. Most kids would rather swim than take a bath. Swimming could thus be used to reward taking baths. Likewise, if you like to talk on the telephone but detest cleaning your room, make telephone calls contingent on cleaning the room. In short, you refrain from engaging in a desirable, frequent activity unless you first perform the less likely behavior you wish to increase.

Sometimes it is better to use a reinforcer that is a special object or event, something you otherwise might not treat yourself to, such as spending a day in the country or attending an expensive concert. This is particularly effective if you are reluctant to spoil yourself with free time or other gifts of the spirit. On the other hand, it is usually more effective to employ reinforcers that are already familiar to you.

It is important to include verbal self-praise along with tangible reinforcers. As children we learned much of our complex behavior by responding to the praise, affection, and hugs of our parents. However, the principle applies equally well to adults. Congratulate yourself: "You've done well! Take a bow!" You deserve praise for accomplishing what previously seemed to be an overwhelming goal. Abundant praise and approval do not spoil people; what spoils them is the inappropriate use of reinforcers. The use of verbal reinforcers will be examined further in the chapter on cognitive self-change techniques.

The reinforcer you choose to change a behavior need not be large or exotic. Sometimes information feedback can function as an alternative to more tangible rewards. One case describes a 59-year-old woman who suffered from an extreme fear of knives (Leitenberg, Agras, Thompson, & Wright, 1968). Four years prior to seeking help it had occurred to her that she could easily kill her bothersome grandchild! Gradually her fear grew and became more obsessive until she literally could not look at sharp knives, and so she totally avoided her kitchen. Among other treatment goals, the therapist attended directly to the knife phobia. A steak knife with a sharp five-inch blade was placed in a drawer. The woman was encouraged to practice opening the drawer to look at the knife for as long as she could without experiencing much discomfort. Whenever she became uncomfortable, she was to close the drawer. Her therapy program consisted of four practice sessions a day; she opened the drawer ten times per session. There was a 45-second interval between each trial. By noting how many seconds the drawer was open, she could monitor her performance and reinforce her progress. The feedback alone provided enough motivation to improve. When she began the program, she could tolerate only four seconds of exposure to the knife. Improving steadily, the woman advanced to 120 seconds after 45 days, and her fear disappeared.

A final principle to consider in selecting an appropriate reinforcer is the principle of *satiation.* It is conceivable that over time or in sufficient quantity some reinforcers may lose their ability to modify your behavior.

Generally speaking, large and significant rewards are more powerful behavior-change agents than small, trivial ones. However, if you reinforce each half hour of studying with a box of chocolates, you are likely to end up with a painful stomach ache and an aversion to your reinforcer! Satiation has been deliberately used for therapeutic purposes—for example, with a hospitalized woman who compulsively hoarded towels (Ayllon, 1963). This woman plagued the hospital staff by hoarding at least 20 towels in her room and on her person at any one time. When other interventions failed, Ayllon resorted to encouraging the hospital staff to regularly flood the patient with towels. At one point in this process she had over 600 towels in her room. As she became satiated with towels their reinforcing value began to diminish, and her towel collecting was reduced to a modest number per day.

CONTINGENCY MANAGEMENT

People often use their potential reinforcers in destructive or random, indiscriminant ways. They laugh at their children when they are spilling food or misbehaving. They smile and say "That's okay" when they mean to reject or refuse. They go on buying binges when the mood strikes them and come to regret their frivolity. However, by applying them discriminatingly, people can use these attractive, highly rewarding behaviors to encourage or maintain minimally occurring or deficit behaviors. The process of coupling problem behaviors with reinforcers to produce behavior change is called *contingency management* (Homme, 1965).

It is essential to the achievement of your goals that reinforcers be presented at the proper time. Remember when you told yourself "I'll do the ironing as soon as this program is over," only to find that this program was followed by that program and the ironing remained crumpled in the cupboard? Or consider the case of the harried executive who comes home to fall into the receptive arms of a martini. In these examples, a crucial principle of reinforcement theory has been violated so that the very behaviors that might be desirable to increase—namely, ironing and relaxing—are not appreciably affected. Since television viewing is preferable to ironing, the ironing remains undone; since relaxation is the reward that follows the martini, the hassled executive may be propelling himself along the road to alcoholism. The ingredients for potent behavioral control are available. However, the sequence of the events is inappropriate for achieving the desired goals. If you tell yourself that, after you have ironed a prescribed number of articles of clothing, you will reward yourself with an hour of television, it will increase your ironing behavior, since ironing is *followed* by a reinforcing event. Likewise, the executive might say to herself "I really want to learn how to relax. And I like to drink a martini after work. Rather than allowing myself to become dependent on my martini to relax me, when I come home, I will first sit down and relax. Then I will reward myself for relaxing with a martini!" The fundamental principle in contingency management is that those behaviors that immediately *precede* the administration of rewards will increase. The effective use of self-reinforcement techniques requires that you follow desirable, deficit behaviors with reinforcers in order to increase the probability of their occurrence in the future.

If reinforcers are to have any impact at all, they should follow the response as closely in time as possible. Such advice is commonly violated —for example, by the mother who says to her obstreperous child "Wait until your father gets home!" This approach not only labels the father as the punitive agent in the eyes of his child, a role he will have difficulty escaping, but also is unsound behavior modification. The same problem exists with the promise of a reward, such as "If you make your bed every morning, Santa Claus will bring you a special present." With the passage of time the link between the original behavior and the reward or punishment becomes vague, and the impact on behavior change diminishes accordingly.

SELECTING TARGET BEHAVIORS

The selection of a target behavior in your self-reinforcement program is also important in determining the success of the therapeutic process. Many people tend to set unrealistic expectations for themselves and then become disillusioned and disheartened when they fall short of their grandiose goals. Weight reduction campaigns that depend on the exertion of will power frequently fail because the person selects an unrealistic goal. When the target weight is not achieved, the individual becomes convinced of the hopelessness of his or her situation.

One out-of-shape woman set her sights on improving her physical condition through jogging (Kau & Fisher, 1974). Since exercise was not intrinsically rewarding to her, she enlisted her husband's help to provide reinforcement. Her goal was 40 points per week, based on the point system developed in Cooper's (1970) *The New Aerobics*. Jogging one mile in 8 to 10 minutes, for example, is worth four points. You receive more points for jogging further in a specified period of time. At the start, she was reinforced for jogging every day irrespective of the points she earned toward her goal. As a reinforcer, she could choose a weekly social activity from a list—for example, going to a movie or going out to dinner. If she did not jog every day she earned no social activity at the end of the week. Her husband also reinforced her with 25 cents immediately after she jogged. After an initial increase in her exercising, she began to level off at about 23 aerobic points per week. At this time she changed the system; she earned a reinforcer for accumulating at least 25 points per week rather than for running every day. She also dropped the payment from her husband, which had by now lost its effectiveness. With this new self-change program she was on her way to reaching her ultimate goal in ten weeks. At that point she had lost some weight, was more energetic, and had more stamina, so that the jogging had become self-reinforcing. A graph of her progress is shown below.

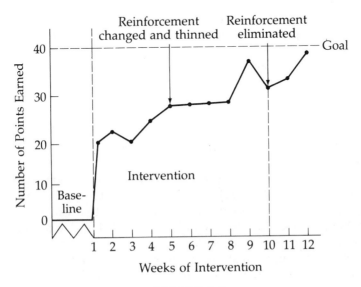

FIGURE 3-5

Reinforcement of exercising. From "Self-Modification of Exercise Behavior," by M. L. Kau and J. Fisher, Journal of Behavior Therapy and Experimental Psychiatry, *1974, 5, 213–214. Reprinted by permission of the author and publisher, Pergamon Press, Ltd.*

It is important that you try to select target goals that are within your reach. You can always work toward a more difficult goal once you have achieved some success with an easier one. If physical conditioning is your aim, select a reasonable goal, such as 15 minutes of exercise each evening, as your first target. Once you have reached this goal, set a new one and continue with your program. If you want to increase the rate at which you study, choose a simple goal such as reading one chapter per day. If you are unsuccessful, do not despair. Merely change the requirements and reward yourself for smaller successes. When you reinforce yourself for small incremental changes in the direction of your goal, you are engaged in the process known as *shaping*.

SHAPING BEHAVIOR

Shaping helps to conceptualize some of the complex processes of human and animal learning. The trainer of an acrobatic porpoise does not wait for the animal to do a double flip and somersault before rewarding it. Instead, he waits for a small movement in the desired direction and rewards that. The next time, he rewards a slightly more complex movement. A showy combination of flips and somersaults must be broken down into discrete behavioral units before the animal can perform successfully. With the possible exception of some addictive and dangerous behaviors, you should try to encourage a desired response or discourage an undesired response gradually. When a person claims that his or her lack of success was due to lack of will power, you can usually translate this to mean that there was difficulty in shaping (Watson & Tharp, 1977).

Shaping your behavior may require that you set up hierarchies of increasingly more demanding tasks and reinforce each task along the way to your final destination. Begin at the level of your current skills and systematically insist on a small gradual improvement prior to each new reinforcement. It is crucial that you begin at a level that is not intimidating or overly challenging and that you withhold reinforcement when no progress is made. For example, the shy man who experiences heterosexual anxiety may select a shaping procedure to reach his target of being able to comfortably meet and relate to diverse women. He must first arrange various subgoals to form a hierarchy, such as sitting down next to a woman in the library, initiating a discussion with her, and, finally, asking her for a date. Since each task is important to achieving his goal, he can justifiably reward himself in a meaningful way for completing each rung up the ladder. Rehm and Marston (1968) have achieved considerable success with clients complaining of interpersonal anxieties in just this way.

The application of shaping has proved invaluable in the treatment of sexual dysfunction. In the last few years a number of manuals on the behavioral treatment of symptoms such as premature ejaculation, erectile failure (impotence), and nonorgasmic conditions have been published (Kaplan, 1974; Masters & Johnson, 1970), and sex clinics utilizing shaping procedures have proliferated.[2] Although most of these techniques require the active participation of both partners in a treatment program, some have been adopted for use by individuals.

LoPiccolo and Lobitz (1972) describe a step-by-step procedure for nonorgasmic women that can be adapted for use in a self-therapy program.

---

[2]The success rates for behavioral treatments of sexual dysfunctions have been impressive, although they are based primarily on uncontrolled case studies. For example, Masters and Johnson (1970) and others report treatment effectiveness at over 90% for premature ejaculation.

Their exercises are for women who have never been able to achieve orgasm (primary inorgasm) or have not achieved orgasm in some time (secondary inorgasm). Of course, there are many reasons why a woman might have difficulty achieving orgasm, including some physiological problems, lack of information, lack of experience, lack of opportunity, anxiety, and fear of losing control. A behavioral self-therapy approach encourages the woman to become more comfortable with her own body, to discover her own sources of sexual pleasure, before focusing on her sexual relationships.

> The first step in the program is for you to become familiar and comfortable with your own sexual parts. Begin by standing naked in front of a full-length mirror and looking at yourself. Using a hand mirror, examine your vagina, clitoris, and the entire genital area until you have a clear conception of the way you are constructed. You might find an illustrated reference book of human anatomy useful to help identify your sexual parts. Many women never take the time to explore themselves in this way.

Masturbation is a universally practiced yet pervasively condemned form of sexual activity. Masturbation is not only a normal, healthy behavior; it is also a helpful adjunct in treating primary orgasmic dysfunction in women (LoPiccolo & Lobitz, 1972). Recent studies have found that virtually all men and up to 85% of women masturbate to orgasm at some point in their lives (Dearborn, 1967). Since masturbation is much more likely than intercourse to produce orgasm, it is a particularly appropriate method for encouraging orgasmic potential.

> The second step of the shaping procedure is to tactually explore your entire body. Although you may experience some apprehension at first, try to become comfortable with the idea of masturbation by touching yourself in the genital area. When you feel comfortable looking at and touching every part of your body, try to discover special areas where you experience the greatest sensations of pleasure. Most of you will find that your clitoris is especially sensitive to touch and produces more intense feelings of pleasure than the vagina itself.

> Next, begin to manually manipulate the genital area where you experience the most pleasure. Practice different kinds of pressure and stroking to maximize your own pleasure. Try changing the pressure and speed of manipulation. Give yourself lots of time and masturbate until "something happens" (LoPiccolo & Lobitz, 1972) or until you become sore. This may take up to 30 minutes. If you still have trouble reaching orgasm manually, try using

erotic fantasies, pornographic literature, vaginal lubricants, or an electric vibrator to enhance your reaction.

By practicing several times a week most primary inorgasmic women will achieve orgasm through masturbation using this shaping procedure (McGovern, Stewart, & LoPiccolo, 1975). Once a woman is able to masturbate to orgasm in private, the focus in behavior-change techniques shifts to generalizing these experiences to settings with a partner. If you have accomplished the goal of orgasm by masturbation or if you are one of the many women who have difficulty experiencing orgasm only with a partner, the next procedural step consists of masturbating while your partner observes you. This helps you to overcome your resistance to letting go in front of your partner and to teach him how to be helpful in facilitating your sexual pleasure. Invite your partner to participate in your orgasm by encouraging him to stimulate you manually. Remember what gives you the most pleasure and try to teach these strokes and touches to him. In effect, you teach your partner to do for you what you have successfully been doing for yourself. LoPiccolo claims that many women have a phobic response to fully expressing their orgasms in what might seem to be an embarrassing, public way. If this is true for you, you might try role playing an imagined orgasm in front of your partner, deliberately exaggerating your moans, screams, and cries. Keep the act going and your anxiety should disappear.

LoPiccolo's treatment program in its entirety consists of a continuing hierarchy of steps leading to the end goal of coitus with orgasm. Because the target goal is too imposing and anxiety-arousing to tackle directly, the shaping procedure, where closer approximations to the target behavior are reinforced, is more effective and more appropriate.

CONTRACTS

Self-reward techniques can be advantageously combined with self-monitoring and record-keeping procedures. The data that are available on a graph provide a clear record of your progress or your lack of it, as well as indicating whether or not your reward has been earned. The use of charts or graphs for monitoring and reinforcing your behavior introduces the system of *contracts*. Contracts are written documents that specify the kinds of behaviors you want to modify and the reinforcement contingencies you will use to reward these behaviors. They have been used extensively, and with significant success, to alter the problem behavior of children and adults alike (Patterson, 1971). The importance of an official-looking contract is that it is more difficult to ignore a signed paper than a verbal commitment. Imagine, for example, that your target goal is to become more punctual. Your contract might look something like this:

Number of late appointments during week	Contingency
0	Going out to dinner on the weekend
1	Going out to lunch
2 or more	Nothing

There are four important elements to consider in a good contract for self-change. First, explicitly describe the precise behaviors in which you are interested. If physical fitness is your goal, describe each exercise or athletic activity you intend to perform. Second, list the rewards and privileges you intend to use as reinforcers for complying with your contract goals. You may want to reinforce yourself with a steak dinner for achieving a goal of one hour's worth of physical exercise and with less extravagant meals for more meager performances. Obviously, you reward yourself after performances, not after making promises to perform. Third, list the sanctions you intend to impose on yourself for failing to meet your target goals. You may decide that having boiled eggs for dinner is sanction enough for lack of compliance with your goals. The last suggestion is that you include a bonus reward for high-level or consistent compliance with your contract goals (Stuart, 1971). You may want to reward yourself with something special for joining a basketball team. Remember that the contract is flexible. It can be renegotiated when it has outlived its usefulness.

The importance of reinforcing responses as closely in time to their occurrence as possible has already been emphasized. However, there are times when this is not possible. In this case, points or tokens can be used to plug the gap between the behavior and the long-range reinforcement. Tokens are "conditional" reinforcers because they have become associated with reinforcing consequences over time. They are exchanged at later dates for more tangible and obvious rewards. Money, for example, is a universal token. So-called "token economies" have frequently been established in institutions such as hospitals, schools, and prisons in order to encourage socialized behavior (Ayllon & Azrin, 1968; Kazdin, 1975). By giving yourself points or tokens for meeting your target subgoals, you bridge the gap between the behavior and the ultimate reinforcer. You can eventually convert the points into more desirable rewards. A shy man, for instance, decided to reward himself with one point every time he interacted with a new woman without stammering. Once he had earned ten points, he treated himself to a skiing trip. It is important to note that this contingency was determined prior to initiating the program.

In Table 3-3 we see an example of a contract that a professor used to reduce his coffee- and cola-drinking behavior. In this case points were based on engaging in the undesirable behaviors. This contract also demonstrates how friends can be involved and promise to supply positive or negative consequences for certain performances.

TABLE 3-3
Self-Contracting to Decrease Caffeine Intake

Behavior	Sunday	Monday	Tuesday	Wednesday	Thursday	Friday	Saturday
Cups of Coffee							
Cola							
Total							

Note: Each cup of coffee or cola consumed = one point
Consequences: 0–14 pts/week—treat myself to a $10 purchase;
15–21 pts/week—receive a body massage from wife;
22–28 pts/week—no reward or punishment;
29–35 pts/week—cook meals and wash dinner dishes for a week;
over 35 pts/week—give wife $50 to spend on clothes for herself.

A more complicated contract is illustrated by the case of a 21-year-old man who complained that his life was quickly deteriorating: his school performance was declining, he never seemed to have sufficient time to complete a task, he was tense and guilty, he went to bed late and slept poorly, he skipped meals and had lost 20 pounds, and his personal habits in general were degenerating (Whitman & Dussault, 1976). First the man drew up a list of behavior goals. These are listed in Table 3-4. Then he picked some reinforcers that were meaningful to him. They seemed to fall in four categories:

Group I	being with girlfriend	25 points/day
Group II	eating a meal out	10 points/day
	reading the newspaper	5 points/day
	reading other nonrequired reading	10 points/day
Group III	listening to the radio or stereo	5 points/day
	watching television	10 points/day
	talking on the phone	5 points/day
Group IV	taking a drive for pleasure	20 points/occurrence
	walking for exercise or pleasure	5 points/occurrence

The points each behavioral goal earned and the points needed to receive a reinforcer were determined by the relative subjective importance of

TABLE 3-4
*Target Behaviors, Their Operational
Definitions, Priority of Importance and
Number of Points Received by Subject for
Achieving Criterion*

Priority Group	Target Behavior	Operational Definition	Points for Criterion Achieved
	Study time:		
	Course A 4–6 hr/wk.	Time spent reading,	20
	Course B 3–5 hr/wk.	writing, and researching	20
	Course C 3–5 hr/wk.	for course assignments	20
	Course D 4–6 hr/wk.	and preparation	20
	*Class attendance	Physical presence at	
	—100% of time	scheduled class	20
I	Class preparation	Completion of required	
	—100% of time	reading and assignments due for the class	20
	Promptness of arrival:		
	Class—100% of time	Arriving at class or work before starting time	20
	Work— 100% of time		20
	Write home—1 time/ week	Writing on at least one side of 9 × 11 paper and mailing letter to parents	20
	Miscellaneous		20
	Work (maximum time on job)	Physical presence on job site	
	Part-time job 16 hr/week		15
	Odd jobs 5 hr/week		15
II	Sleep 6 hr/day minimum	Time spent in bed sleeping or trying to sleep	15
	Eating meals:		
	Breakfast 7 times/ week	Consumption of juice and toast and cereal or eggs	15
	Lunch 7 times/week	Consumption of liquid and one or more sandwiches	15
	Dinner 7 times/ week	Consumption of liquid, prepared meat or fish, and vegetable or soup	15
	Up at alarm 6 times/week	Arising with alarm, and not going back to bed	10
	Shower 3 times/ week	Washing with soap and water the entire body, excluding hair, and subsequent drying	10

TABLE 3-4 (continued)
Target Behaviors, Their Operational
Definitions, Priority of Importance and
Number of Points Received by Subject for
Achieving Criterion

Priority Group	Target Behavior	Operational Definition	Points for Criterion Achieved
III	Wash hair 1 time/ week	Shampooing and rinsing hair	10
	Shave 3 times/week	Removing all facial beard and trimming sideburns	10
	Groceries 1 time/ week	Buying all staples necessary for preparation of meals	10
	Social contact:	Being in social situation for ½ hr or more	10
	With males 3 times/week		10
	With females 2 times/week (other than girl friend)		10
	Miscellaneous		10
IV	House duties: Make bed 1 time/day	Tucking in sheets, putting blanket, pillow and sleepware in place	5
	Pick up 1 time/ day	Placing all clothes in appropriate place; drawer, closet, or laundry bag	5
	Dishes 1 time/ day	Washing, drying and putting away all dishes used that day	5
	Laundry 1 time/ week	Separating, washing, drying and folding all clothes; returning to proper place	5
	Ironing 1 time/ bi-weekly	Ironing of shirts, pants and other miscellaneous articles of clothing	5
	General cleaning 1 time/week	Scrubbing sink, using dust mop, taking out trash and newspapers	5

*Because of the normal fluctuation of behavioral requirements during a given week, some of the goals are stated in terms of percentages rather than in terms of absolute frequencies.

From "Self-Control Through the Use of a Token Economy," by T. L. Whitman and P. Dussault, Journal of Behavior Therapy and Experimental Psychiatry, 1976, 7, 161–166. Reprinted by permission of the publisher, Pergamon Press, Ltd.

the items to the man and their frequency of occurrence. He obtained this information in part by recording his activities for four weeks and keeping a baseline. Once he began the program, he decided that points earned in Group I could only be spent on a Group-I reinforcer, since being with his girlfriend was far and away his favorite prize. The other three groups were regarded as interchangeable. He also did not allow himself to spend points that he had not yet earned, nor could he save up points for the following week. By using this comprehensive contract, the man was able to bring some order into his life, and he improved in all categories.

One would hope that, once behaviors are learned and developed, they will become effortless and self-sustaining without programmed reinforcement. This is often the case with many prosocial responses such as dating, studying, and losing weight, adaptive behaviors that generate their own positive consequences and become intrinsically pleasant. On the other hand, washing dishes and taking out the garbage may never become too intrinsically satisfying and may require more constant contingency management. You can reduce your self-reinforcement schedule—that is, reward yourself less frequently—after your target goal has been achieved. Intermittent schedules of reinforcement are especially likely to maintain behavior change over long periods of time. After all, gamblers keep coming back to the roulette wheel, which pays off all too seldom. The same principle applies to the maintenance of self-change.

SELF-CHANGE TECHNIQUE 11:
SELF-PUNISHMENT

The use of aversive stimuli to elicit change has a firmly entrenched role in psychology. To the general public reference to this method generally conjures up images of demonic doctors zapping their clients with electric shock. In Stanley Kubrick's film *A Clockwork Orange*, for example, a young hoodlum is forcefully injected with a nausea-producing drug and coerced into watching filmed acts of violence to change his antisocial behavior. The actual successes of punishment in recorded behavior change, however, are not nearly so spectacular.

Of course, the use of punishment to modify the behavior of others carries monumental ethical implications. In one particularly egregious example, an American psychiatrist in South Viet Nam attempted to eliminate patient apathy by giving patients a choice of either working in the fields or receiving electroconvulsive ("shock") therapy (Cotter, 1970)! Fortunately, most therapists who use aversive control devices, such as electric shock or chemical agents that induce nausea, *are* cognizant of ethical issues and abide by a concrete code of ethics that ensures that clients voluntarily submit to treatment, that safeguards are taken to ensure their ultimate safety, and that aversive techniques are used only as a last resort.

Psychologists have had some success using aversive techniques in eliminating behavior that is demonstrably harmful to the client, such as the head banging or face scratching of the autistic child (Lovaas, Koegel, Simmons, & Long, 1973). Chemical treatment and electric shock have also been used to treat maladaptive behavior that has proved resistant to other procedures, such as alcoholism (Davidson, 1974), sexual fetishes (Marks & Gelder, 1967), and even uncontrollable sneezing (Kushner, 1968). Milder forms of punishment, such as prescribed tasks or loss of privileges, have been used effectively with numerous behavioral problems (Patterson, 1971). Although ethical concerns are less obvious when aversive methods are applied either to a volunteer or to oneself than when they are applied to an unsuspecting subject, punishment is probably still best considered as the treatment of last choice.

Self-punishment can bring about rapid behavior change. A variety of creative and grandiose self-punitive schemes utilizing intricate apparati have been popularized. For example, there are machines that blow exhaled smoke back into the smoker's face (Lichtenstein, Harris, Birchler, Wahl, & Schmal, 1973) and cigarette lighters that contain a noxiously malodorous chemical. Self-administered shock has been found to have some impact on smoking, alcoholism, and sexual deviations (McGuire & Vallance, 1964). However, these devices may not be suitable for the average person who conscientiously wishes to work on his or her own problems. Most people rely on their own good sense and are not particularly willing to inflict much pain on themselves. The effects of these devices are often temporary, and there is one other issue to consider. Many of us have been brought up in the school of "sin and suffer." Consequently, self-punishment in the wake of symptomatic behavior may seem like a just reward and, paradoxically, *increase* the future likelihood of the behavior.

Now that you are aware of some of the disadvantages of self-punishment techniques, you can consider some applications of the procedure that may prove effective for you. There are two general categories of self-punishment techniques. In the first category, an aversive stimulus is immediately presented following the undesirable response. In the second category, a reward or positive reinforcer is *removed* following an undesirable response. As in the other self-change techniques we've discussed, it is important to be specific in detailing the target response that you wish to decrease and the particular contingencies that you intend to establish between behavior and punishment.

THE USE OF AVERSIVE CONSEQUENCES

> To use self-punishment directly, choose an aversive consequence that is easily administered, that is sufficiently potent to terminate the behavior it follows, and that does not have an enduring effect. Ask yourself what negative consequence is apt to discourage or reduce your problem behavior. Settle on a punishing consequence that you will be willing to deliver to yourself. Smokers, for instance, have been helped by committing themselves to the aversive contingency of tearing up a dollar bill after each cigarette consumed (Axelrod, Hall, Weis, & Rohrer, 1971).

For individuals who are troubled by obsessive ruminations,[3] Mahoney's (1972) innovative technique involving the use of a rubber band worn around the wrist has proven effective. After each obsessional thought, the individual is required to snap the elastic against his or her wrist. This technique has also been successfully used to eliminate self-destructive habits that have not been receptive to more positive approaches. It was applied, for example, to the case of a 15-year-old girl who had been compulsively pulling her hair for 2½ years (Mastellone, 1974). The habit was so serious that the pulling, which occurred while she spoke on the telephone or watched television or read, had resulted in bald spots on her scalp. She was instructed to wear a loose-fitting rubber band on one wrist and to administer a stinging snap to the underside of her wrist as punishment for hair pulling. Each time she pulled a strand of hair out, or had an urge to do so, she used the rubber band. This simple intervention proved effective in eliminating the habit. It is, of course, difficult to know if the effectiveness of the treatment was due to the minor pain of the snapping rubber band or to increased awareness of her relatively unconscious habit for which the rubber band became a cue. In a similar case of compulsive hair-pulling (trichotillomania), an embarrassed man significantly reduced his habit by following his therapist's instructions and mailing any hairs he pulled to him (Bayer, 1972)! In yet another case of hair pulling, a woman did 15

---

[3]Obsessions are persistent and repetitive thoughts that can be neither terminated nor controlled. They may be mundane, such as the consistent subvocal repetition of a popular tune, or they may be more disturbing, such as thoughts of your plane crashing or a loved one becoming involved in an accident.

sit-ups at home each time she pulled her hair or had the urge to do so (MacNeil & Thomas, 1976).

> After you have settled on a specific aversive consequence, use it immediately and consistently. Parking tickets are only moderately effective at discouraging illegal parking because you only get caught a percentage of the time. The punishment must follow the target behavior each and every time. Invoke the negative consequence as early in the behavioral chain as possible. If you want to discourage late-night snacking, punish the act of opening the refrigerator. If you wait until you reinforce yourself with chocolate cake and whipped cream, your task of reducing the unwanted behavior will be much more difficult.

WITHDRAWAL OF REINFORCERS

The second category of self-punishment involves withdrawing positive rewards following an undesirable behavior. When positive reinforcers are removed for a prescribed period of time, the procedure is called "time-out" (from reinforcement). Sometimes these rewards are social reinforcers —for example, when the young child screams and has tantrums to get the attention of the adults in the room. If the child is removed from the room for a short period of time, the social reinforcers in the form of attention are no longer available, and the tantrums will tend to dissipate. In fact, consistently ignoring negative behaviors proves to be a powerful change technique. Time-out has been shown to be effective in altering antisocial behaviors (Burchard & Tyler, 1965), self-stimulation (Pendergrass, 1972), and facial tics (Barrett, 1962). It seems to be important to withdraw reinforcers consistently and for only brief periods of time.

A "response-cost" intervention, used quite often in token economy programs, involves the loss of a certain amount of reinforcers or the payment of a penalty. For example, patients may be asked to pay fines for their misbehavior using their accumulated tokens. Unlike time-out, there is no time restriction with response cost. A common example of response cost is the payment of fines for driving violations. Loss of tokens or privileges as a mild punishment can be a very effective behavior-change invention, although not much empirical research has accumulated on response-cost procedures. One potential problem in applying the technique is the risk of losing more points or tokens than you have earned.

> Be sure that the penalty you pay for undesirable behavior is something you can afford to lose. You can punish yourself by withdrawing reinforcers such as watching television, eating

dessert, or going to the movies. If you fail to do your exercises in the morning, deny yourself the privilege of your daily martini. As a penalty for not hanging up your clothes, you might agree to pick up your clothes from the floor plus vacuum the entire house.

A sophisticated contract for changing your behavior could easily include a punishment component.

> If you cannot get yourself to your appointments on time, you may want to include self-punishment in your contract. For example, you might contract to reward yourself with an hour of television viewing for arriving within 15 minutes of the appointed time, permit yourself no television if you arrive between 15 and 30 minutes late, and suffer the punishment of washing five windows in your home if you arrive more than 30 minutes late. To discourage smoking, a notoriously difficult target behavior, you might reduce the positive consequences of smoking by going to the basement to smoke and increase the negative consequences by donating some money to charity each time you finish a pack of cigarettes. The principle is simple enough: first define your behavioral goal and then formalize a contract incorporating both positive and negative consequences. This will encourage progress toward your goal.

SUGGESTIONS FOR USING SELF-PUNISHMENT

Should you settle on self-punishment techniques, be certain that the new behavior receives an increasing number of positive reinforcers so that the punishment regime can eventually be supplanted. Reinforcement for your behavior that arises spontaneously from the environment is especially potent. An increase in social interactions, for example, will probably be maintained easily since most people ultimately find it pleasant and rewarding to interact with others.

> It is not sufficient to punish negative behavior. You also need to encourage alternative, more desirable behaviors by reinforcing them. For each target behavior you choose to punish, try to identify an incompatible, positive behavior to encourage and reward. If you have decided to follow your compulsive talking with aversive consequences or penalties, try to increase your listening skills by arranging reinforcing contingencies for listening behavior.

Sometimes self-punishment and self-reinforcement can be effective when used in fantasy. In one interesting case, a 27-year-old anxious and depressed woman complained about her very ritualized performance of household chores (Wisocki, 1970). She would spend literally hours folding and refolding clothes, making beds, and putting groceries away and would become very upset by any small change in her routine. She would take five or ten minutes to fold a single item of clothing, take it to a drawer, return and recheck the item, and often fold it once more. The treatment she received punished her compulsive clothes folding and reinforced incompatible responses. She was told to close her eyes, relax and imagine the following scene:

> You're in the laundry room. There is a pile of clothing in front of you. You take one thing . . . it's a towel . . . and you fold it once and put it aside. You look over at it and think that it's not quite wrinkle-free and you decide to refold it. As soon as you have that thought, you get a queasy feeling in the pit of your stomach. Vomit comes up into your mouth. It tastes bitter and you swallow it back down. Your throat burns. But you take the towel and start to refold it anyway. Just as you do that, your stomach churns and vomit comes out of your mouth—all over the clean clothes, your hands, the table, over everything. You keep vomiting and vomiting. Your eyes are watering; your nose has mucus coming out of it. You see vomit all over everything. You think that you should never have tried to fold that towel a second time—a few slight wrinkles make no difference—and you run from the room. Immediately you feel better. You go and clean yourself up and smell fresh and feel wonderful [p. 236].[4]

The woman practiced visualizing the scene whenever she thought about folding clothes, prepared to fold clothes, or performed the folding. As she imagined the details of the scene several times a day, the problem behavior began to develop an aversive quality. After visualizing an aversive scene, she would imagine refraining from the folding ordeal and engaging in an antagonistic behavior, such as folding an item only once, stacking clothes quickly, and closing a drawer without rechecking it. Immediately afterward she would indulge in a reinforcing fantasy, such as practicing

[4]From "Treatment of Obsessive-Compulsive Behavior by Covert Sensitization and Covert Reinforcement: A Case Report," by P. A. Wisocki, *Journal of Behavior Therapy and Experimental Psychiatry*, 1970, *1*, 233–239. Reprinted by permission of the publisher, Pergamon Press, Ltd.

ballet, drinking tea, eating Italian food, playing golf, or taking a walk in the woods. After eight two-hour sessions of this covert-sensitization procedure, the woman overcame her difficulty. She folded clothes quickly and spent minimal time on housework.

The pairing of unpleasant scenes (usually nausea and vomiting) with scenes of an unwanted behavior has also been effective with cases of alcoholism, obesity, and other maladaptive habits (Cautela, 1967). The use of reinforcement of incompatible behaviors to acquire a proportional decrease in an aversive behavior was discussed in the section on self-reinforcement. In the next section, the use of alternative behaviors as a specific self-change strategy will be discussed more fully.

SELF-CHANGE TECHNIQUE 12: ALTERNATE RESPONSES

Behavioral self-change techniques function by encouraging and sustaining desired behaviors or discouraging and inhibiting unwanted behaviors. These interventions may consist of restructuring preceding environmental events, as in stimulus control, or altering the contingencies of existent behaviors, as in self-reinforcement and self-punishment. This section will describe the use of alternate responses as substitutes for unwanted behaviors. Two types of alternate response will be considered. The first type of alternate response inhibits or slows down the series of actions that culminates in the problem or target behavior. The second kind of alternate response, introduced briefly in previous sections, is the use of responses that are directly incompatible with the behavior to be eliminated.

INHIBITING AND DISTRACTING RESPONSES

Inhibiting responses involve the introduction of pauses in an established chain of events in order to establish opportunities to avoid the temptation of automatically continuing with a well-ingrained yet aversive behavioral pattern.

If you are trying to diet, interrupt your compulsive eating pattern by putting your eating utensils down on the table between each bite of food. Concentrate on chewing the food in your mouth thoroughly before swallowing. Pick up your fork for another bite only after you have swallowed that mouthful. The effectiveness of the interruption is based on the probability that, as an overeater, you probably eat automatically, without paying much attention to your food. As you slow down your eating, you begin to attend more fully to your eating behavior. Perhaps more importantly, you increase the interval between the response (eating) and the reinforcement (swallowing the food).

Inhibiting responses can function as helpful distractors from fear or anxiety. People who are afraid of flying, for example, a fear shared to some extent by about 25 million Americans, can decrease their anxiety by substituting irrelevant thoughts and activities for more fear-inducing preoccupations. Smith (1977) recommends making use of the "orienting reflex," the automatic way in which attention is drawn to interesting and novel stimuli, to inhibit fear. A flight-phobic man can distract himself from his discomfort by deliberately rating the attractiveness of the cabin attendants, guessing the occupations of the passengers, counting objects in the plane, and taking deep breaths as in the relaxation response. Likewise, the acrophobic woman may be able to inhibit the anxiety she feels while standing on a bridge or overpass by focusing on some activity, such as pitching stones into the water below.

Men have been using distracting responses for centuries to reduce the heightened sexual arousal that leads to premature ejaculation. Thoughts of neutral events, such as football games and reading assignments, may help to postpone passing the threshold of excitability. Masters and Johnson (1970) recommend the "squeeze technique" for dealing with premature ejaculation. In this approach, the woman is encouraged to help her partner diminish the sensation of imminent orgasm by placing her thumb on the underside of the penis and her first two fingers on either side of the coronal ridge on the upper side of the penis. Application of rather strong pressure for three or four seconds, followed by sudden release, will cause the man to experience an immediate loss of the urge to ejaculate. The squeeze technique can be applied several times during the course of love-making to extend the period of mutual pleasure. The Semans stop-start technique is another alternate-response intervention for eliminating premature ejaculation (Kaplan, 1974). In this technique the man is encouraged to concentrate on the sensations preceding orgasm as his partner stimulates him. As his arousal increases, the partner ceases stimulation until he improves control. The exercise is repeated until he acquires more and more control over his orgasms. Both the stop-start and the squeeze technique have been extremely successful in treating premature ejaculation.

Inhibiting responses are also useful in behavior chains involving anger or frustration. Shelton and Ackerman (1974) suggest the technique of warning others when you feel ready to explode. A warning by the anger-prone individual might be a telephone call from work saying "I've had a rough day. Please have a calm house available when I come home." This same person can also manage his or her anger better by taking a few minutes at home alone to unwind before interacting with other family members. Wise and sensitive family members will graciously give those few minutes rather than meeting the volatile kin with interpersonal sparks. Physical exercise or long walks are other alternate responses for dealing with frustration. These actions help to absorb tension that has already developed and to forestall a more impulsive, destructive expression of emotion. In the same vein, couples who want to quell arguments may adopt a "cooling off" period, a deliberate pause before responding (Bach, 1969).

Here are some guidelines for selecting appropriate distractors or orienting stimuli (Smith, 1977):

> Prepare your distracting responses ahead of time. Do not wait until you are actually confronted by the feared situation. Have a sufficient number of responses available to carry you through the situation. Use responses that are novel and interesting. Try to involve all of your senses—seeing, hearing, smelling, touching, tasting. Use activities that take some mental effort, that make you think and make choices. Consider enlisting the aid of a friend who can distract you by interacting with you, asking you questions, and providing you with challenges.

Distracting responses can be used in almost any anxiety-provoking situation to help you cope, as long as your total attention is not required for survival. For instance, psychological experimentation has shown distractors to be useful in minimizing pain from physical trauma (Kanfer & Goldfoot, 1966). If you try to *not* attend to the pain you are experiencing, you may in fact feel less pain. The response of pain or anxiety is heavily influenced by your individual expectations and interpretations of ambiguous stimuli. The apprehension of pain is often worse than the pain itself. That is why the physician or nurse will try to engage you in conversation while sticking a needle into your arm. That is also why some dentists use music as a distractor for patients having their teeth drilled.

One good example of a distracting response is the Lamaze psycho-prophylactic method of childbirth (Lamaze, 1970). Fernand Lamaze, a French obstetrician, was one of the modern proponents of the view that childbirth need not be accompanied by excruciating pain and that physical and psychological education of the pregnant woman can result in relatively painless childbirth. Basically, lessons in the Lamaze technique teach the pregnant woman to substitute relaxation and breathing responses for any experience of pain that might accompany uterine contractions during labor. A contraction becomes a stimulus to begin active relaxation rather than to tense the body. The woman learns to isolate muscle sets, such as the pelvic-floor muscles, and either contract or relax them with control. As she is taught to maintain an active and conscious control of her relaxation, she learns to control her breathing. One breathing exercise is intended for early labor and involves slow, deliberate chest breathing. A second type of breathing is called accelerated decelerated shallow breathing and is used if there is difficulty controlling contractions with slow chest breathing. A final type of breathing consists of short, superficial breaths coupled with a short blowing out and is effective for intense contractions. With practice, contractions signal breathing and controlled relaxation rather than pain.

Other distracting responses work in other situations. Individuals who become anxious during long drives can prepare for their trips by bringing along appetizing foods, counting license plates, or listening to the radio. However, if they are driving, they must still be able to concentrate on the road to avoid accidents. For agoraphobics, who usually fear being away from home or out among people, a number of distracting responses are viable. They may try wearing themselves out physically by exercising before leaving the house. This helps change their preoccupation from an incipient panic attack toward muscular discomfort or fatigue (Smith, 1977).

Making a list of tasks to complete before returning home can help the agoraphobic to minimize anxious ruminations. Likewise, if you know you are going to be in a stressful situation, such as waiting for a job interview, it would be shrewd to have a well-prepared distracting response available for yourself. Relaxation instructions may serve this purpose, as might knitting, reading, counting tiles, or imagining your favorite vacation spot. Some people seem to be perpetually distracted and may be using this device to avoid adaptive problem-solving behavior. To sidestep this possibility, it is recommended that you develop an effective distracting response for use as a coping skill only when stress is unavoidable and unendurable. In this way you can learn to cope with extreme anxiety and to circumvent such consistent avoidance responses as not showing up at all for job interviews.

INCOMPATIBLE RESPONSES

A second type of alternate response is the *incompatible response*. The use of an incompatible response involves determining a behavior that cannot readily coexist with the problem behavior and practicing it. Lady Macbeth, who felt a compulsive need to wash away the guilt from her hands, would not have been able to engage in ritualistic handwashing if she had always worn gloves. If you want to stop compulsively cleaning the house whenever you are anxious, try visiting a friend or taking a bicycle ride instead. If you are a compulsive talker, practice the incompatible behavior of improving your listening skills. A fast-paced, "hurry-up" man could introduce an incompatible response such as devoting a predetermined period of time to spend at an activity. For example, he could budget 30 minutes for grocery shopping and then be sure to spend at least that long in the store. Or he could count each step as he walks to make it more difficult to run between appointments.

A clever incompatible response was suggested to a client who urinated many more times a day than he really needed or wanted. Urination had become part of the ritual every time he walked into the bathroom. His therapist instructed him to walk deliberately into the bathroom several times during the day, perform some behavior other than urination, and walk out congratulating himself for withstanding the temptation (Watson & Tharp, 1977). Over time, the automatic association between bathroom and urination was gradually eradicated.

Bothersome habits are among the problems that can be discouraged using an incompatible response. In one case a 21-year-old woman suffered for years from an unpleasant, itchy rash on her hands and arms and behind her knees (Watson, Tharp, & Krisberg, 1972). The symptoms could be partially controlled by drugs and medications, but the rash would flare up again during times of stress. Her scratching would then lead to inflamed skin, more ugly rashes, and periodic infections. To initiate her self-change program, the woman carried a small card in her purse and noted each time she scratched. The baseline frequency was 9.8 times per day. She decided that stroking and patting her limbs might substitute for scratching whenever she itched. These patting and stroking responses were a first step in greatly reducing the frequency of her scratching.

It was somewhat more difficult for the woman to reduce her nighttime scratching since she was not aware of her behavior during sleep. Consequently, she decided that she would have to learn to wake up when she scratched. She practiced by deliberately waking herself and scratching an unaffected area of her skin just as she was ready to fall asleep. For two weeks she practiced scratching and waking for at least one minute and then substituted stroking in place of scratching. Although this program was effective in greatly reducing her scratching at night, she added a self-reinforcement component to help eliminate the problem completely. Basically, she awarded herself points when she stroked instead of scratched. The points were used for allowing herself to take a bath or to study. After 20 days this diligent woman had eliminated all daytime scratching, stroking, and patting, and the itching had disappeared as well.

Virtually all nervous habits start as normal behaviors that become altered in form. Head jerking, nail biting, thumb sucking, and similar habits may begin so subtly that the movements are hidden from awareness until they become so frequent as to be problematic. It should not be difficult to think of a behavior that would be incompatible with a given nervous habit. Hair brushing and scalp massaging are incompatible with hair pulling. Fist clenching is incompatible with thumb sucking. Grasping an object is incompatible with nail biting. Tensing the neck is incompatible with head jerking. Azrin and Nunn (1973) have developed an entire habit-reversal program for encouraging the self-modification of nervous habits. The first step is to become aware of each occurrence of the habit through self-monitoring. The idea is to interrupt the behavioral chain as early as possible and institute the incompatible response before engaging in the habit. The incompatible movement should be opposite to the nervous movement, be capable of being carried out for several minutes, produce heightened awareness by involving tensing of the muscles used in the movement, be socially inconspicuous and thus practical in everyday activities, and help strengthen the muscles antagonistic to the nervous habit. For instance, if you are a nail biter, you might make a fist and squeeze until you experience tension in the arms and hands. Practice the incompatible response for about three minutes following either the temptation to perform the habit or the actual occurrence of the habit. Azrin and Nunn have had enviable success using these exact principles when treating clients.

SELF-CHANGE TECHNIQUE 13:
PARADOXICAL TECHNIQUES

Sometimes the wisest self-therapy strategy is not to fight a symptom head-on but to go with it and actually try to increase it either in frequency or in magnitude. This approach is called *paradoxical*. A paradox is something that seems absurd or contradictory but that also reveals valuable insights. In the therapeutic use of paradox a client who wants to change either is instructed *not* to change or is required to change in an apparently self-defeating direction. Paradoxical techniques are particularly effective with behaviors that are experienced as being truly uncontrollable, such as obsessions, compulsions, and psychophysiological problems.

MASSED PRACTICE OF AN
UNWANTED BEHAVIOR

Practicing an uncontrollable habit can paradoxically diminish the behavior. One example of using massed practice with a repetitive dysfunctional behavior was the case of a 22-year-old man who had suffered a clonic neck jerk for 15 years (Nicassio, Liberman, Patterson, Ramirez, & Sanders, 1972). It was determined that his neck tic stemmed from psychological origins rather than physical injury and that it increased with self-reported emotional stress. The client used a small notebook to record the frequency of his neck jerk. After recording a baseline frequency for two days, he was instructed to conscientiously practice the tic for ten minutes six times per day and to record the spontaneous frequency of the tic outside of the practice sessions. During a ten-minute session he was able to practice the tic 35 to 50 times. During the second day of practice the frequency of the tic declined, and it continued to decrease at an accelerated rate.

Before instituting the program, the young man recorded about 200 tics per day. After one week of treatment the number was down to 50 tics per day. He also began to enjoy several hours of "tic-free" time, which had never been the case before treatment. In about two weeks of massed practice the tics were almost completely eliminated. A year and a half later the tic had not returned (and treatment was well over), and no other symptom or undesirable behavior had taken its place.

Another example of the paradoxical approach involves a 20-year-old woman who still suffered shock from an attempted rape when she was 13 years old (Wolff, 1977). She was babysitting when a stranger bound and gagged her and tried to force intercourse on her. He ejaculated before intromission, however, and hastily fled. Although the woman worked out her negative feelings about men after a few years, she retained a pronounced fear about spending a night alone. She sought treatment when one of her roommates was moving and her other roommate was working evenings. In therapy she practiced systematic desensitization for overcoming her difficulty in sleeping alone in her apartment. In addition, she used a paradoxical technique to deal with the elaborate checking ritual she had developed when she entered her empty apartment. Typically she would go through 13 steps in a set order, looking in the kitchen, checking under beds, and looking in the closets every time she came home. Her treatment consisted of unlocking the apartment door, taking off her coat, deliberately going through the 13 steps, putting on her coat, leaving the apartment, and locking the door—and repeating this ritual *five* times. After one week of complying with these instructions she could perform the checking if she chose, but she had to do it five complete times. She soon terminated her unreasonable compulsive behavior while retaining normal safety precautions.

THE BLOW-UP TECHNIQUE

A provocative example of the paradoxical approach describes a man who experienced an excessive and debilitating fear of fire breaking out whenever he frequented a theater or movie house (Lazarus, 1971). The man realized that his anxiety was unreasonable, yet he panicked and could not sit still unless he had canvassed the entire movie house including the men's room several times for signs of fire. In therapy the client was instructed to remain in his seat; then the therapist asked him to imagine that a fire had broken out in the theater and to picture the fire mushrooming in intensity and scope as it spread from the men's room through the lobby, until the entire theater was a raging inferno. He was then asked to carry the fantasy further, imagining the fire department helpless in the face of the disaster, which soon engulfs the entire neighborhood, then the whole city, until the world itself is totally in flame! "Blowing up" the symptom (in the above case, a phobia) to ludicrous proportions adds a touch of humor to the gravity of the obsession and far surpasses the client's own worst fears about the potential danger.

In the blow-up approach the client is asked to imagine the worst thing that could possibly happen in a situation that he or she fears and to pursue that fantasy. The "worst fear" is often a fantasized antisocial act. For instance, a woman client used to avoid cocktail parties because she was afraid that she would spill a drink on somebody or dump a tray of hors d'oeuvres in someone's lap. The blow-up intervention required that she imagine herself acting in that antisocial way, embellishing her fantasy of dropping food and drinks on the guests. In a short time she began to *enjoy* the experience of gratifying her impulse in fantasy.

> Schedule a particular time to worry about some anxiety-provoking issue. Imagine yourself in the fearful situation. Allow yourself to pursue your worst fantasy. If other people are involved, imagine them responding in the worst possible way. Ruminate about the fantasy from every imaginable perspective. Now exaggerate the fears beyond their usual unpleasant level. Be sure to repeat the images until you feel the anxiety shrinking. Otherwise you may make yourself *more* sensitive to them. You will likely begin to smile and laugh as you think about your worst fear. If you feel guilty because you are enjoying such insensitive, antisocial behavior, remember that there is a world of difference between a fantasy experience and an action with consequences in real life. Thinking about dropping a glass is not the same as dropping a glass.

A variant of the blow-up technique is to use deep muscle relaxation prior to imagining your worst fear. In one case (Feather & Rhoads, 1972) a client suffered from a severe driving phobia in which he feared running over pedestrians. Unsuccessful with systematic desensitization, the client was asked to imagine, while in a state of relaxation, *deliberately* hitting someone and to fantasize enjoying the experience. This treatment proved effective in overcoming the fear, in part, most likely, because the man learned to discriminate between fantasy and reality and to gratify his antisocial impulses purely in fantasy. The focus of treatment was not the external fear of driving but the underlying anxiety associated with his hostile impulses. Repeating and embellishing the real source of anxiety will help you adapt to it, and relaxation helps make it easier to endure the experience. As a further example, imagine that you are terrified about the possibility of being in a compromising situation where you must either perform sexually or retreat shamefully. Understandably, you might deny your fear to yourself; you may attribute your feelings of loneliness and alienation to your extreme selectivity in women, you may claim that you are overburdened by work, or you may complain that people overstress the role of sex in human relations. In this case, blowing up your worst fear would be useful after you have identified the underlying anxiety regarding sex.

When you exaggerate a symptom, you develop a heightened awareness of—and some control over—a previously involuntary behavior. Some behaviors, like sleeping and sex, go from bad to worse if we try too hard to achieve success. The young man who is worried about being rejected by women may exert considerable effort in devising sure-fire dating "lines" until he loses all spontaneity and ends up being rejected even more. It is not uncommon to hear such "helpful" advice as "Stop being nervous." It is doubtful, however, that such advice will have a positive impact on you. On the other hand, if I suggest that you try to be as tense as possible and make yourself even more nervous, you may be surprised by the outcome. I know that in those situations in which I am most fearful and apprehensive I have tended to try to hide my fear from others in the hope that it will disappear by itself. I now find that giving in to the fear, perhaps by exaggerating the shaking and trembling, is the quickest way to overcome it.

> The next time you find yourself feeling anxious in a situation, try not to flee but instead to exaggerate your symptoms of anxiety to their extreme. Experiment with deliberately confronting feared situations. Try to do exactly what you fear you will do. If you are afraid you might faint, "try" to faint. Ask yourself "What is the worst thing that can happen in this situation?" Then imagine that outcome in vivid detail.

PARADOXICAL INTENTION

Lazarus' blow-up technique was presaged by the techniques of paradoxical intention and reflection created by Victor Frankl (1975). Frankl, a highly regarded existential therapist, focuses on the power of paradoxical

TABLE 3-5
*Some Common Applications of Behavioral
Methods of Self-Change*

	Paradoxical Techniques	Alternate Responses	Self-punishment	Self-reinforcement	Stimulus Control	Self-monitoring
Addictions			X			X
Anger		X			X	
Anxiety		X				
Behavioral deficits				X		
Compulsions	X					
Eating				X	X	
Habits and tics	X	X	X			X
Impulsivity		X				
Insight and self-awareness						X
Obsessive thoughts						X
Physical pain		X				
Sexual difficulties					X	
Smoking			X	X	X	
Studying				X	X	

instructions to grant clients some detachment from their symptomatic behavior, some behavioral control over it, and the ability to laugh at themselves. (Neurotics typically have a great reluctance to laugh at themselves and tend to take themselves very seriously). Frankl's approach to paradoxical techniques makes them quite amenable to self-change applications. He cites an example of a client who felt paralyzed by fear prior to an important examination. Rather than try to deny the anxiety, the client was instructed to say to himself "Since I am going to fail anyway, I may as well *do my best at failing!* I'll show this professor a test *so* bad, that it will confuse him for days. I will write down total garbage, answers that have nothing to do with the questions at all! I'll show him how a student *really* fails a test . . . " (Frankl, 1975, p. 221). After he had defused his anxiety wrapped up with the fear of failing, each exam question seemed crystal clear to the student and he breezed through the test totally relaxed. The worst possible outcome had been envisioned to the point of ridiculousness. Consequently, the stakes attached to success or failure had been reduced and the anxiety dissipated.

In another example, a depressed woman was deeply enmeshed in a pattern of hopeless thoughts and sleepless nights. After a number of days of trying unsuccessfully to pick herself up and talk herself into feeling optimistic, she said to herself "I'll see how depressed I can get." She imagined herself crying great rivers of tears until the entire room, and the whole house, was filled with tears rolling off her face. As she stepped up the fantasy, she began to see the situation as more and more preposterous until her crying changed to laughter. Only by deliberately crying could she gain access to her laughter. Alternatively, the woman might have "scheduled" times for intentionally crying or thinking hopeless thoughts. When clients who are prone to ruminating obsessively, for instance, are instructed to worry only in a particular place at an appointed time, they often find that they are not as able to upset themselves as they used to be.

Paradoxical intention is useful in situations in which anxiety prevents you from engaging in desired behavior. One application is the area of sex. Frankl has reported using paradoxical techniques with clients complaining of sexual difficulties. For example, a client who suffered from premature ejaculation was told to concern himself only with his own pleasure since he would be unable to do anything about his problem anyway. His attempts to prolong ejaculation were doomed to failure because he was obsessed with the need to succeed and to please his partner. Such anxiety can inhibit sexual potency. By shifting the focus from pleasing his partner to satisfying only himself, he was paradoxically able to attain effective control (*and* please his partner). Similarly, when a sexual relationship is plagued by excessive anxiety, the couple may be instructed to have close physical contact but, for a period of time, be absolutely forbidden to engage in sexual intercourse. By giving permission *not* to perform, the onus on performance is removed and the anxiety response is allayed. Many of the newer therapies for overcoming sexual dysfunctions implicitly acknowledge the same paradox: to succeed in reaching the goal is to give up the struggle to get there.

Paradoxical interventions have frequently been applied to treating families since they disrupt the family's ordinary way of perceiving the symptomatic behavior of others and introduce a helpful detachment. Hare-Mustin (1976) treated a family that had been driven up the wall by a disobedient eight-year-old son. Since the parents had been unable to think of any good behavior Billy engaged in, the therapist shifted the focus by suggesting that they encourage Billy to be bad all day long. If their son tried to be good, the parents were to remind Billy to be bad. When the family returned to the therapist the next week, the parents reported that Billy had not been bad. Although the family had not cooperated completely with the therapist's directions, the mother insisted that they had indeed tried. Billy's response as to why he had not been bad was "There was nothing to be bad about." A most instructive comment!

In another family, parents were concerned about their 14-year-old daughter's frequent crying. The therapist reassured the parents that adolescents cry (relabelling a previously unwanted behavior as desirable or tolerable) and gave the girl "permission" to cry, asking her in fact to do a little crying every day. Not surprisingly, the crying diminished and the girl became more able to discuss her troubles directly with her mother.

In many cases, family and friends may perpetuate our problems in the course of trying to solve them (Weakland, Fisch, Watzlawick, & Bodin, 1974). When you feel depressed, the more your family tries to encourage you or cheer you up, the more likely you are to feel misunderstood and the more hardened you may become in the depressive cycle. The more the wife of the alcoholic nags her husband to change his behavior and hides his bottles, the more his drinking remains at the forefront of his mind. Paradoxically, interventions that are meant to eliminate problems often serve to aggravate them. Encouraging or prescribing your own symptomatic behavior or that of others may actually bring it under control by interrupting this vicious, reinforcing cycle.

REFERENCES

Adler, A. *Understanding human nature.* New York: Greenberg, 1927.
Ayllon, T. Intensive treatment of psychotic behavior by stimulus satiation and food reinforcement. *Behavior Research and Therapy*, 1963, *1*, 53–61.

Ayllon, T., & Azrin, N. *The token economy.* New York: Appleton-Century-Crofts, 1968.

Axelrod, S., Hall, R. V., Weis, L., & Rohrer, S. Use of self-imposed contingencies to reduce the frequency of smoking behavior. Paper presented at the Fifth Annual Meeting of the Association for the Advancement of Behavior Therapy, Washington, D.C., September 1971.

Azrin, N. H., & Nunn, R. G. Habit-reversal for habits and tics. *Behavior Research and Therapy.* 1973, *11*, 619–628.

Bach, G. R., & Wyden, P. *The intimate enemy.* New York: Morrow, 1969.

Barrett, B. H. Reduction in rate of multiple tics by operant conditioning methods. *Journal of Nervous and Mental Disease,* 1962, *135*, 187–195.

Bayer, C. A. Self-monitoring and mild aversion treatment of trichotillomania. *Journal of Behavior Therapy and Experimental Psychiatry,* 1972, *3*, 139–141.

Bellack, A. S. Behavior therapy for weight reduction: An evaluative review. *Addictive Behaviors,* 1975, *1*, 73–82.

Burchard, J. D. & Tyler, V. O. The modification of delinquent behavior through operant conditioning. *Behavior Research and Therapy,* 1965, *2*, 245–250.

Cautela, J. R. Covert sensitization. *Psychological Reports,* 1967, *20*, 459–468.

Cooper, K. H. *The new aerobics.* New York: Bantam, 1970.

Cotter, L. H. Operant conditioning in a Vietnamese hospital. In R. Ulrich, T. Strachnik, & J. Mabry (Eds.), *Control of human behavior,* Vol. 2. *From cure to prevention.* Glenview, Illinois: Scott, Foresman & Co., 1970, 100–105.

Davidson, W. S. Studies of aversive conditioning for alcoholics: A critical review of theory and research methodology. *Psychological Bulletin,* 1974, *81*, 571–581.

Dearborn, L. W. Autoeroticism. In A. Ellis & A. Abarbanel (Eds.), *The encyclopedia of sexual behavior.* New York: Hawthorn Books, 1967.

Feather, B. W., & Rhoads, J. M. Psychodynamic behavior therapy: II. Clinical aspects. *Archives of General Psychiatry,* 1972, *26*, 503–511.

Ferster, C. B., Nurnberger, J. I., & Levitt, E. G. The control of eating. *Journal of Mathetics,* 1962, *1*, 87–109.

Foxx, R. M., & Azrin, N. H. Restitution: A method of eliminating aggressive-disruptive behavior of retarded and brain-damaged patients. *Behavior Research and Therapy,* 1972, *10*, 15–27.

Frankl, V. E. Paradoxical intention and dereflection. *Psychotherapy: Theory, Research, and Practice,* 1975, *12*, 226–237.

Frederiksen, L. W. Treatment of ruminative thinking by self-monitoring. *Journal of Behavior Therapy and Experimental Psychiatry,* 1975, *6*, 258–259.

Goldiamond, I. Self-control procedures in personal behavior problems. *Psychological Reports,* 1965, *17*, 851–868.

Haley, J. *Strategies of psychotherapy.* New York: Grune & Stratton, 1963.

Hare-Mustin, R. T. Paradoxical tasks in family therapy: Who can resist? *Psychotherapy: Theory, Research, and Practice,* 1976, *13*, 128–130.

Herbert, E. W., & Baer, D. M. Training parents as behavior modifiers: Self-recording of contingent attention. *Journal of Applied Behavior Analysis,* 1972, *5*, 139–149.

Homme, L. A. Perspectives in psychology: XXIV. Control of covariants, the operants of the mind. *Psychological Record,* 1965, *15*, 501–511.

Kanfer, F. H. The many faces of self-control, or behavior modification changes its focus. In R. B. Stuart (Ed.), *Behavioral self-management*. New York: Brunner/Mazel, 1977.

Kanfer, F. H. Self-regulation: Research, issues and speculations. In M. R. Goldfried & M. Merbaum (Eds.), *Behavior change through self-control*. New York: Holt, Rinehart, & Winston, 1973.

Kanfer, F. H., & Goldfoot, D. A. Self-control and tolerance of noxious stimulation. *Psychological Reports*, 1966, *18*, 79–85.

Kaplan, H. S. *The new sex therapy*. New York: Brunner/Mazel, 1974.

Kau, M. L., & Fisher, J. Self-modification of exercise behavior. *Journal of Behavior Therapy and Experimental Psychiatry*, 1974, *5*, 213–214.

Kazdin, A. E. *Behavior modification in applied settings*. Homewood, Ill.: Dorsey Press, 1975.

Kushner, M. The operant control of intractable sneezing. In C. D. Spielberger, R. Fox, & I. Masteron (Eds.), *Contributions to general psychology*. New York: Ronald Press, 1968, 361–365.

Lamaze, F. *Painless childbirth*. Chicago: Henry Regnery Co., 1970.

Lazarus, A. *Behavior therapy and beyond*. New York: McGraw-Hill, 1971.

Leitenberg, H., Agras, W. S., Thompson, L. E., & Wright, D. E. Feedback in behavior modification: An experimental analysis of two phobic cases. *Journal of Applied Behavior Analysis*, 1968, *1*, 131–137.

Liberman, R. Behavioral approaches to family and couple therapy. *American Journal of Orthopsychiatry*, 1970, *40*, 106–118.

Lichtenstein, E., Harris, D. E., Birchler, G. R., Wahl, J. M., & Schmal, D. P. Comparison of rapid smoking, warm, smoky air, and attention placebo in the modification of smoking behavior. *Journal of Consulting and Clinical Psychology*, 1973, *40*, 92–98.

Lichtenstein, E., & Keutzer, C. Experimental investigation of diverse techniques to modify smoking: A follow-up report. *Behavior Research and Therapy*, 1967, *7*, 139–140.

LoPiccolo, J., & Lobitz, W. C. The role of masturbation in the treatment of orgasmic dysfunction. *Archives of Sexual Behavior*, 1972, *2*, 163–171.

Lovaas, O. I., Koegel, R., Simmons, J. Q., & Long, J. S. Some generalizations and follow-up measures on autistic children in behavior therapy. *Journal of Applied Behavior Analysis*, 1973, *6*, 131–165.

Lovaas, O. I., & Newsom, C. D. Behavior modification with psychotic children. In H. Leitenberg (Ed.), *Handbook of behavior modification and behavior therapy*. Englewood Cliffs, N.J.: Prentice-Hall, 1976.

MacNeil, J., & Thomas, M. R. Treatment of obsessive-compulsive hairpulling (trichotillomania) by behavioral and cognitive contingency manipulation. *Journal of Behavior Therapy and Experimental Psychiatry*, 1976, *7*, 391–392.

Mahoney, M. J. Research issues in self-management. *Behavior Therapy*, 1972, *3*, 45–63.

Maletzky, B. M. Behavior recording as treatment: A brief note. *Behavior Therapy*, 1974, *5*, 107–111.

Marks, I. M., & Gelder, M. G. Transvestism and fetishism: Clinical and psychological change during faradic aversion. *British Journal of Psychiatry*, 1967, *119*, 711–730.

Mastellone, M. Aversion therapy: A new use of the old rubberband. *Journal of Behavior Therapy and Experimental Psychiatry*, 1974, *5*, 311–312.

Masters, W. H. & Johnson, V. E. *Human sexual inadequacy.* Boston: Little, Brown, 1970.

McFall, R. M. The effects of self-monitoring on normal smoking behavior. *Journal of Consulting and Clinical Psychology,* 1970, *35,* 135–142.

McGovern, K. B., Stewart, R. C., & LoPiccolo, J. Secondary orgasmic dysfunction: 1: Analysis and strategies for treatment. *Archives of Sexual Behavior,* 1975, *4,* 265–275.

McGuire, R. J., & Vallance, M. Aversion therapy by electric shock, a simple technique. *British Medical Journal,* 1964, *1,* 151–153.

Nicassio, F. J., Liberman, R. P., Patterson, R. L., Ramirez, E., and Sanders, N. The treatment of tics by negative practice. *Journal of Behavior Therapy and Experimental Psychiatry,* 1972, *3,* 281–287.

Nolan, J. D. Self-control procedures in the modification of smoking behavior. *Journal of Consulting and Clinical Psychology,* 1968, *32,* 92–93.

Patterson, G. R. *Families.* Champaign, Ill.: Research Press, 1971.

Pendergrass, V. E. Time-out from positive reinforcement following persistent, high-rate behavior in retardates. *Journal of Applied Behavior Analysis,* 1972, *5,* 85–91.

Premack, D. Reinforcement theory. In D. Levine (Ed.), *Nebraska Symposium on Motivation: 1965.* Lincoln: University of Nebraska Press, 1965, 123–180.

Rehm, L. P., & Marston, A. R. Reduction of social anxiety through modification of self-management: An instigation therapy technique. *Journal of Consulting and Clinical Psychology,* 1968, *32,* 565–574.

Rozensky, R. H. The effect of timing on self-monitoring behavior on reducing cigarette consumption. *Journal of Behavior Therapy and Experimental Psychiatry,* 1974, *5,* 301–307.

Rutner, I. T., & Bugle, C. An experimental procedure for the modification of psychotic behavior. *Journal of Consulting and Clinical Psychology,* 1969, *33,* 651–653.

Shelton, J. L., & Ackerman, J. M. *Homework in counselling and psychotherapy.* Springfield, Ill.: Charles C Thomas, 1974.

Skinner, B. F. *Science and human behavior.* New York: Macmillan, 1953.

Smith, M. J. *Kicking the fear habit.* New York: Dial Press, 1977.

Stuart, R. B. Behavioral contracting within the families of delinquents. *Journal of Behavior Therapy and Experimental Psychiatry,* 1971, *2,* 1–11.

Thoresen, C. E., & Mahoney, M. J. *Behavior self-control.* New York: Holt, Rinehart & Winston, 1974.

Wallace, I. Self-control techniques of famous novelists. *Journal of Applied Behavior Analysis,* 1977, *10,* 515–525.

Watson, D. L., Tharp, R. G., and Krisberg, J. Case study in self-modification: Suppression of inflammatory scratching while awake and asleep. *Journal of Behavior Therapy and Experimental Psychiatry,* 1972, *3,* 213–215.

Watson, D. L., & Tharp, R. G. *Self-directed behavior: Self-modification for personal adjustment.* Monterey: Brooks/Cole, 1977.

Weakland, J. H., Fisch, R. I., Watzlawick, P., & Bodin, A. M. Brief therapy: Focused problem resolution. *Family Process,* 1974, *13,* 141–168.

Whitman, T. L., & Dussault, P. Self-control through the use of a token economy. *Journal of Behavior Therapy and Experimental Psychiatry,* 1976, *7,* 161–166.

Wisocki, P. A. Treatment of obsessive-compulsive behavior by covert sensitization and covert reinforcement: A case report. *Journal of Behavior Therapy and Experimental Psychiatry,* 1970, *1,* 233–239.

Wolff, R. Systematic desensitization and negative practice to alter the aftereffects of a rape attempt. *Journal of Behavior Therapy and Experimental Psychiatry,* 1977, *8,* 423–425.

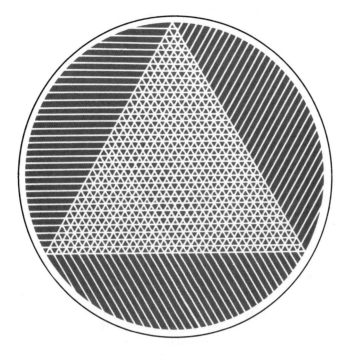

4

COGNITIVE METHODS OF SELF-CHANGE

Curiously enough, when people examine their problems in living, they often neglect the role of thinking as a source of personal disturbance. Most of us attribute our symptoms and complaints to affective variables, such as uncontrollable anxiety, helplessness, or disillusionment, to behavioral variables, such as the misguided actions of ourselves or others, or to coincidence, to poor genes, or even to astrological signs. However, it is most often our perception or our interpretation of our feelings and actions, rather than emotions and behaviors per se, that determines their impact on personality functioning. In fact, there is considerable evidence to suggest that our cognitive interpretations of events actually precede our emotional reactions to them. For instance, imagine receiving a letter from the Internal Revenue Service. Your emotional reaction to that event will probably be based on your cognitive interpretation of what the letter might contain: a tax rebate or a request for an audit. The emotional reaction might be prefaced by an internal dialogue in your head: "Oh, oh, I knew I shouldn't have claimed so many days of my vacation as a business expense." These thoughts are idiosyncratic. No two people interpret the same stimulus in the same way, and consequently no two people have the same emotional response.

For example, an instructor cautions two students who are gossiping in a classroom "If you have anything to say, share it with the rest of us or else be quiet." For one student the emotional response is anger, and for the other student it is fear. Beck (1967, p. 44) suggests that the first student interprets the instructor's message as an attempt to control or belittle her, whereas the second student feels caught and criticized. For the first student, a warning by an authority figure is interpreted as an attempt to control or coerce; for the second student it equals exposure and guilt.

In contrast to treating affective experiences of distress or overt problematic behaviors, the cognitive approach focuses on changing cognitive variables such as thinking, reasoning, imagining, and problem solving. (Refer to Table 4-1 for some common applications of cognitive self-change techniques.) In many ways, it is the dimension of thinking and reasoning that sets humankind apart from its evolutionary predecessors. In part, the task of living involves constructing your world as accurately as possible, assessing your strengths and liabilities, conceptualizing difficulties as they occur, and organizing clear and appropriate ways to deal with obstacles. If we are concerned about the mental health of the pilot of the 747 we're flying in or of the carpenter who's building our house, it is not his or her feelings and emotions that are important to us but the ability to think clearly and make critical judgments. Cognitive psychologists stress that humans are reasoning animals and that, when people experience psychological problems, their thoughts are apt to be distorted or incorrect. Commonly, when people are in the midst of depression or anxiety or when they have just experienced a crisis in their lives, their judgment is affected.

George Kelly, probably more than anyone else, is responsible for the cognitive focus in psychotherapeutic practice. Kelly (1955) maintained that people use a variety of alternatives or *constructs* for interpreting or construing the world. Consequently, in order to understand a person it is important to understand the constructs he or she uses to anticipate and interpret events that occur in the world. One person, for example, may be very sensitive to anger and to rejection by others. An important construct in his or her core system might be the kindness/hostility dimension, whereby the actions of others are automatically characterized along that axis. When a person finds that her constructs are failing her, because they no longer make the world safe and predictable, she may suffer from anxiety; and when her entire belief system is challenged she may experience threat. For Kelly, psychotherapy, whatever the particular techniques employed, consists of cognitive reconstruction. His *fixed-role therapy* encourages clients to "try on" a new personality in an atmosphere of experimentation.

The cognitive techniques presented in this chapter are self-generated approaches for changing a negativistic construct system into a more satisfying way of viewing the world. The common assumption shared by these procedures is that it is not the world that is too limited to tolerate alternate beliefs and behaviors but people who lock themselves into a particular way of seeing the world with a set of limited options. To be sure, all people have areas in which they act appropriately and effectively and other areas of vulnerability where reasoning falters and they act inappropriately and unrealistically. The following techniques should be particularly useful in situations in which your thinking is not as clear as you would like or your problem-solving ability is hampered.

SELF-CHANGE TECHNIQUE 14: LINGUISTIC CHANGES

Language is a highly structured medium for representing our experience. Although we are rarely conscious of the process of selecting words and phrases that best communicate our experience, we all follow rules that govern our use of language. Alfred Korzybski (1958), renowned semanticist, states "We do not realize what tremendous power the structure of a habitual language has. It is not an exaggeration to say that it enslaves us through the mechanism of semantic reactions. These structural assumptions and implications are inside our skins—if unravelled, they become conscious; if not, they remain unconscious." Because language functions as a cognitive interpretation of experience, the way we use language is directly related to our perceptions of the world, which is clearly influential in generating our behavior. Each person's perception of the world is biased in the direction of his or her unique developmental experiences. A woman who grew up in the company of extremely critical, demanding family members, for instance, may perceive benign comments or suggestions from others as unusually harsh and rejecting. A man who was reared in a highly competitive family atmosphere may develop a model of the world as a jungle in which only the fittest survive.

At a cultural level the Whorfian hypothesis (Whorf, 1956) suggests that language mediates our world view, that people who speak different languages transform and construct their experiences differently and, consequently, live, quite literally, in different worlds. The Innuit, a tribe of Eskimo who live in Northern Canada, for example, have many more words for snow that we do in the English language. As a result, they are able to discriminate nuances of snow conditions we cannot. At a psychological level our self-perception is mirrored by our choice of words. Out of our experience we generate representational models of the world that we then use to interpret future experience and that govern our behavior (Bandler & Grinder, 1975). Psychotherapy functions to alter a client's model of the world into a richer, more enlightened, and more rational representation of reality.

The way we speak is so much a reflection of the way we think that, when we experiment with our linguistic habits, behavioral and affective changes often ensue. Over time stylistic word usage becomes quite resistant to change. The following is a list of expressions that are commonly misused in the English language and thus lead to ambiguity and confusion in communicating (Rudestam, 1978). See if you can diagnose yourself in terms of the frequency of your use of these expressions. If you deliberately attempt to express yourself differently, you may be able to create change at other levels of functioning.

1. *Should, ought.* The use of the word "should" or "ought" implies the existence of an authority structure that governs your behavior. For the child this authority was very much present in the form of parental expectations and wishes, but for the adult this authority is not always clear or appropriate. The statement "I should go now" is quite different from "I want to go now" or "I am going now," yet these three expressions are often used

interchangeably. When you use "should," you give up your power and deny your responsibility for your behavior; you imply that there is some other person or standard that you must please. When you use either of the other two expressions ("I want to go" or "I am going"), you state clearly and directly that you have the ability to choose and to act on your choice. The ultimate effect of this kind of communication is to restore your sense of control. Try asking yourself "According to whom?" in response to a "should" phrase. This question can help shed some light on the identity of the original authority.

2. *Can't, won't.* The word "can't" implies inability or a limitation in ability and is often used inappropriately when the issue is not one of competence but one of motivation. Habitual use of the word "can't" is related to a very limited view of the opportunities you have to choose, act, and function in the world. When you change a sentence such as "I can't get up before 10 in the morning" to "I won't get up before 10 in the morning," you take responsibility for your behavior and therefore make change easier and more likely.

3. *Let me.* Prefacing a sentence with the words "Let me" suggests that you are asking for permission, usually in contexts where such requests are superfluous. A woman may say "Let me tell you about my husband." Such terminology reflects an underlying feeling of insecurity about the right to express yourself verbally or behaviorally. This insecurity leads to seeking approval rhetorically from the perceived authority figure. A more honest, direct translation of the "let me" semantic structure would be "I want to tell you about my husband."

4. *Apologizing.* Obviously, the appropriate use of apologies such as "I'm sorry," "I regret," "I didn't mean to" has a worthwhile function in social situations. However, if you find yourself constantly downgrading yourself by sprinkling apologies throughout your speech, you may be trying to protect yourself in advance from the rebuke of others. It is almost as if you were saying "I apologize for existing." Try to consciously control the number of inappropriate apologetic statements you make, as a step toward acknowledging your right to have opinions, values, and actions as an independent being.

5. *It.* A more subtle form of communication in common usage is the unreferenced "it," as in "It hurts," "It's so sad," or "Damn it!" The vagueness of the pronoun "it" allows you to avoid responsibility by refusing to identify with or own your beliefs and feelings. An appropriate translation of "it" phrases is to own the feeling, by saying "I hurt," or "I'm so sad," or "Damn you!" If you change "it" statements to "I" or "you" statements, your behavior can become less sterile and detached.

6. *Commands.* Commands have little place in adult/adult exchanges unless role requirements call for them (as in teacher/student or employer/

employee interactions). Frequent use of commands between couples can breed considerable resentment. Nobody likes to be told what to do. Try to rephrase inappropriate commands into sentences beginning "I would like you to . . . " or "Would you be willing to . . . " This structure suggests an implicit recognition of the right of the listener to accept or reject the invitation and your willingness to take the risk of being turned down.

7. *But.* The word "but" can be used inappropriately in a variety of ways. In a sentence such as "I like your dress, *but* your hair is a mess," the speaker may intend to articulate two separate thoughts of equal value. However, the presence of the "but" clause tends to drown out the first thought and highlight the second. In general, everything before the "but" goes right out the window, and the listener focuses on the second clause. Sometimes you really want to communicate the second idea but are using the first as a sort of palliative to soften it (as in "I love you, but you're not quite right for me"). Try substituting the word "and" for the word "but" as often as possible. Bandler and Grinder (1975) suggest that one function of "but" is as an implied causative (for example, "I want to leave home, but father is sick"). In this case, the implication is that the father's illness prevents the speaker from leaving or forces him or her to stay. Explore this kind of sentence construction to see if the two clauses in these sentences are, in fact, causally dependent. "I want to go, but it costs so much money" often does mean that it costs a lot of money, but there may be other, more valid reasons why you would prefer not to go.

8. *Unclear pronouns.* One quite obvious form of undesirable speech is to speak as if you can read someone else's mind (for example, "I know you didn't mean what you said about your father" or "We aren't angry in this family"). Not only do most people resent being spoken for, but you may in fact be incorrect and miss an opportunity to learn something new about another person. There are other uses of unclear pronouns, such as "People get upset by . . . " or "You can't do that . . . ," in which the incompletely specified referent usually turns out to be "I." A simple rule in most group or family therapies is to speak only for yourself. This may be risky, since you may invite the conflict that you are trying to disguise by implying knowledge or agreement. It may be a lonelier experience to speak only for yourself, but it can help you to own your ideas and feelings, emancipate yourself as a unique person, and experience others as autonomous and independent.

9. *Okay, all right.* Take note of those times when you respond to someone's invitation by answering "Okay" or "All right" rather than a simple "Yes" or "No." "Okay" or "all right" appear to be more tentative, ambiguous, and guarded responses. They seem to indicate that you are willing but not necessarily eager to comply. Although most people will not call you on this response and will merely assume that your reply means

"yes," using a more direct and straight answer again puts you in touch with your own feelings and keeps you from doing things against your will.

10. *Feel, think.* Very commonly people substitute thoughts for feelings (for example, "I feel that you are unfair to me" or "I feel that I am worthless"). There is a difference between identifying and exploring one's feelings and reasoning clearly and unambiguously. Feelings are gut sensations that you experience ("I feel angry, glad, hungry, confused, light-headed, drained" and so on). Thoughts are conclusions you reach through cognitive appraisal and reasoning ("I think you are kind" or "I think you are being unfair").

Discriminating between thoughts and feelings can help you expand your capacity to recognize and label your emotions, as well as ascertain thinking errors that are semantically camouflaged as statements of feeling. In this way, you are in a position to appropriately use affective self-therapy techniques with feelings and cognitive self-therapy techniques with beliefs.

11. *You make me feel.* Have you ever been told that you are making someone feel awful? Although you probably experienced guilt as a result of it, this expression is meaningless in the sense that, literally, no one can create an emotion in another person. You can be sensitive to the behavior of others and experience particular feelings such as anger, jealousy, or joy as a result. You can also know that some of your behaviors make it likely that someone else will have a particular emotional experience. The "you make me feel" semantic structure, however, provides the speaker with an excuse for avoiding some share of responsibility for his or her feelings by assigning them to external forces. Different people react in different ways to the behavior of others. It is important that you realize that there are alternatives to the feelings you have in a given situation. If your boss fires you, you may feel relief, anger, humiliation, or some other emotion. However, it does not necessarily mean that the emotional response was caused by the act of being fired. Similarly, if you are the boss and you fire one of your workers, your behavior cannot be held to be totally responsible for creating the worker's emotional response. If you can control your use of such phrases as "you make me feel . . . ", you will stop delivering messages to people that induce guilt and resentment.

This list of undesirable language habits is certainly not complete. You may think of some additions from your own speech patterns, a particular phrase or sentence structure that you recognize as a defense guarding you against feelings of helplessness, responsibility, or anxiety. Focusing exclusively on language expression would be very sterile and intellectualized self-therapy, but judicious intervention can help clarify your communications. Bear in mind that there is a reciprocal relationship between your language and your thought, so that the habitual use of a particular semantic structure can also influence your thoughts and feelings.

SELF-CHANGE TECHNIQUE 15:
COGNITIVE RESTRUCTURING

Cognitive restructuring, or altering maladaptive thoughts, refers to a set of techniques for exploring and manipulating the fallacious reasoning that underlies symptomatic behaviors. Albert Ellis (1962) was probably the first psychologist to assert that people needlessly restrict themselves by holding on to self-defeating philosophies of life that perpetuate their unpleasant emotions. Ellis maintains that most of our negative emotions are the result of our own thinking and that, consequently, it is possible to learn to reappraise our thinking and to choose more rational attitudes. In this respect even affective problems may stem from faulty cognitions. Research concerning the power of thinking in creating emotional pain has demonstrated that the way a person interprets events and situations actually precedes and influences his or her emotional reactions to them (see, for example Schachter & Singer, 1962). The woman who experiences fear when she sees a shadow does so only after she interprets the shadow as menacing and potentially threatening. The same shadow interpreted as that of her lover who is arriving might lead to feelings of surprise and elation. The sleeper who is awakened by a sound in the middle of the night will have different feelings depending on whether he or she assumes it is coming from a stranger stalking the living room or a window slamming in the wind. Sometimes people we do not understand clearly, such as members of different cultural or racial groups, or mental patients, or homosexuals, engender feelings of anxiety in us only after they are identified as belonging to the member group. It is likely that the same people with identical behavior would not be threatening at all had we not been aware of their status and subsequently attributed mysterious or destructive motives to them.

Generally speaking, people are surprisingly able to ignore important realities such as war in a neighboring country or poverty in a neighboring household when they feel that they would experience some discomfort by acknowledging them. In other cases, however, their idiosyncratic interpretations of events actually serve to create uncomfortable and problematic feelings. The student who feels criticized when a teacher corrects her is operating on her own assumption that all corrections by authority figures are criticisms. Another person reads belittlement into and feels humiliated

after each occasion when someone laughs at a remark he makes. In either case a particular set of assumptions has been applied to ascertain, perhaps incorrectly, the significance of someone else's actions.

Aaron Beck (1967) maintains that specific, predictable emotions are most often associated with specific and related interpretations of an experience. For instance, you feel sad when you realize that something of value has been lost and euphoric or joyful when you perceive that something of value has been or will be gained. Anxiety and fear are preceded by the anticipation of imminent damage or danger. Anger is most commonly experienced when you perceive that you have been attacked on your own territory. The attack could be symbolic if, for example, your standards or values are being violated or questioned. More anger could be expected if the attack is seen as intentional and direct. With a persistent negative appraisal of events, momentary sadness, anxiety, or anger can develop into more lasting, even characterological, states of depression, anxiety, or paranoia.

IRRATIONAL BELIEFS

We each have our own unique and sometimes irrational way of interpreting and understanding events. Ellis (1973, p. 37) has noted some beliefs that consistently generate emotional disturbance. He cites the following patently illogical ideas as especially common and destructive:

1. The idea that it is a dire necessity for an adult human to be loved or approved by virtually every significant other person in his life.
2. The idea that one should be thoroughly competent, adequate, and achieving in all possible respects to consider oneself worthwhile.
3. The idea that certain people are bad, wicked, or villainous and that they should be severely blamed and punished for their villainy.
4. The idea that it is awful and catastrophic when things are not the way one would like them to be.
5. The idea that human unhappiness is externally caused and that people have little or no ability to control their terrors and disturbances.
6. The idea that it is easier to avoid than to face life's difficulties and self-responsibilities.
7. The idea that one's past history is an all-important determiner of one's present behavior and that, because something once strongly affected one's life, it should definitely continue to do so (Ellis, 1973, p. 37).

According to Ellis, whenever you are in psychological distress, you are probably holding on to one of these persistent and illogical beliefs.

Reread Ellis' list of illogical ideas and ask yourself to what extent you adhere to these beliefs. Do you believe, for instance, that school, work, relationships, or some other thing *has* to be difficult? Or do you believe that one *should not* act depressed, sexy, silly, or some other way? Try to discover the belief that is most fundamental for you. In therapy, Ellis helps clients trace their "magical thinking" and question their inviolate hypotheses about themselves and the world.

In order to use the cognitive-restructuring technique, it is important that you identify your self-defeating thoughts and record them in writing. Negative thoughts occur automatically and involuntarily at key moments. At first, these thoughts are uncritically accepted as valid. Only on further analysis can they be identified as unreasonable and destructive. Record your upsetting thoughts as precisely as possible, in one of these ways (Beck, Rush, Shaw, & Emery, 1978): (1) Immediately after a negative thought occurs, write it down. Keep a list of such self-defeating thoughts as "I'm a social disaster!" and "I'm a lousy lover." (2) Keep track of these thoughts by recording them on a regular basis; for example, spend 15 to 20 minutes each evening writing them down. (3) Identify stressful situational events, and note the negative thoughts associated with them. As you monitor your thoughts you may find that certain cognitions frequently recur at times of painful affect.

Ellis and Harper (1976) have coined the word "musturbation" to refer to certain kinds of cognitions that result in much emotional disturbance. The word derives from the "shoulds," "oughts," and "musts" that we maintain to punish ourselves with: "I *must* do well or I am a worthless human being"; "You *must* treat me kindly and you are *rotten* if you don't"; "The world *must* make life easy for me or else!" Quite clearly, these irrational ideas do not stand up to objective analysis and reflective reasoning. Also, by being pre-occupied with the idea, you tend to make yourself feel anxious or upset. It is perfectly normal to be sad or annoyed; it is unnecessary (and somewhat melodramatic) to become horrified or devastated by most events. The man who has just been rejected by his lover needs to realize that, although it may be undesirable and indeed painful, such a rejection is not *inherently* awful. It does not in any way indicate that he is worthless, but he may erroneously maintain that he *should* have been able to keep the relationship going. To take the example a step further, it is difficult enough to readjust after a painful divorce without labeling oneself a bad person for being unable to maintain the marriage or punishing oneself for having failed to successfully carry through one's commitments.

ELLIS' A-B-C METHOD

The rational-restructuring method encourages you to trace your anxieties back to the specific beliefs from which they emanate and to examine the rationality of those beliefs. You need to learn to "think straight." Self-application of Ellis' analysis of negative thinking consists of three steps in an ABC paradigm.[1] C is the Emotional Consequence (or conditioned response), such as feelings of anxiety, worthlessness, or depression. You probably think that you know the cause of this unpleasant emotional response and attribute it to A, the Activating Experience. A usually refers to some kind of interpersonal disappointment. For example, you may believe that your depression was caused by your lover rejecting you. However, Ellis insists that A cannot possibly cause C; the external event cannot create a gut feeling. Otherwise everyone who experienced rejection, let us say, would be devastated in a similar way, and clearly that is not the case. The task, then, is to analyze B, the Belief System (also referred to as "bull shit!"), which shapes C, the emotional response, more directly. The Belief System has both a rational component and an irrational component. The rational component is the real sense of loss and misfortune that accompanies any rejection and the realization that it would take great effort to regain the lost love or to obtain a substitute for it. The rational aspect of the Belief System is empirically valid and is a positive coping response. The rational belief leads, of course, to some feelings of disappointment, regret, and sorrow as a result of A but probably not to intense feelings of worthlessness, devastation, or depression. These feelings are reserved for the irrational component of the Belief System. This component creates worthless evaluations of the self and hopelessness about the future as a result of rejection. After her relationship with Bill breaks up, Suzanne says to herself "Not only has Bill rejected me but I am a worthless human being, incapable of attracting any desirable man!" This belief is unrealistic, since it suggests that Suzanne should *never* lose a lover. In fact, it serves mainly to maximize her pain. This particular example, of course, reflects the irrationality of the first belief in Ellis' list, the belief that one should be loved and approved by all significant people. And this belief is not uncommon; it is so prevalent that it is reflected in such current popular song lyrics as "I can't live if living is without you" and "You're nobody 'til somebody loves you."

An exaggerated need for approval may be a function of not fully trusting yourself. It may lead to such self-defeating, approval-seeking behaviors as changing your opinions to please others, hiding your true feelings, apologizing for your views, becoming upset when someone disagrees with you, and being easily intimidated. Take another example: Your boss has criticized you for slow production (point A); you feel awful (point C). What are you telling yourself at point B? Perhaps it is something on the order of "Not only did I not finish my assignment on time, but I am basically,

---

[1]Ellis was one of the first to adopt an ABC model of change. His abbreviations, however, refer to a therapeutic analysis of cognitions, whereas the model introduced in this book is a global conceptualization of the parameters of change.

fundamentally, and irrevocably incompetent." The irrational component of the Belief System maintains "I *should* be able to be so competent that I *never* disappoint my boss on the job."

Identification of those situations in which you feel extreme shame, anxiety, anger, sadness, guilt, or depression is a process similar to functional analysis. After the situation is identified, you fill in the picture by pinpointing the messages or ideas that you indoctrinate yourself with and that are part of an irrational belief system that defines the way you think you and others *ought* to be. After identifying maladaptive thoughts, you can replace irrational beliefs with more accurate judgments of your behavior that ultimately have less destructive consequences. Suzanne may change her irrational belief to a more reasonable understanding of her situation, such as "Isn't it sad that Bill doesn't love me anymore. That's disappointing, and I'll miss him. But I'm still a likable person." Or you may tell yourself "Yes, I wish I were a little faster on the job. And perhaps I can learn to be. In the meantime I still do other things well, and I don't have to get an ulcer worrying about disappointing my boss."

Ten sufferers of tension headaches were treated with systematic applications of the cognitive-restructuring method (Holroyd, Andrasik, & Westbrook, 1977). Tension headaches, which create a band of pain around the head lasting for hours, weeks, or even months, are considered to be stress related. Treatment for these ten people consisted in part of determining their cognitive responses to stress-eliciting situations. They were encouraged to discuss the unreasonable expectations they had for themselves and to attribute their headaches to their own thoughts rather than to personality traits or to some external factor. They listed stressful situations (Activating Experiences), noting the cues that triggered their tension, which presumably led to their headaches (Consequences). They then explored the thoughts they had before, during, and after experiencing the tension (Beliefs). Through self-monitoring, they learned to identify the cognitive components of their distress. Thereafter they learned to interrupt the thought sequence early and use the impending distress as a signal for other cognitive strategies. They began to reappraise their thoughts by asking themselves "What are the facts?" and "What is the evidence for this belief?" They also used incompatible responses such as relaxation and fantasies of lying on a beach. As can be seen in Figure 4-1, the group benefited greatly from eight 45-minute sessions of cognitive restructuring; by contrast, a "wait-list control" group received no treatment and had a slight increase in headaches.

To use the cognitive-restructuring technique, follow these steps:

1. Note the extreme, uncomfortable emotional response that you experience (C, the Emotional Consequence).

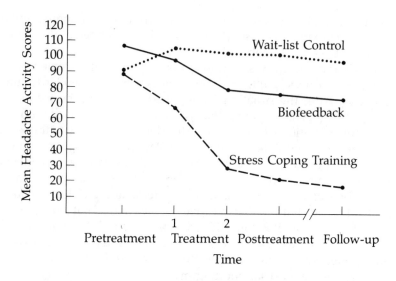

FIGURE 4-1
Mean weekly headache activity scores in two-week blocks. From "Cog-
nitive Control of Tension Headache," by K. A. Holroyd, F. Andrasik,
and T. Westbrook, Cognitive Therapy and Research, *1977, 1(2),*
121–133. Copyright 1977 by Plenum Publishing Corporation. Re-
printed by permission.

2. Determine the activity, event, or person to which you attribute
   your emotional response (*A,* the Activating Experience).
3. Explore the rational Belief resulting from that event ("How
   unfortunate that I was fired from my job").
4. Identify the irrational Belief ("It is catastrophic that I lost my
   job, and life can't go on").
5. Try to identify the demands underlying the irrational Belief
   ("Must I *always* do well at a job? Is it impossible to live a
   fulfilling life without this particular job?").
6. Dispute your irrational Belief ("Can I still be a worthwhile
   person without that job? Am I really destroyed by the loss of
   the job?"). The cognitive impact of this reappraisal will be that
   you admit the inconvenience of the job loss but dispense with
   the definition of yourself as a hopeless incompetent as a result.
   This cognitive reappraisal will help to alleviate destructive
   feelings as well as prevent you from behaving defensively by
   blacklisting the boss for firing or laying you off. It also has the
   positive behavioral impact of preventing you from becoming
   anxious about upcoming job interviews.

ADDITIONAL HINTS FOR USING
COGNITIVE RESTRUCTURING

When you dispute your irrational beliefs, you should examine the evidence for and against them. Remember that originally you experienced these thoughts as incontrovertible facts, whereas there are, of course, alternative interpretations to the event to consider. Try to substitute more reality-oriented interpretations for your negative cognitions. Consider listing your alternative interpretations in the following manner (Beck et al., 1978):

Situation	Feelings	Cognitions	Alternatve Interpretations
Professor did not call on me in the seminar.	Depressed and embarrassed	He thinks I'm stupid. (Moreover, I am stupid and worthless!)	He did not see me. He ran out of time. He already knew my point of view. He wanted to include other students in the discussion.

Imagery can be used to visualize the problem situation more intensely. Maultsby and Ellis (1974) suggest the use of negative imagery, in which the unpleasant Activating Events are fantasized in great detail.

> Imagine, as realistically as possible, being in the painful or fearful situation. Next, try to fully experience the upset and discomfort that come with reliving the event without blocking or inhibiting the disturbed feeling. Once you have the intense feelings of anxiety, depression, guilt, or hostility, try to moderate them to feelings of disappointment, annoyance, or irritation. In this way, you learn to feel displeased rather than upset. Finally, examine any changes in your Belief System that accompany the more manageable emotions. Try to identify the thoughts that helped to produce the new, more adaptive feelings.

> The flip side of the negative imagery technique is to fantasize the unpleasant Activating Event at its worst. Then, when you see the irrational Belief, dispute and argue with it vigorously. Imagine the new feeling that would ensue if you were to give up the Belief and replace it with a rational alternative.

The last phase of cognitive restructuring is the analysis of the beliefs (usually a variant of Ellis' tenets of irrational living) and their replacement with a realistic and constructive appraisal of the situation. The student who feels devastated by the mere thought of opening her mouth in a new social situation might replace the irrational thoughts (I'll be stupid and make a complete ass of myself, and no one will like me at all") with a more valid evaluation of reality ("Well, they'll probably think I'm shy or perhaps not too well informed on this topic, but they probably won't reject me totally. Even if they do, I'm still an O.K. person who doesn't need their love to get along").

In one unusual case, a 46-year-old compulsive gambler was taught to use cognitive-restructuring methods to overcome his habit (Bannister, 1977). For years he had bet on sporting events and was heavily in debt. He viewed his gambling as a disease that was out of his control whenever the "urge" came over him. Therapy consisted of trying to provoke some sense of inner control in him by dissecting his use of language and developing negative associations with his gambling. As an illustration, the therapist helped him explore his thinking in the following way:

Event:	I bet $200 on Alabama over Notre Dame in the Orange Bowl.
Irrational Self-Talk:	I knew I didn't have money to spare, but something came over me. Besides, gambling is a disease with me.
Emotions:	Guilt, anxiety.
Other Consequences:	Increasing debts; my wife is threatening to leave; I might lose my job if my boss finds out.
Rational Challenges:	"Something" didn't come over me. I chose to gamble. I feel out of control by saying that gambling is a disease. I have a choice each time.

Use of this intervention several times a week for three weeks, combined with a covert sensitization procedure whereby he was encouraged to imagine negative, noxious consequences for gambling, helped the man overcome his habit. Two and a half years after the termination of treatment he was making a good adjustment to his job and marriage and had broken his gambling habit.

COMMON ERRORS IN REASONING

In the diagnosis of irrational aspects of thought processes, the following kinds of errors in reasoning are particularly common (Brown, 1972):

1. Magnification. This occurs when you exaggerate an event so that its impact becomes much more extreme than the situation might warrant. Receiving a summons to appear in court can be a stressful occurrence, but it is not the end of the world.

2. Selective abstraction. This refers to looking at negative, destructive features of a situation out of context and exaggerating their significance while overlooking or minimizing other, more positive features. This tendency is exemplified by the woman who is flattered by a list of compliments about herself but feels insulted by one minor criticism and focuses solely on the negative comment. For example, a good friend might say "I like your dress very much. You seem to have lost weight, and it fits so nicely. Your suntan also highlights your appearance. Your hair always has such great body to it, but isn't it a little too short?" In selective abstraction, the last comment is the one attended to. This principle is also illustrated by the anecdote of the woman who gave her nephew two shirts for his birthday. The next day, when he wore one of the shirts in her presence, her guilt-inducing response was "What's the matter? Didn't you like the other shirt?"

3. Overgeneralization. This is the tendency to draw far-reaching conclusions on the basis of very little data. The man who is turned down for a date may assume not only that this woman is not interested in him but also that no woman is apt to be attracted to him. The man who has difficulty maintaining an erection after his first sexual experience with a woman and runs to his doctor for a physical checkup to account for his impotency is exhibiting overgeneralization. Other examples of overgeneralization are common ungrounded beliefs such as "all woman drivers are bad" or "all women make good mothers."

4. Thinking in extremes. This refers to the tendency to see your environment, and perhaps yourself, in absolute terms. Behavior is either all bad or all good, all right or all wrong. The woman who catches her husband in a lie may decide that there is no longer a speck of good in him; the woman who has a ribald sexual fling may vilify herself as being completely bad and worthless. In the real world, of course, people are never so simple. Behavior is a complex function of many variables; it cannot be labeled in absolutes. It is not necessarily "bad" or "wrong" for a young woman to walk the street at night, but it may be unwise or self-destructive in some situations. It is perfectly acceptable to be a friend to someone and still disagree with that person on occasion. In short, the words "always" and "never" should be viewed with a great deal of skepticism.

A fifth category might be added to Brown's list of errors in reasoning:

5. Excessive reliance on other people's judgment. This type of faulty reasoning is not as clearly associated with logical structure as the previous examples, but reliance on the belief systems of others is not a good basis for evaluating your own behavior (Lazarus, 1971). Referring to "what the neighbors will think" is a powerful control device that easily generates insecurity and distrust of one's own judgments. If you live your life trying to please everyone, you end up pleasing no one. If the most popular girl in school does not like you, this does not mean that you are a bad person. Sometimes

the judgment of others is used to win an argument in a particularly detestable way: "Not only do I think you are aloof, but Joanne (plus 10 others, or 100 others) thinks so too!"

One way to rationally reevaluate a response that has led to emotional upset is to follow Arnold Lazarus' (1971) advice and imagine confronting a group of your peers with the following question: "What would you consider a reasonable response under the circumstances?" The following is a sample internal dialogue of a client trying to combat fallacious reasoning and an emotional over-reaction: (Lazarus, 1971, pp. 179–180):

Client:	Is it irrational to feel upset about losing my job?
Observer:	No, there are a number of inherent frustrations about which you probably can't help telling yourself some realistically negative things. So to feel "rather frustrated" under the circumstances is a logical reaction. But you feel more than "rather frustrated." Look at yourself. To feel so dreadful about it surely means that you are compounding the facts with irrational assumptions.
Client:	Losing one's job is more than "rather frustrating."
Observer:	Why? Is it a catastrophe? Would you say that losing one's job is worse than losing an eye?
Client:	Losing an eye is far worse.
Observer:	But your grief and anguish seemed to fit the situation of someone who had just lost both eyes, 50% of his hearing, plus an arm and a leg, and who was in acute physical agony from his festering wounds.
Client:	Well, at least he'd have everyone's sympathy, whereas everyone will know that I am a failure.
Observer:	It sounds as though you want to be pitied? However, are you a total failure or have you merely failed in a few specific situations?
Client:	Well, it is very upsetting.
Observer:	*It* is not so upsetting. *You* are upsetting yourself.
Client:	So then what would be a rational course of action?
Observer:	First, start looking for another job. Second, try to determine what acts of omission or commission caused you to lose your last job. Third, try to correct these errors in the future. And above all, stop telling yourself that you are worthless, useless, and a complete failure.[2]

[2]From *Behavior Therapy and Beyond*, by A. A. Lazarus. Copyright 1971 by McGraw-Hill Book Company. Reprinted by permission.

SELF-CHANGE TECHNIQUE 16: SELF-INSTRUCTION TRAINING

Whereas some therapists focus on identifying maladaptive self-statements and changing them, Meichenbaum (1977) suggests the use of coping self-statements to offset the negative impact of anxiety-eliciting or gloomy self-talk. Meichenbaum notes that young children automatically correct and perfect their behavior by talking to themselves. In the same way that a child might say "Ball here" to guide his or her motor performance, self-statements can be prepared for coping with and monitoring your progress in difficult situations. The anxiety experienced in such situations can act as a cue for initiating a coping statement, together with or independent of a relaxation response. The following instructions illustrate "stress-inoculation training," a means of safeguarding yourself by rehearsing coping skills to counter the negative, self-defeating patterns you anticipate in anxiety-eliciting situations (Meichenbaum, 1977):

> When you know a stressful situation is coming up, prepare for it
> by coaching yourself. Tell yourself "Take it easy. You can
> manage. Just relax and think rationally." If you feel your fear and
> anxiety mounting, say to yourself "Don't worry about the fear;
> just keep it manageable. It will probably rise a little. You can
> expect that. But focus on what you have to do." Finally, each time
> that you do manage to cope successfully, reinforce yourself with
> positive self-statements such as "It worked; you did it! You're
> making good progress. You're great!"

Meichenbaum and Cameron (1973) maintain that a behavioral approach to skill training can be made more effective by including cognitive techniques of self-instruction training. Coping statements can augment the effects of behavioral techniques at several stages in the self-change process:

1. Preparing for a stressor
   Suitable self-statements might include: "Just focus on what you have to do"; "Don't worry"; "Just think clearly."
2. Confronting and handling a stressor
   Suitable self-statements might include: "You can handle this situation"; "You're feeling a little tense. That's okay"; "You're in control."

3. Coping with the feeling of being overwhelmed
   Suitable self-statements might include: "Just stay in the here and now"; "It's predictable that your fear will rise; just be aware of it."
4. Reinforcing self-statements
   Suitable self-statements might include: "You're improving. It wasn't so bad"; "Congratulations! You made it!"

EXAMPLES OF SELF-INSTRUCTION TRAINING

Successful self-instruction training has been documented for cases of multiple phobias, evaluation anxiety, interpersonal anxiety, anger, and pain (Meichenbaum & Turk, 1976). Clients typically learn about the role of cognitive factors in maintaining their problem, rehearse coping skills, and practice coping statements in actual stress conditions. The coping statements reflect the four stages of overcoming stress described above.

Meichenbaum and Turk (1976) have applied self-instruction training as part of a stress-inoculation package for the relief and toleration of physical pain. Motivational and cognitive factors seem to be as important as the sensory input in accounting for the experience of pain (Melzack, 1973). Subjects were first offered a number of techniques to control the sensory component of pain through relaxation and deep-breathing exercises and the motivational component through diverting attention to irrelevant stimuli, focusing attention on bodily processes, and transforming the experience of pain by means of fantasy. At a cognitive level, subjects were encouraged to conceptualize the pain experience as composed of several phases. Self-statements were introduced for each phase: preparing for the painful stressor ("What is it you have to do?" "Don't worry; you have lots of different strategies you can call upon"); confronting and handling the stressor ("Don't think about the pain. Just do what you have to do." "This tenseness can be an ally, a cue to cope"); coping with feelings at critical moments ("Don't try to eliminate the pain totally. Just keep it manageable." "When the pain mounts, you can switch to a different strategy; you're in control"); self-reinforcement for successful coping ("Good, you did it," "You knew you could do it!").

Subjects rehearsed the self-statements by imagining themselves in stressful situations. After one hour of training they were able to tolerate a significantly greater amount of physical pain (in this case, pain induced by wearing a tight tourniquet on the upper arm). Apparently self-instructions affect behavior by helping the person to become aware of the behavior and then to interpret and experience physiological arousal differently. The task was a challenge, and the positive, task-relevant self-instructions facilitated adaptive coping and reduced negative, inhibiting self-appraisals. The researchers also point to the value of having a choice of self-management techniques available, recognizing that a successful intervention is often dictated by personal preference.

Self-instruction training has typically been used with people who are clearly deficient in verbal self-control, such as children and schizophrenics. Adults with anxiety-based problems, on the other hand, may be characterized as using too many critical or inappropriate self-statements. Cognitive self-change procedures can be used to eliminate unreasonable expectations and negative thinking. If you are overly anxious in social situations, you may lack specific behavioral skills. On the other hand, you may possess the knowledge and skills but be telling yourself that you can't succeed or "make it." It has been found, for example, that male university students who rarely date and report a great deal of interpersonal anxiety rate their social performance as ineffective but actually have as many social skills as high-frequency daters (Glasgow & Arkowitz, 1975). The issue may be one of thinking differently rather than acting differently. In one study, men who were shy and ill at ease with women were asked to write down their immediate thoughts and feelings when they were in problematic social situations (Glass, Gottman, & Shmurak, 1976). For instance, a student might call up a recent acquaintance and ask her for a date, only to have her ask him to repeat his name. Tempted to hang up, the socially anxious person might think "She is clearly not interested, or she would have remembered my name." The therapy program consisted of identifying problem situations and replacing self-defeating thoughts with more adaptive, positive self-statements. One value of the cognitive approach over direct social-skills training is that it seems to generalize better to novel situations that have not been previously encountered (Glass et al., 1976).

HINTS FOR USING SELF-TALK STRATEGIES

It is important when using coping self-statements to have the appropriate affect and to internalize the meaning of each situation rather than perform the task in a routine or mechanical way. One of the drawbacks of very general, positive self-statements such as "Day by day, in every way, I'm getting better and better" is that they become automatic and lose their emotional content over time. Also, of course, such universal banalities are not individualized enough to be optimally effective.

One way to make the practice of coping statements richer and more evocative is to introduce visual imagery into behavioral training. By imagining a threatening situation in advance and then rehearsing guided self-statements, you will experience a more life-like replication of the problem situation, thereby augmenting emotional involvement. This fantasy also serves to make the task more familiar when you encounter it in real life. By sitting back, for example, and visualizing the day you give your speech before a large audience or confront your parents with a touchy subject and practicing positive self-talk, you help to reduce the threat associated with the actual experience.

In this context, Schneider (1974) has developed an ingenious technique for encouraging children to practice cognitive coping methods. First, the children are taught to relax to the cue words "do turtle," which means to generate a visual image of a turtle drawing into its shell and relax when the imaginary turtle has withdrawn its head. During problem-solving tasks, the kids are told to "do turtle," and, given a moment's pause, they are able to use the self-instructions to relax before they tackle the problem before them.

Imagery techniques are not devoted solely to the resolution of intrapsychic conflicts. Suinn (1976) has developed a *visuo-motor behavior-rehearsal* program, an imagery technique intended to improve the performance of athletes or to help others increase their skills in a wide variety of areas. Suinn suggests beginning with relaxation training prior to using imagery. The visuo-motor behavior-rehearsal technique rests on the assumption that the repeated practice of behaviors in fantasy leads to a kind of muscle memory that facilitates the behavior afterwards.[3] Suinn's experience with competitive skiers suggests that motor performance can be improved by repeatedly imagining in detail each component of a successful combination of physical postures and movements. Similar principles have recently been employed to help people become better tennis players. In *The Inner Game of Tennis*, Gallwey (1974) encourages tennis players to focus their attention on the here and now, reduce movements to slow motion, and concentrate on feeling, watching, and listening to each muscle rather than on thinking and evaluating. The possibility exists for extending the technology to other self-initiated behavior change. You might, for instance, work at improving a particular social skill by imagining each movement involved over and over prior to initiating the change behaviorally.

The final step in the self-instruction training procedure is to practice the skill in a wide variety of situations. The more situations in which you try to use the method, the more generalizable and automatic it will become. The procedure may be most effective when it is used in association with some very threatening events in the rehearsal stage and then with somewhat less

---

[3]This point has also been made by Feldenkrais (1972), who helps people gain improved awareness of their physical movements by using memory techniques.

formidable real-life events. You can inoculate yourself even more by imagining failure and preparing to cope with it calmly and rationally. Even a disaster can be a learning experience.

SELF-CHANGE TECHNIQUE 17: PROBLEM SOLVING

Problem solving is a cognitive self-change procedure that involves generating a variety of potentially helpful response alternatives for tackling a problem and increases the probability of choosing the most effective response from among these alternatives (D'Zurilla & Goldfried, 1971). Problems are an inevitable component of daily living. Some people seem to respond to problems as challenging to tinker with, and they delight in being consulted to problem solve. Many successful business executives are attracted to a corporation when its profits are low, morale is poor, and problems appear to be overwhelming. Once they have proved themselves instrumental in turning the company's fortunes around, they tire of the smooth-sailing operation and go in search of more problems to attack. At the other extreme there are those who appear to be baffled and undone by the smallest of decisions—whether to buy black shoes or brown, whether to allow a teenage son to borrow the car, or how to tell Aunt Shirley that she is not welcome to spend the summer with the family.

You can teach yourself to solve or cope with problems more effectively and creatively by using the following five steps:

1. *General orientation.* Problems are both inevitable and normal. You can learn to cope with them more effectively, even at times when you feel overwhelmed by a flood of significant problems—a lost job, a failed course, a rejecting wife, an unappreciative child, ill health—by inhibiting your temptation to act impulsively. When you are confronted with a problem, move slowly and cautiously.

2. *Problem definition and formulation.* At this early stage the trick is to translate your problem from the abstract to the concrete. If your problem is that you are not receiving enough love, try to reconceptualize it in concrete behavioral terms. What does this problem really mean to you? Do you want to receive more

compliments from men? Do you want more sex? Would you feel better loved if family members volunteered to help with household chores more frequently? Or perhaps your problem is that you don't like your job. Try to specify those aspects of the job that displease you. Is it the location? The salary? The tasks? The coworkers? The boss?

3. *Generation of alternatives.* "Brainstorming" is a process frequently used in organizations and "T-groups" to generate a variety of potential strategies. In brainstorming, you list any and every strategy that occurs to you *without* evaluating its quality or practicality. Focus on quantity rather than quality. Keep a list of your ideas, and try to generate as many solutions as possible. If you need a new roommate, you might brainstorm such alternatives as advertising in the paper, hanging notices on bulletin boards, asking friends, calling agencies, wearing a button that says "I'm available," playing the role of a village crier, and so on. Try to list all the solutions you can think of no matter how nonsensical they appear to be at first.

Another example may be helpful. If you are becoming increasingly distraught because your roommate neglects to pick up clothes that he habitually scatters through the house, consider as many alternative actions as possible without regard to practicality. First of all, you might consider simply yelling louder and more frequently. You might refrain completely from reminding him to see if that generates results. You might ask for a family meeting to discuss your case and solve the problem using the consensus of family members. You might leave your own clothes lying around the house to show him how insensitive he is. You might try reinforcing him when he picks up his clothes without being reminded by cooking extravagant meals. You might deprive him of sex until he shapes up. You might use his scattered clothes as dusting rags. You might put up with the agony of defeat and learn to relax in a more disordered house. The list of potential alternatives is as unlimited as your own creativity.

4. *Decision making.* At this point, go back and review all the potential solutions you have listed, and consider the desirability of the various outcomes. Consider first the personal consequences, the impact of each solution on you. Then examine the effect of the solution on significant other people in your life—that is, consider the social consequences. Next consider the consequences from the point of view of time. Look at the short-term outcomes. Will your life be improved in the short run?

Finally, look at the long-term consequences. Make sure that a short-term solution will not come back to haunt you over time.

5. *Verification.* In the last step, you act on the decision that seems to have the best utility. Remember that it is unlikely that any solution will have all positive outcomes. If it did, it wouldn't be a conflict! After acting on your decision, be sure to check the outcomes to note whether your hypothesized consequences did, in fact, occur. This step is important for guiding your future problem-solving activities. Frequently we assume that the worst will happen, only to find that the situation was not nearly so bad as we had predicted. For example, consider the apprehension we feel when we reveal negative aspects or secrets about ourselves, only to discover that the other person is not disgusted nor devastated but reacts sensitively to our disclosures.

Problem-solving skills make use of the preceding steps in a systematic fashion. Most real-life problems will, in fact, succumb to logical reasoning.

Research in experimental psychology warns that creative problem solving requires a flexible, open-minded approach. Your solutions are likely to be uninspired if you are consistently rigid and fail to consider alternative strategies. Of course, it is very difficult to think of issues from a totally fresh perspective once you have seen them in a particular way. This phenomenon, known as *functional fixedness,* is illustrated by problems that require cognitive flexibility to arrive at a solution (Duncker, 1945). Here is an example of the role of functional fixedness as an impediment to effective problem-solving. Connect the dots using no more than four straight lines and without lifting your pencil from the page. (You must go beyond the boundaries implied by the nine dots in order to solve the puzzle.)

$$\begin{matrix} \bullet & \bullet & \bullet \\ \bullet & \bullet & \bullet \\ \bullet & \bullet & \bullet \end{matrix}$$

To conclude, it may be especially important for you to develop problem-solving skills if you have become passive and dependent on others to make decisions and solve conflicts for you. These skills not only provide you with a structure for taking more initiative and solving dilemmas more productively, but they can also help you to overcome emotional inhibitions about tackling new challenges more independently and assertively. They are also valuable if you will be facing some particularly tough challenges in the near future.

SELF-CHANGE TECHNIQUE 18:
THOUGHT STOPPING

The role of self-generated negative thoughts in maintaining un-wanted behaviors has already been discussed. In some cases, the self-generated thoughts and ruminations can be considered symptoms because the individual has difficulty controlling them. At one end of the continuum of unnecessary worrying is the obsessional neurotic whose waking thoughts are constantly drawn to impending catastrophe and danger. At the other end of the continuum, even the most normal individual sometimes worries unnecessarily about going crazy, being unable to perform a task, or doing something with serious, negative consequences that in reality is unlikely to occur, such as throwing the baby out the window. When irrational thoughts make it difficult for you to concentrate on anything else, you need a method for handling those cognitions.

One straightforward technique for dealing with persistent thoughts that make you miserable is called "thought stopping." Thought stopping involves having the client concentrate on the ruminative, anxiety-producing thoughts for a period of time, until the therapist suddenly and definitively says "Stop!" or makes some loud noise. The intervention, of course, inter-rupts the thought sequence and makes it virtually impossible to continue it. The procedure is repeated until the association between the stop cue and the obsession is strengthened and the client takes over for the therapist and intervenes with his or her own subvocal "stop" as soon as he or she becomes aware of being involved in the obsessional sequence.

Perhaps you are a mother who spends half the night fretting about the safety of your son when he stays out late. The first step in applying this technique is to determine the extent to which your worrying is reason-able and constructive and to what extent it is irrational and unnecessary. In other words, you may be concerned when the clock strikes a certain hour, especially if your son is unreliable or in unreliable company. But even in that situation your actual worrying probably functions merely to prevent your own sleep and serves no useful purpose. Some of your thoughts may actually be unrealistic, however, such as imagining the grisly details of an automobile accident or a knife fight.

In one study ten outpatients with a diagnosis of obsessive-compulsive neurosis used a thought-stopping intervention (Hackman & McLean, 1975). Each patient closed his or her eyes and imagined a particular situation that was usually related to the occurrence of obsessive rituals or thoughts. When the client indicated that he or she was thinking about the situation and had started obsessing, the therapist shouted "Stop!" This procedure was repeated until the person could keep his or her mind blank for 30 seconds after the "stop" interruption on three consecutive attempts. Thereafter, the therapist merely spoke the word "stop" rather than shouting it until they had achieved three successful trials. Gradually the client took complete responsibility for interrupting himself or herself. He or she was first encouraged to interrupt the obsessional sequence by shouting "Stop!", then by saying the word, next by whispering it, and finally by using the cue subvocally. After eight sessions the procedure proved effective in controlling the obsessions.

For example, one outpatient, a 20-year-old student, consistently failed to complete any assignments at school because he had to ensure that he understood every single word that he read, heard, or wrote. For over two years he had pored over the dictionary looking up every new word he encountered and rechecking those he wasn't positive about. In another case, a 31-year-old woman had a three-year history of intrusive thoughts about Jesus, the Virgin Mary, and other religious figures engaging in sex. Each time a sacrilegious thought occurred she would wash her hands. The therapists in these cases found thought stopping especially helpful for intervening with the ideational or obsessional part of the problem and less helpful whenever an avoidance behavior was the focus of concern. For instance, persistent worries about coming in contact with dirt or germs might be more easily treated with flooding or desensitization methods.

HINTS FOR USING THOUGHT STOPPING

As a self-therapy procedure, thought stopping is used to interrupt an ongoing, aversive sequence of thought. It is particularly appropriate for disturbing thoughts that seem out of control or that involve behaviors that could have harmful social consequences (Cautela & Wisocki, 1977).

> You will need a kitchen timer or alarm clock, or, if you prefer, have a friend assist you. Set the timer to interrupt you in two or three minutes. Then close your eyes, and obsess in your usual way. Continue to set the timer to interrupt your obsessing until your thoughts are effectively blocked. Once this is accomplished,

begin to control your unwanted ruminations without the use of
the alarm or the friend. Again, focus on the aversive thought and
then say "Stop!" out loud in a strong, authoritative voice. Since
you really cannot go around yelling "Stop!" in many public
places, your overt interruption needs to be replaced by a covert
interruption. After you are able to effectively block your thoughts
by saying "Stop!" overtly, try a subvocal interruption. Focus on
the aversive ruminations, wait 15 seconds, and then say "Stop!"
silently to yourself to terminate the thought sequence. Practice the
technique for 10 minutes twice a day, about 20 trials per session.

An unusual case history involves a 37-year-old woman suffering
extreme pain with a severe case of psoriatic arthritis (Cautela, 1977). She
experienced generalized pain all over her body, especially in her knees and
toes. She often needed help to mobilize herself, used a wheelchair to get
around, and had her knees drained of fluid twice a month. To combat her
pain she took large doses of aspirin, pain relievers, and antidepressants. In
therapy she was encouraged to develop some self-control over her pain
as an alternative to relying solely on medication. First she learned some
muscle-relaxation skills. Then she adopted a thought-stopping procedure to
interrupt herself whenever she became aware of pain. Each time she successfully distracted herself with a "stop" command, she invoked her relaxation response and visualized a pleasant scene. To increase the probability of
using the thought-stopping technique, she practiced imagining particularly
troublesome situations, such as getting out of a chair, walking across the
room, and turning a door handle, *without* experiencing pain, and then
reinforced herself by imagining a pleasant scene. She rehearsed each situation five times a day in order to fully dissociate these activities from a pain
response. Her therapist also instructed her not to complain about her pain
and told her husband and children to ignore her complaints to avoid reinforcing them. Her total self-therapy program relied heavily on the thought-
stopping technique and was successful in alleviating some of her distress.

The thought-stopping intervention can also be used to control antic-
ipatory thoughts prior to an unwanted or feared behavior. An unwanted
behavior such as eating sweets is often preceded by a thought such as "I'd
love a chocolate bar," which can be interrupted using the technique. A
feared behavior such as going to a party might be anticipated by a worri-
some thought such as "What if I say something stupid and make a fool of
myself?" In either case, thought stopping is not a way to avoid facing problems but a method for terminating unconstructive thoughts. As such, you
may need to supplement the technique with other methods such as systematic desensitization, which can modify the disturbance that initiates
the negative thoughts. Thought-stopping will shift your attention away
from your distress and give you a sense of control over such thoughts.

COVERT ASSERTION

Rimm and Masters (1974) have added a component to the thought-stopping technique to improve its long-term effectiveness. They suggest including a positive, assertive statement along with the subvocal interruption of obsessive thoughts. This intervention, called *covert assertion*, is used to further reduce the anxiety associated with the unwanted rumination and to strengthen competing, assertive responses. The mother who lies awake fitfully worrying about her son's safety might try to use a variety of assertive statements after mastering the covert "stop" procedure. The statements should be realistic, such as "My son is perfectly responsible" or "He's just having a good time." First, learn the "stop" procedure well. Thereafter, each time you use the technique and successfully terminate the obsessive ruminations, immediately follow your success with a forceful assertive statement, first overtly and then covertly. The content of the assertive response may be directly antagonistic to the obsessive thoughts. For example, if you are plagued by the thought that you are having a mental breakdown, you might say to yourself "To heck with it! I'm perfectly normal!" If you are the kind of person who envisions his or her plane disintegrating and all the passengers being killed, you might tell yourself "These 747's are super-safe airplanes."

In one study (Hannum, Thoresen, & Hubbard, 1974), three self-critical teachers were encouraged to monitor their positive and negative self-thoughts during a specific hour each day. A positive self-thought might be "I'm patient with the children," and a negative self-thought might be "I'm just too old for teaching." The thought-stopping technique, using the subvocalized word "stop," was applied to the unwanted thoughts, and the high-probability response of looking at the wall clock was used to help cue a positive self-thought. The results suggest that this combined procedure led to fewer negative self-evaluations and may actually have helped increase the self-esteem of the participants.

SELF-CHANGE TECHNIQUE 19: DIRECT DECISION THERAPY

One of the most straightforward and productive cognitive approaches to psychotherapy is Harold Greenwald's (1973) direct decision therapy. Greenwald insists that a person would not develop symptoms unless those symptoms served a number of useful purposes. A problem in the present was probably instituted as a way of coping with an untenable situation sometime in the past. It is not easy for people to realize that there is often a "method to their madness" and that bizarre, nonsensical, uncontrollable, "insane" behaviors may actually make a great deal of sense if their function can be comprehended. The ultimate cure, according to Greenwald, requires that the troubled person make a decision to give up the symptom in the same way that the original decision was instrumental in creating it.

Decision therapy attempts to increase our awareness of choices we originally made to conduct our lives in a particular fashion. Some of us made a decision to always act smart and sound intelligent because such behavior generated positive attention for us as children. A child who is ridiculed for his or her remarks, on the other hand, learns to keep quiet unless it is totally safe to open up. One client talked of wanting to maintain an intimate relationship with his girlfriend and at the same time experiment with relationships with other women (Greenwald, 1973). The only trouble was that he could not tolerate his girlfriend adopting the same behavior. He needed to recognize a decision behind his jealousy, the decision that he should always be thought of as a nice person and be perfect. Any woman who was also interested in other men must obviously find him imperfect. On recognizing that this early decision was now interfering with his functioning in relationships, he was able to change the decision and view his relationship with his girlfriend in a less binding, possessive way. Ironically, as his jealousy diminished, he was able to commit himself to her much more fully.

In the same way, nonorgasmic women may have indirectly made the decision not to have orgasms (Greenwald, 1973). "Indirectly" in this case implies that a woman may have decided not to give a man the satisfaction of pleasing her, or she may have decided never to let go because of self-consciousness about her sexuality and performance in lovemaking. The prescribed redecision is to allow oneself the luxury of being swept away by passion and start enjoying sex. The orgasms will usually ensue.

For self-therapy purposes you can gain an increased understanding of the symptoms you experience by following the steps that Greenwald typically uses with his clients.

The first step, true of virtually all the procedures that have been discussed, is to clearly conceptualize your problem in concrete terms. Next, examine the decisions you made in the past that may have helped to create the problem. This will require careful self-exploration. Try looking back to past instances of trouble with the problem behavior to find a point at which a volitional decision or choice was made to act in that way. They may be the times when you decided to whine rather than ask for something directly, the times when you decided to keep smoking, or the times when you decided to sacrifice your needs for those of your family. Take the example of the woman who consistently chooses the "wrong" men, those who eventually cause her a great deal of agony and remorse. Long ago, on the basis of an early traumatic rejection or a parental message, she made the decision that men are fundamentally rotten, and her subsequent behavior is consistent with this conclusion.

The third step in direct decision therapy is to identify the payoffs, or advantages, of the past decisions that were instrumental in the development of the problem. It may strike you that there are no advantages in having the unpleasant symptom you possess, but don't be too sure. Most symptoms are accompanied by secondary gains that would surely be missed if the symptoms were relinquished. The ordinarily self-reliant and independent woman who has a driving phobia receives a powerful payoff from the service and companionship of friends who are willing to drive her across town. The depressed person who ordinarily feels compelled to meet all of life's responsibilities with diligence finally has an excuse to slow down and rest. In fact, almost any psychological disorder has the secondary gain of eliciting some concern and attention from family members and friends, a response that might be more difficult to obtain without the symptom or problem.

A young woman complained about feeling shy with men and uncomfortable asserting herself in their presence. By examining her problem, she discovered that the decision underlying her shyness was a resolve that she would never make a fool of herself. She could, in fact, recall an episode very early in life when she had risked being bold and ended up feeling humiliated and foolish. This single early decision had persisted since then in the form of a behavior pattern of shyness that she wished to change but that appeared quite resistant to change. When she tried to determine the advantages of her shyness in the present, she found that men needed to take the initiative in seeking out her company. Consequently, the men she generally encountered were rather aggressive, which she liked.

The fourth step in Greenwald's system is to examine alternatives to your past decisions. Try to think of some healthier ways to achieve the same payoffs. At this point, you need to forcefully redecide and then support yourself in carrying off the new decision. In this context, self-reinforcement strategies are very applicable.

The woman with the driving fear, for instance, could have the company of her friends or request their assistance without using an uncontrollable symptom as bait. Consider the case of the graduate student who suffers with considerable anxiety, especially when she feels powerless or without control. The decision she had made long ago was always to be in charge. In this way she defended herself from being vulnerable to the whims of other people, as she had been in her early childhood. Now, when she cannot meet her need to be in control, such as in interactions with her research supervisor, she becomes panicky and anxious. She might consider some alternatives that would involve seeking other outlets for her independence or her ability to be in control that do not have the disadvantage of creating conflicts for her at work. A realistic alternative with her supervisor would be to play the graduate-student game and not take her research position quite so seriously. The consequent advantage would be that she would have more fun at work while channeling her need to be in charge to other parts of her life.

> The last step in Greenwald's approach is to choose one alternative and put it into practice. You might want to establish a self-reinforcement contract to encourage the new behavior. The woman who enjoys the company of assertive men can attempt to meet such men without playing helpless. She can decide to take the risk of being more aggressive and implement some new behaviors that are consistent with this alternative.

The systematic exploration of past decisions and payoffs, coupled with an active redecision, can have a significant impact on your life. The bored and unhappy housewife, tired of the ritualized pattern of shopping, cooking, cleaning house, and playing bridge, can make an active decision to become involved outside of the home. Quarreling spouses who battle to maintain a one-up position can decide to stop fighting and approach each other with the intention of solving a mutual problem. The frustrated businessman, doubtful of his ability to succeed at something else, can decide to leave his "safe" position and try a new career.

As a final illustration of the power of direct decision making to effect major behavioral and attitudinal changes, here is a segment of an interview conducted by Greenwald with a hospitalized woman with an unkempt appearance and an explosive manner (1978, pp. 32–33):

> "What would you like? How can I help you?"
> Her answer was, "Get me out of this crazy place."
> I asked, "Are you sure?"

She said, "Yes, I'm sure. I want to get out of this crazy place."

I said, "If you really do, Marie, you have to make a very simple decision."

"What's that?" she asked.

I said, "Just decide to act sane. But before you do, let me ask you some questions."

"Okay, do that. At least, I think *you* might understand what I'm telling you, not like these other idiots here," she said, pointing at the staff sitting behind the table with me.

I asked, "Marie, when did you decide to act crazy?"

She replied, "That's an easy question. I don't know why nobody ever asked me that before. When I was five years old I was having an argument with my mother and she said, 'You're crazy,' and I thought to myself, if you think I'm crazy now, I'll show you what crazy is. And after that I was terrible. I became worse. I was taken to every doctor in town. This is the third hospital I have been in. They have given me all kinds of pills but all they do is make me worse."

"Marie," I said, "are you sure you want to give this up? Aren't you getting anything out of it?"

She looked at me and said, "I thought you had some sense. Of course I get things out of it. For one, I have complete social security. I never have to work in my life if I don't want to. I can stay here and they will take care of me for the rest of my life. Another thing is that I don't have to look for a job. I don't have to go to work. They will always take care of me. The third thing is I don't have to listen to my mother say, 'Why don't you go out like other girls do,' because there are enough crazy guys here. I meet them down in the boiler room and we have a good time. And furthermore, most important of all, I can say whatever I want to my mother. I can even kill her because I'm crazy."

So I asked her, "If you can do all of those things and you're getting so many great payoffs from being crazy, why should you stop?"

She said, "I want to be a part of life."[4]

---

[4]From "A Case History Illustrating Direct Decision Therapy with a Labeled Schizophrenic," by H. M. Greenwald, *Voices: The Art and Science of Psychotherapy*, 1978, 14(2), 31–37. Copyright 1978 by the American Academy of Psychotherapists. Reprinted by permission.

SELF-CHANGE TECHNIQUE 20: TRANSACTIONAL ANALYSIS

Much has been written about Transactional Analysis, an approach to psychotherapy pioneered by Dr. Eric Berne (Berne, 1961a; James & Jongeward, 1973; Steiner, 1974). Although some of the techniques associated with TA make use of affective or behavioral interventions, the method focuses on acquiring insight and understanding. One of the virtues of TA is the relatively straightforward language it employs, which makes it a useful and comprehensible system for the lay person. When TA is used in a therapist/ client context, the client contracts for various changes with the therapist. The most relevant aspects of TA for self-therapy purposes are probably the analysis of personality structure and the identification of life scripts.

EGO STATES

Berne conceived of the human personality as composed of three different "selves," or ego states, which interact with one another in many different ways. The fundamental distinction in personality functioning is in terms of *Parent, Adult,* and *Child* components. The Parent ego state consists of those beliefs and feelings you hold and those behaviors you engage in that are based on early messages from parental figures.[5] These parental messages, which may be either critical or nurturant, continue to influence the way you think and feel and interact with others.

> To contact your Parent, identify those behaviors that were characteristic of your parents and that you sometimes use. Consider the way that each of your parents might have responded to a baby crying in the night, to a panhandler at the door, to a teenager who has become pregnant, or to a relative needing care. By imagining the ways in which your mother and father would have reacted in these or similar situations, you can get a better idea of the parental attitudes you have adopted.

[5]In a strict structural analysis of ego states, Parent behavior can come from Adult and Child ego states as well, depending on the way it was learned and incorporated by the individual (James, 1977).

The Child ego state consists of the unsocialized, naturalistic impulses that you had as a child. When you act and feel as you did when you were a youngster, you are in your Child ego state.

What do you do now that resembles your childhood behavior? When you want to have things your own way or when you manipulate others, you are probably relating from your Child ego state. Do you hold back your feelings, or ingratiate yourself with others, or hold grudges and seek revenge, or act helpless a lot? These are typical legacies from early childhood. Another way to reach your Child is to ask yourself how you respond when someone relates to you in a parental manner, by criticizing, directing, scolding, or advising you. Are you apt to coweringly comply or deviously rebel?

Finally, the Adult ego state is a purely cognitive, data-gathering state. It takes in information, adds up the observations, and provides an output that is dispassionate and rational. The Adult ego state is recognized any time you are thinking clearly and dealing with reality in an objective way.

To illustrate the distinctions among Parent, Child, and Adult, the various ego states might respond in the following way on a hike in the country:

Parent: Careful you don't step in the water!
Adult: I notice a hummingbird in the tree.
Child: Wow! The sun feels hot!

Or, in a more transactional context, these are the reactions to a friend who has arrived late for an appointment:

Parent: He should know better than to keep someone waiting.
Adult: I wonder why he's late so often.
Child: I wish *I* felt free to ignore the time.

Virtually any situation can elicit Parent, Adult, or Child ego-state responses. Ask yourself how your Parent, Adult, or Child might respond if you won the state lottery, if you witnessed a mugging in the street, if you lost your job, or if a friend criticized you. List the things you did or said recently that: (a) were rationally considered and based on factual information (Adult); (b) were similar to what one of your parent figures once did or said (Parent); or (c) were similar to your behavior as a child (Child) (James & Savary, 1977).

Psychological ego states are important because of the way they influence relationships or transactions with other people. Every person has a Parent, Adult, and Child ego state, and each is differentially stimulated by certain, predictable situations. We were all innocent, self-gratifying children at one point (Child ego state), we all observed and imitated our parents (Parent ego state), and we all have to make sense out of the world to meet our own needs (Adult ego state).

The phenomenological reality of Parent, Adult, and Child ego states was brought home to a 34-year-old housewife who had experienced short depressions of sudden onset for 15 years (Berne, 1961a). In addition to her depressions, which lasted two or three days, she complained about difficulties in controlling her 13-year-old son and in getting along with her husband. She also felt insecure at times about walking, a symptom that she labeled "walking high." One of her first comments to her therapist was "Like a little girl I want approval from my husband, even though I rebel against what I have to do to get it. I think that's the way I used to feel with my father. When my father and mother separated, I thought 'I could have kept him.' I was devoted to him" (Berne, 1961a, p. 161). Her behavior as a mother, an adult, a little girl who wants approval, and a little girl who rebels can easily be translated into Parent, Adult, compliant Child, and rebellious Child, respectively. Even the walking symptom, in which she would stumble and get up, could be likened to the walk of a child. The woman, in fact, later recalled a childhood memory of not wanting to go to day nursery while her mother worked and refusing to walk until her parents forced her. The woman learned to differentiate her Parent, Adult, and Child ego states. She began to consciously, rather than defiantly, acknowledge her child and to encourage her Adult to maintain control.

TYPES OF TRANSACTIONS

Most often when we relate to another adult, our communication originates from our Adult ego state, and we expect a complementary response from the Adult of the other person. For example, you ask the plumber how much her work costs, and she tells you $20 an hour. At other times you may justifiably relate in a Parent-Parent way, although some people are "top-heavy" and have great difficulty escaping the Parent role. Sally says to Stewart "That table is a mess," and Stewart responds "Don't bother me right now." Complementary transactions between Child ego states tend to be playful, as when one person says "You're cute" and the other responds "You're quite a beauty yourself!" Complementarity also occurs when one of your ego states deliberately engages a different ego state of another person and you receive a response from that level. For instance, in a time of need you might say "I'm really upset about what happened at work today" (Child to Parent), and your husband replies "Sit down and I'll get you a drink" (Parent to Child).

Sometimes transactions with other people do not lead to pleasant, predictable outcomes but instead generate ill will, resentment, or hostility in you or the other person. Perhaps you have become expert at sabotaging your interactions in this way. When this happens, it may be that your transactions are "crossed" with regard to psychological ego states, and an accurate analysis of how you become "hooked" by another person becomes critical. The following transactions are illustrative:

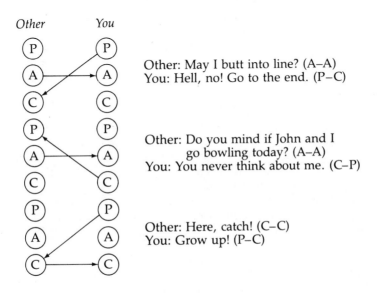

Other   *You*

Other: May I butt into line? (A–A)
You: Hell, no! Go to the end. (P–C)

Other: Do you mind if John and I
      go bowling today? (A–A)
You: You never think about me. (C–P)

Other: Here, catch! (C–C)
You: Grow up! (P–C)

These are examples of crossed transactions, which typically create feelings of hurt or bewilderment. In each case a statement was directed at one ego state and responded to by another. The initiator anticipates a complementary response and ends up feeling put down because he or she hooked a sensitive spot or weakness in the other person.

An even more insidious type of transaction is called "ulterior." In an ulterior transaction two messages are communicated: one message occurs on an overt, social level, while another, more subtle, message is communicated covertly and often nonverbally. The door-to-door salesman says "This vacuum cleaner is the biggest and best, but it's probably too expensive for you." On the surface this may appear to be a complementary transaction from his Adult to your Adult; below the surface, however, he may hook your insecure, status-conscious Child. If the transaction were really complementary, your response might be "Yes, you're right, that does cost too much for me." However, when the transaction is ulterior, you might defensively respond with a statement such as "No, I'll take it, that's the one I want."

You may be engaging in ulterior transactions if you try to solicit indulgence or criticize others indirectly while not admitting it. A martyr-like statement such as "I'm sure the chicken wasn't very good" may appear to be an Adult statement directed to another's Adult. But below the surface it is probably a Childish whine seeking to receive a Parental response like "Of course not, dear, it was great chicken." An Adult comment such as "Nobody in my family ever did it that way" sounds like an objective statement of fact. But couched within it there is probably a Parental judgment implying that the other person must be stupid to try it that way. Transactions that are ulterior at a psychological level and that inevitably lead to a payoff of negative feelings are called "games" and have been indexed by such colorful labels as "Kick Me," "I'm Only Trying to Help You," and "Wooden Leg" (Berne, 1961b).

> To analyze the nature of your relationships using the framework of TA theory, try to enumerate those transactions you engage in that lead to less than satisfactory outcomes: the "discussions" you have with your children, the arguments you have with your spouse, the interactions you have with your coworkers. People often develop "favorite" ego states based on psychological-survival experiences in childhood, so that some constantly act like controlling or caring parents with their acquaintances, some get what they want with tantrums or tears, and some learn to think of themselves and be self-sufficient. Ask yourself how often you are in each ego state during a typical day. A general rule of thumb is that your psychological symptoms are a result of responding too frequently or inappropriately either in a critical way from your Parent or in a helpless way from your Child rather than in a thoughtful way from your Adult. When someone directs a transaction to you from his or her Parent ("Take the garbage out"), do you instantly jump in with a helpless Child response ("Why do I always have to take out the garbage?"), or do you retort with another Parent statement ("Take it out yourself!"). On the other hand, maybe you avoid being hooked and respond in an Adult fashion ("I believe it is your turn today, and I'm busy right now"). When others relate to you from their Child, are you able to discriminate between those times when it is appropriate to be either a nurturant Parent or even a critical Parent and those times when a Parent response merely encourages someone else's helplessness or reinforces your role of constant responsibility? When your mate admits "Gee, I can't seem to fix this faucet," do you respond with "Sounds like it's a difficult task" (Adult) or with a resentful "Okay, I'll do it" (Parent)?

EGOGRAMS

One way of diagnosing the psychological energy that a person has invested in his or her respective ego states at a given time is by using an "egogram" (Dusay, 1978). Egograms visually represent how you appear to others. They depict the relative strengths of five basic ego states. The Parent ego state has been functionally divided into a Critical Parent, which tries to control another person's way of being, and a Nurturant Parent, which expresses tenderness and caring. The Child ego state is divided into a Free Child, which acts spontaneously without regard for the reactions of others, and the Adapted Child, which uses learned patterns of behavior to get along with others. By intuitively developing your own egogram you can get an idea of how you may wish to change in certain ego states. Ego states are not good or bad; rather it is important to establish a balance among them so as to be able to use all of them productively. Each person's ego state is different; a nuclear physicist's egogram would probably not be like that of a pop singer.

The egogram shown in Figure 4-2 is that of a woman who has a high Adapted Child, reflected in acting helpless and stupid much of the time and blaming herself for her difficulties. Her Free Child is also quite high and can be seen in her playfulness and creativity. Her Nurturant Parent is exemplified in her benevolent concern for the reactions and conditions of others, and her relatively low Critical Parent is shown in that she rarely complains about other people. Finally, her Adult ego state is particularly low, indicating that she spends little effort thinking for herself and developing her decision-making and judgment capacities.

The purpose of Transactional Analysis is to become sensitive to and aware of which ego state you are responding from and then to act flexibly and appropriately to meet your needs and be sensitive to those of others. One man suffered from sexual potency problems and was a habitual premature ejaculator, which was creating considerable frustration and disappointment in his marriage (James, 1971). He was sexually inexperienced at the time of his marriage; his parents had told him that he would learn about sex after marriage. His wife was now criticizing him for not knowing what she wanted sexually. In TA terminology, this man's Natural (Free) Child wanted gratification; his Adapted Child hadn't learned to delay gratification; his Adult needed to acquire more information about female sexuality in order to retrain his Adapted Child, and his Parent had to be decommissioned from expressing the belief that women are sex objects to be used for a man's pleasure.

The first goal of TA is often to strengthen Adult ego-state boundaries to eliminate any contamination by the Parent or Child; that is, for some individuals rational problem solving becomes obscured by inflexible Parent opinions and prejudices. Most women in our culture have overdeveloped their rescuing and nurturant Parent at the expense of their rational, com-

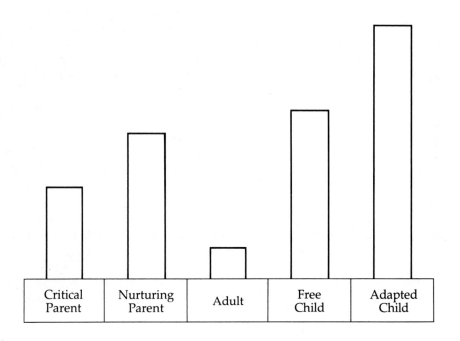

FIGURE 4-2
An egogram

petent Adult (Steiner, 1974). For others, thinking clearly is inhibited by the unrealistic expectations, magical solutions, or inherent "stupidity" of the Child. You can decontaminate your Adult by learning how to collect accurate information about yourself and the world and reinforcing yourself for using your capabilities. Incidentally, most men have a strong Adult but need to develop a nurturing Parent and begin to accept the feelings of their natural and spontaneous Child.

SCRIPT ANALYSIS

Another element of TA that holds great promise for self-therapy is script analysis. Scripts are personal life plans chosen at an early age in response to your own interpretation of situational events. A script refers to a role that the individual feels compelled to act out, as if he or she were a character in a play written by someone else or by the hand of God. Scripts often exist outside our range of awareness, and yet by their very nature they exert a powerful influence on our ongoing behavior. Although it would be oversimplified to try to understand all of a person's behavior as a function of life scripts, the script does in part determine the individual's course of life. As long as your script is a positive one, based on good feelings about yourself and others, you are in luck. Unfortunately, most of us are operating under much more constricting or destructive life scripts.

Scripts originate in early parent/child relationships through the ongoing communications from parents about one's basic worth and role in life. If your parents communicated a sense of your worth in their words and actions, handled you affectionately, and reasoned with you lovingly and appropriately, you probably learned to feel that you were "OK" and developed a constructive life script. More destructive scripts occur when parents give their love conditionally, as when their child's behavior meets their standards of excellence, or when parental attention is totally negative or unavailable. Some scripts are cultural or familial and apply to the entire family system. The family message might be "This family has always been into farming and always will" or "In this family, Father's word is law." Other messages are much more individualized. They are instructions that the child feels obligated to follow, because generally speaking it is the only way to ensure some measure of parental love and comfort. Consider, for instance, a child raised in a family that discourages and punishes all overt displays of aggression and insists on having a child who is regarded as "sweet and nice." The child picks up nonverbal messages about mother or father's discomfort with aggressiveness and resolves to stifle all his or her spontaneous protests and anger responses. As Steiner (1974) puts it, the child adopts a script for life when he or she modifies personal expectations to meet the realities that others have created. Although scripts are initiated by parent figures, the child, even before he or she is capable of considering things rationally, makes a decision about the kind of script to adopt, and the Adapted Child carries the scripted behavior into adulthood.

Generally speaking, scripts reflect one of the four basic psychological life positions (Berne, 1972):

1. *I'm OK–You're OK* is a confident position, indicating that you are basically a positive, winning individual and that the world is also basically good, trustworthy, and interesting.
2. *I'm OK–You're not–OK* is a superior or paranoid position, indicating that you are solid and worthy while other people are not.
3. *I'm not–OK–You're OK* is an anxious or depressed posi-

tion, indicating that other people are adequate and competent, but you are not.

4. *I'm not–OK–You're not–OK* is a hopeless position, indicating that you and the world share an inability to trust, cope,
   or exist.

There is no end to the kinds of early parental messages that form the
basis for scripts. Among commonly communicated themes are:

> You'll never amount to anything.
> You'll never be a man.
> You'll be famous some day.
> Don't ask anyone for anything.
> Get lost.
> Be beautiful.

Repetitive messages then become internalized scripts such as:

> I'm a loner.
> I'll never trust anyone again.
> I need a woman to take care of me.
> I'm a warm person.
> I'm clumsy.

Although most parents relate a host of messages and expectations
with varying degrees of constructiveness and destructiveness, the most
debilitating "injunctions" are communicated by parents out of their own
pathology. In any case, the script is a restriction on the free, spontaneous
behavior of the Child and, subsequently, the Adult, because it reflects
the fears, wishes, and expectations of one's parents as interpreted by the
child. Most people need some illusions to face the risks involved in living, and scripts can serve this end. Unfortunately, they have a driven quality so that the person may experience recurrent feelings of dissatisfaction
and disillusionment.

If your scripts are not apparent to you, there are many techniques
available that can help you identify them.

> Think about the kind of lives your parents led and the rules they
> adhered to or at least espoused. Did they have some slogans for
> living that you as a dependent, gullible child simply assumed to
> be necessary and true?

Berne (1972) suggests that favorite fairy tales, remembered from childhood,
often give valuable clues to scripts. Little Red Riding Hood, for example,
communicates the message "Be a good, helpful girl," with the implication
that she will ultimately be rewarded for her efforts. Women who live this

fairy tale tend to gradually wither away while being cute, indulged, and victimized by others. They may protest their script (because, after all, even the most disabled of us have some push to growth and autonomy) by adopting depressive symptoms, turning their anger against themselves while making life miserable for others in the process. To overcome her script, Red may have to begin to think of herself first, stop acting like a cute kid, and achieve a balance between giving and taking.

> Consider the following questions for identifying your script:
> What did you have to do to get your parents to smile?
> How did your parents react when the going got tough?
> What happens to people like you?
> If you go on as you are now, what will be the logical outcome?
> What will other people say about you when your life is over?
> What would your epitaph read?

MINISCRIPTS

Most people have more than one script. People reinforce their main life scripts through their ongoing behavior and very brief rehearsals called "miniscripts" (Kahler, 1977). To use the miniscript as a clue to internal processes, you need to become aware of words, tones, gestures, facial expressions, and postures that you adopt before engaging in not-OK or scripted behavior. One kind of miniscript is called a "driver." The five most common drivers are: *Be Perfect, Try Hard, Please Me, Hurry Up,* and *Be Strong.* The "Be Perfect" person believes that the way to make it is merely by trying hard at all times. The "Please Me" person thinks that he or she is responsible for other people feeling good or bad. The "Hurry Up" person thinks that he or she must always be in a rush in order to be OK. The "Be Strong" person believes that people are emotionally fragile and that he or she must maintain a strong facade and hide vulnerabilities. These five drivers, together with cues for their detection and behaviors that exemplify them, are provided in Table 4-1.

> Consider these drivers and see whether any of them conform to
> early parental messages you heard or experienced. If they do, try
> to identify their relevance for you. For example, you may believe
> that you are OK only as long as you comply with your drivers.
> Drivers can have a crippling impact on your self-esteem when you
> are an adult, since it is patently impossible to always be strong,
> perfect, or fast enough, or to please all people, or to try hard
> enough. As long as your efforts fall short of your drivers, you will
> experience not-OK feelings about yourself. To combat these

TABLE 4-1
Driver Chart

| Drivers: | Compliance (Inner Feelings) | | | Important Behavior | | | | |
	Physical	Psychological: Internal Discount	Words	Tones	Gestures	Posture	Facial Expressions
1. *Be Perfect*	Tense	"You should do better."	"Of course." "Obviously." "Efficacious." "Clearly." "I think."	Clipped, righteous	Counting on fingers, cocked wrist, scratching head	Erect, rigid	Stern
2. *Try Hard*	Tight stomach, tense shoulders	"You've got to try harder."	"It's hard." "I can't." "I'll try." "I don't know."	Impatient	Clenched, moving fists	Sitting forward, elbows on legs	Slight frown, perplexed look
3. *Please Me*	Tight stomach	"You're not good enough."	"You know." "Could you." "Can you." "Kinda."	High whine	Hands outstretched	Head nodding	Raised eyebrows, looks away
4. *Hurry Up*	Antsy	"You'll never get it done."	"We've got to hustle." "Let's go."	Up and down	Squirms, taps fingers	Moving quickly	Frowning, eyes shifty
5. *Be Strong*	Numb, rigid	"You can't let them know you're weak."	"No comment." "I don't care."	Hard monotone	Hands rigid, arms folded	Rigid, one leg over	Plastic, hard, cold

Fig. 1 "Driver Chart" (p. 224) in "The Miniscript," by Taibi Kahler, from *Transactional Analysis After Eric Berne.* Copyright ©1977 by Graham Barnes. By permission of Harper & Row, Publishers, Inc.

drivers, try to be open and trusting, to make mistakes, to take your time, to please yourself, and to do things rather than just trying to do them. Experiment with behaviors that oppose your drivers by giving yourself permission to violate them.

TA CONTRACTS

The long-range goal of TA therapy is to dispense with the scripts that inhibit you and to work toward greater volition and self-determination. The short-range goal is to set up contracts for yourself that fly in the face of your scripted behavior.

> If you are the kind of person who believes that you are OK only if you are strong, you need to give yourself permission to be weak on occasion. Start with something minimal that will succeed. Contract with yourself that you will ask for help once a day, for instance, until you can spontaneously allow yourself the luxury of not always going it alone. If you have a need to be perfect, experiment with admitting small deficiencies and see how that feels. It may be a welcome load off your shoulders. If you always need to hurry up, try slowing down in a very concrete way—for example, by walking more slowly between appointments. You may find that you begin to meet more interesting people as you deliberately slow down your pace. If you are scripted to please people (a very common script for women in our culture), try saying "No" to requests or implied requests. Finally, if you have a need to always try harder, experiment with yielding or making do.

From a transactional standpoint, as you contract for change you begin to develop your nurturant Parent and to disengage the Critical Parent, which gives your drivers their meaning and impact.

Contract goals should be as specific as possible. Most goals are in the direction of combatting scripted behavior. They might also be in the direction of strengthening Parent, Adult, or Child ego states.

> There are seven ingredients for a good TA contract (James & Savary, 1977). Complete the following statements to create a meaningful and valuable contract for self-change:
> What I want that would enhance my life is . . .
> What I would need to change to get it is . . .
> What I'm *willing* to do to make it happen is . . .
> Others would know about the change I'm making when or
>   if I . . .
> I might sabotage myself by . . .

TABLE 4-2
*Some Common Applications of Cognitive
Methods of Self-Change*

	Transactional Analysis	Direct Decision Therapy	Thought-Stopping	Problem-Solving	Self-instruction Training	Cognitive Restructuring	Linguistic Changes
Anger					X	X	
Anxiety					X	X	
Communication problems	X						X
Decision-making	X	X		X			
Depression	X					X	
Guilt						X	
Impulsivity				X	X		
Insight and self-awareness	X	X				X	X
Interpersonal conflicts	X	X			X	X	
Intrapersonal conflicts	X	X				X	
Major life changes	X	X					
Obsessive thoughts			X				
Phobias					X		
Physical pain					X		
Unclear and faulty thinking						X	X

> Therefore, my agreement to change, stated clearly and
>   reasonably, is . . .
> When I achieve my contract, the meaning it will give my
>   life is . . .

Once a script is acquired, a person tends to act in ways that reinforce and maintain it. The person who has been told "You can't trust anybody" invariably chooses friends and confidants who are completely untrustworthy, thereby proving that people are basically no good. The scripted individual is habitually saying "Why does this always happen to me?" as he or she makes the same mistakes with relating to boyfriends or girlfriends, with being clumsy, or with failing to meet challenges. The way out of this vicious cycle is to identify your dysfunctional conclusions and scripts and contract with yourself to redecide your fate by beginning to act in ways that counter your typical pattern. The phobic, for example, can be viewed as living out an early decision in response to a parental injunction (Goulding, 1977). A man who is afraid of heights may have had the childhood experience of not being caught once when he fell. The young boy interprets the fall as a "Don't be" message from his neglectful parent; he forgets the source but stores the injunction in his Child as a "I had better be careful" self-statement. A combination of redecision work and desensitization might be used to overcome the phobia rapidly (Goulding, 1977). The man must decide that he would *never* fall or jump and that he need not be scared if he is reasonably careful and operates from his Adult. He might climb the first step of a ladder and assertively declare that he is not going to fall or jump off. Gradually he would continue his climb and repeat his assertive declaration. He could also role play making this announcement to his parents.

In its short history, Transactional Analysis has changed its emphasis on cognitive interventions to include more affective and behavioral techniques. This brief overview of the method should provide some idea of its application to self-change. For a more detailed description of TA, you are encouraged to seek out original sources.

REFERENCES

Bandler, R., & Grinder, J. *The structure of magic.* Palo Alto: Science and Behavior Books, 1975.
Bannister, G., Jr. Cognitive and behavior therapy in a case of compulsive gambling. *Cognitive Therapy and Research,* 1977, *1,* 223–227.

Beck, A. T. *Depression.* Philadelphia: University of Pennsylvania, 1967.

Beck, A. T., Rush, A. J., Shaw, B. F., and Emery, G. *Cognitive therapy of depression: A treatment manual.* Copyright by Aaron T. Beck, 1978.

Berne, E. *Transactional analysis in psychotherapy.* New York: Grove Press, 1961. (a)

Berne, E. *Games people play.* New York: Grove Press, 1961. (b)

Berne, E. *What do you say after you say hello?* New York: Grove Press, 1972.

Brown, B. M. The multiple techniques of broad spectrum psychotherapy. In A. A. Lazarus (Ed.), *Clinical behavior therapy.* New York: Brunner/Mazel, 1972.

Cautela, J. R. The use of covert conditioning in modifying pain behavior. *Journal of Behavior Therapy and Experimental Psychiatry,* 1977, *8,* 45–52.

Cautela, J. R., & Wisocki, P. A. The thought stopping procedure: Description, application, and learning theory interpretations. *Psychological Record,* 1977, *27,* 255–264.

Duncker, K. On problem-solving. *Psychological Monographs,*1945, *58,* (5, Whole No. 270).

Dusay, J. M. The evolution of transactional analysis. In G. Barnes (Ed.), *Transactional analysis after Eric Berne.* New York: Harpers College Press, 1977.

Dusay, J. M. *Egograms.* New York: Harper & Row, 1978.

D'Zurilla, T., & Goldfried, M. Problem solving and behavior modification. *Journal of Abnormal Psychology,* 1971, *78,* 107–126.

Ellis, A. *Reason and emotion in psychotherapy.* New York: Lyle Stuart Press, 1962.

Ellis, A. *Humanistic psychotherapy.* New York: McGraw-Hill, 1973.

Ellis, A., & Harper, R. A. *A new guide to rational living.* Hollywood: Wilshire Book Company, 1976.

Feldenkrais, M. *Awareness through movement: Health exercises for personal growth.* New York: Harper & Row, 1972.

Gallwey, W. T. *The inner game of tennis.* New York: Random House, 1974.

Glasgow, R. E., & Arkowitz, H. The behavioral assessment of male and female social competence in dyadic heterosexual interactions. *Behavior Therapy,* 1975, *6,* 488–498.

Glass, C. R., Gottman, J. M., & Shmurak, S. H. Response acquisition and self-statement modification approaches to dating skill training. *Journal of Counseling Psychology,* 1976, *23,* 520–526.

Goulding, R. L. No magic at Mt. Madonna: Redecision in marathon therapy. In G. Barnes (Ed.), *Transactional analysis after Eric Berne.* New York: Harpers College Press, 1977.

Greenwald, H. *Decision therapy.* New York: Wyden, 1973.

Greenwald, H. M.: A case history illustrating direct decision therapy with a labeled schizophrenic. *Voices,* 1978, *14,* 31–37.

Hackman, A., & McLean, C. A comparison of flooding and thought-stopping in the treatment of obsessional neurosis. *Behavior Research and Therapy,* 1975, *13,* 263–269.

Hannum, J. W., Thoresen, C. E., & Hubbard, D. R., Jr. A behavioral study of self-esteem with elementary teachers. In M. J. Mahoney and C. E. Thoresen (Eds.), *Self-control: Power to the person.* Monterey, Calif.: Brooks/Cole, 1974.

Holroyd, K. A., Andrasik, F., & Westbrook, T. *Cognitive Therapy and Research,* 1977, *1,* 121–133.

James, M. M. Curing impotency with TA. *Transactional Analysis Journal,* 1971, 1, 88–93.

James, M. *Techniques in transactional analysis.* Reading, Mass.: Addison-Wesley, 1977.

James, M., & Jongeward, D. *Born to win: Transactional analysis with Gestalt experiments.* Reading, Mass.: Addison-Wesley, 1973.

James, M., & Savary, L. *A new self.* Reading, Mass.: Addison-Wesley, 1977.

Kahler, T. The miniscript. In G. Barnes (Ed.), *Transactional analysis after Eric Berne.* New York: Harpers College Press, 1977.

Kelly, G. A. *The psychology of personal constructs* (Vol. 1). New York: Norton, 1955.

Korzybski, A. *Science and sanity: An introduction to non-Aristotelian systems and general semantics* (4th ed.). Lakeville, Conn.: International Non-Aristotelian Library Publishing Co., 1958.

Lazarus, A. A. *Behavior therapy and beyond.* New York: McGraw-Hill, 1971.

Maultsby, M. C., Jr., & Ellis, A. *Technique for using rational-emotive imagery (REI).* New York: Institute for Rational Living, 1974.

Meichenbaum, D., & Turk, D. The cognitive-behavioral management of anxiety, anger, and pain. In P. O. Davidson (Ed.), *The behavioral management of anxiety, depression and pain.* New York: Brunner/Mazel, 1976.

Meichenbaum, D. *Cognitive-behavior modification.* New York: Plenum Press, 1977.

Meichenbaum, D., & Cameron, R. Training schizophrenics to talk to themselves: A means of developing attentional controls. *Behavior Therapy,* 1973, 4, 515–534.

Melzack, R. *The puzzle of pain.* Harmondsworth, England: Penguin, 1973.

Rimm, D. C., & Masters, J. C. *Behavior therapy.* New York: Academic Press, 1974.

Rudestam, K. E. Semantics and psychotherapy. *Psychotherapy: Theory, Research, and Practice,* 1978, 15(2), 190–192.

Schachter, S., & Singer, J. E. Cognitive, social and physiological determinants of emotional state. *Psychological Review,* 1962, 69, 379–399.

Schneider, M. Turtle technique in the classroom. *Teaching Exceptional Children,* Fall 1974, pp. 22–24.

Steiner, C. *Scripts people live.* New York: Grove Press, 1974.

Suinn, R. M. Visual-motor behavior rehearsal for adaptive behavior. In J. Krumboltz & C. Thoresen (Eds.) *Counselling methods.* New York: Holt, Rinehart & Winston, 1976.

Whorf, B. L. *Language, thought, and reality: Selected writings.* J. B. Carroll (Ed.). Cambridge, Mass.: Technology Press of MIT, 1956.

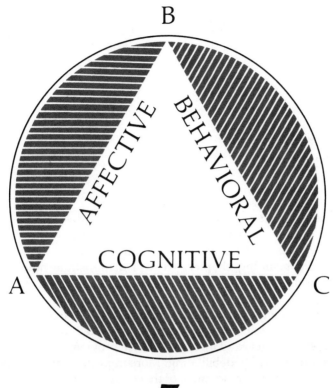

5

INTEGRATING AFFECTIVE, BEHAVIORAL, AND COGNITIVE METHODS

ASSERTIVENESS PROBLEMS
DEPRESSION
ANGER
INSOMNIA

In the last three chapters, we defined and described a variety of self-change techniques that fall into three categories: affective, behavioral, and cognitive. Table 5–1 summarizes these approaches.

In this concluding chapter, we will demonstrate how these self-therapy methods can be effectively integrated into viable treatment packages and applied to a number of psychologically based problems in living. For the purpose of illustration, four problem areas that frequently motivate people to seek professional help have been selected: assertiveness problems, depression, anger, and insomnia. These problem areas are very common and potentially quite debilitating. More important, they all have been shown to benefit from a broad range of therapeutic interventions. No single treatment method has been proven 100% effective or appropriate with any of these problems. As a matter of fact, in practice it is quite likely that therapists of different theoretical persuasions would take decidedly different, even contradictory, approaches to dealing with a person complaining of unassertiveness, depression, explosive anger, or chronic insomnia. And each orientation would probably prove effective with a large number of cases.

TABLE 5-1
A Summary of the ABC Approaches

Affective Methods	Behavioral Methods	Cognitive Methods
1. Relaxation training	8. Self-monitoring	14. Linguistic changes
2. Meditation	9. Stimulus control	15. Cognitive restructuring
3. Systematic desensitization	10. Self-reinforcement	16. Self-instruction training
4. Focusing	11. Self-punishment	17. Problem solving
5. Awareness and fantasy	12. Alternate responses	18. Thought stopping
6. Dream work	13. Paradoxical techniques	19. Direct decision therapy
7. Flooding		20. Transactional analysis

The kinds of problems that can be alleviated by self-therapy methods are not limited to these four syndromes, of course. Virtually all self-defeating behaviors can be modified in some way by systematically applying one or more of the self-change techniques we have discussed. A partial list of manageable problems might include: fears and avoidance patterns; dependent or passive behaviors; feelings of inadequacy, confusion, or helplessness; social ineptness; lack of impulse control; self-injurious habit patterns; problems in experiencing joy; psychosomatic aches and pains; sexual problems; suspicion or distrust; feelings of apathy and emptiness, and so on. Again, remember that, although the procedures introduced in these chapters are widely prescribed by professional therapists, in some instances the rigorous scientific experimentation that would provide the definitive word on their effectiveness with serious psychological problems has not yet been conducted. The best approach for the time being is to try the self-therapy techniques for your personal problems and to seek professional guidance if you reach a plateau and can go no further by yourself.

Success with self-change techniques may depend on the variety of techniques used and the perseverance with which they are applied over time (Lazarus, 1976). Generally, people who are successful at changing their own self-defeating patterns and in eliminating their own symptomatic behaviors have used a greater number of techniques than have people who are not successful. The techniques themselves are differentially effective depending on the particular problem for which they are used. Desensitization procedures, for example, have been found to be particularly helpful with phobic conditions. Other interventions, meditation and linguistic changes being two prime examples, have very general applicability to personality change and are less well suited for resolving specific target problems. Of course, there are also individual differences, differences between and among people. The techniques that appeal most to you and may work the best for you are not necessarily the ones that will attract or be effective for someone else. As you studied the procedural description for each method, no doubt some approaches seemed more shallow or limiting than others. Some may even have appeared totally absurd. Yet some reader will find the very approaches that you reject especially helpful!

The technique you use for working toward self-change is only part of the story. People who persevere for a long time are more likely to be successful. Consequently, a major determinant of the effectiveness of any particular method for you will be the strength of your own motivation to change. A person whose adjustment is based on manipulating others and who benefits from that exploitation—the so-called "psychopath"—is someone with limited motivation to change, and professional therapeutic failures to modify him or her attest to that fact.

The efficacy of any treatment design depends on recognizing and incorporating all three levels of change, the affective, the behavioral, and the cognitive. Although one modality may be sufficient to deal with some types of problems (for instance, if you suffer with pervasive feelings of anxiety, you might focus exclusively on the affective dimension), the majority of psychological difficulties involve unwanted feelings, bothersome behaviors, and unclear or irrational thinking processes. An integrated approach to self-change makes use of all three perspectives in a total treatment package. There is no prescribed order in which to use the techniques. You may have to experiment somewhat with the timing or application of the methods to suit your particular life-style and circumstances.

Finally, bear in mind that initial failures are not at all uncommon. In fact, they are to be expected. If an intervention does not appear to be effective at first, you may be tempted to discard the approach. You may even be prompted to label your problem as more serious and yourself as much crazier than you had initially believed. So anticipate difficulty. Allow yourself a reasonable amount of time. Assess your problem thoroughly, refine your self-change approach so that it suits you best, and persist. The majority of failures in using self-help interventions occur because the individual has not set clear goals or has not been methodical and persistent in creating and following through with a plan. The value of a professional psychotherapist lies in his or her ability to establish an environment that encourages new behaviors, thoughts, and emotional responses. If you can muster the necessary motivation and apply yourself to solving your own problems, you may be able to construct a similarly facilitative situation.

ASSERTIVENESS PROBLEMS

Assertive behavior has been defined as "behavior which enables a person to act in his own best interest and to stand up for himself without undue anxiety and to exercise his rights without denying the rights of others" (Alberti & Emmons, 1974). The infant has no reservation about screaming out to dramatize his or her needs. However, as the child matures, he or she learns to suppress such feelings in order to avoid confrontations with those who seem to be more powerful. The natural ability to act assertively is slowly stamped out as the child becomes more compliant. In fact, adults may find themselves feeling anxious and guilty when they fail to comply with the wishes of others. One leading psychotherapist estimates that 75% of his patients can be characterized as lacking in assertiveness (Fensterheim & Baer, 1975).

During the 1970s there has been an apparent preoccupation with assertiveness. Although some people might consider such self-awareness as narcissistic self-indulgence, on a more moderate level learning to identify and act on our rights provides us with greater confidence and freedom. In fact, assertiveness can be seen as the focus of such historical tracts of emancipation as the Declaration of Independence. Problems in assertiveness can be effectively treated with affective, behavioral, and cognitive techniques, and appropriate assertiveness can be relearned by applying the ABC self-therapy methods.

> There are many ways to determine whether you are less assertive than you could be. A number of scales have been constructed to assess deficits in assertive behavior. One representative scale is the Rathus Assertiveness Schedule (Rathus, 1973). However, a look at your own behavior and feelings in specific situations can give you valuable clues. How well do you do in situations that demand standing up for your personal rights and expressing yourself in open and appropriate ways? Do you habitually apologize for your behavior, thoughts, and feelings? Are you oversensitive to disapproval? Do you have difficulty expressing angry feelings? Tender feelings? If a salesclerk shortchanged you, would you request the correct change and insist on receiving it? Can you refuse to purchase a magazine subscription from a salesperson at the door? Would you refuse a second helping of food that you did not want? Can you request that someone who squeezed in line in front of you go to the end? Would you refuse a supervisor's request to work overtime if you did not want to work on the weekend? Can you ask your mate to experiment with you in a novel approach to lovemaking? Are you able to talk about yourself without feeling that you are imposing yourself? Can you comfortably accept compliments from others? Can you ask for clarification if you don't understand? Can you be persistent if you don't receive an acceptable answer the first time or if your appeals are ignored or minimized?

You can also gauge your reluctance to act assertively by looking at specific indices in your speech, such as the length of time it takes you to respond, the loudness of your voice, the extent to which you are compliant, and your willingness to request others to change their behavior relative to you (Eisler, Hersen, & Miller, 1973). Moreover, many clients seek out psychotherapy because of symptomatic anxiety, interpersonal problems, or somatic complaints when their most salient difficulty is their inability to act

Gaffer

assertively. Headaches, dizziness, tension, or arguments may be the results of avoiding assertive encounters.

Some people confuse assertiveness with aggression, thinking that if they stand up for their rights they are being aggressive. As a matter of fact, one must be a little careful not to behave aggressively as a way of compensating for a previous nonassertive style. Aggression is an act violating the rights of others by domination, humiliation, or degradation. True assertiveness is based on a respect for oneself *and* for the other person; aggressiveness is based not on respect but on the goal of winning the interpersonal encounter. For example, your housemate turns on the TV while you are trying to study. A nonassertive response might be to say nothing, brood, and become resentful. An aggressive response might sound like, "Turn that damn thing down . . . can't you see I'm studying?!" An assertive response states "I'm studying right now, and the sound of the TV interferes with my concentration. Please turn it down or off."

Assertiveness has the value of increasing your viable options and the control you have over your life. With this change comes increased self-respect. The more you act assertively, the more you will respect yourself and

the higher your self-esteem will be. Realize that you do n
sively exercise your rights for the sake of principle. As y
able with the idea that you do have certain rights to ex⌐
thoughts, feelings, and beliefs, remember that you can choose v.
when to insist on those rights. Having the potential to act assertiv
different from always behaving assertively, since assertive behavior may no᷍
necessarily be appropriate in every situation.

COGNITIVE METHODS

Before you can overcome the affective symptoms of anxiety or fear
that prevent you from acting in assertive ways and before you can acquire
new behavioral skills that may be lacking, you need to become aware of and
to accept your personal rights as a human being (see Self-Change Technique
15, Cognitive Restructuring). Smith (1975) lists ten principal rights of all
people:

1. You have a right to judge your own behavior, thoughts,
   and emotions and to take the responsibility for their
   initiation and consequences on yourself.
2. You have the right to offer no reasons or excuses to justify
   your behavior.
3. You have the right to judge whether you are responsible
   for finding a solution to other people's problems.
4. You have the right to change your mind.
5. You have the right to make mistakes—and be responsible
   for them.
6. You have the right to say "I don't know."
7. You have the right to be independent of the goodwill of
   others before coping with them.
8. You have the right to be illogical in making decisions.
9. You have the right to say "I don't understand."
10. You have the right to say "I don't care."[1]

Cognitive interventions, of course, focus on altering self-damaging
thoughts. Actually, both assertive and nonassertive people can generally
identify what an assertive response would be in a given situation. However,
people with low assertiveness are less apt to exercise an assertive response
when threatened (Schwartz & Gottman, 1974).

[1]From *When I Say No, I Feel Guilty,* by Manuel J. Smith, Ph.D. Copyright
©1975 by Manuel J. Smith. Reprinted by permission of THE DIAL PRESS.

Try to identify specific situations in which you are able to behave assertively and those in which you would like to act assertively but tend not to do so. Record these situations in a diary, focusing on *what* happened, *when, where,* and *with whom.* Write down the context, your response, and the result, including how you felt. Such systematic observations will help you diagnose areas of strength and weakness, establish target goals, and gauge improvement.

As you think about acting assertively, what are your thoughts? Do you become self-conscious? Self-accusatory? Do you imagine what others are thinking of you? Nonassertive people tend to use a higher ratio of negative self-statements to positive self-statements than do assertive people (Schwartz & Gottman, 1974). The nonassertive person is more apt to say "If I say this, the other person will be hurt" or "What would he think of me if . . . ?" The assertive person says "I'm free to say 'no' " or "It's reasonable to have a choice." Overconcern for someone else's reactions is a predictable obsession in nonassertive people. You do have the right to be assertive even if someone else's feelings may be injured in the process. Deliberately injuring their feelings or being insensitive to them, however, is aggressiveness, not assertiveness. Moreover, although you may not insist that other people respond or behave in particular ways, you can request that they do. *Asking* is always legitimate, because it implies that others can be assertive too and that they have the option to decline. As a general guideline, if you are not prepared to deal with a person's response, then it might be preferable not to ask your question.

In cognitive restructuring, you make a careful analysis of your self-talk and your actual rights in a given situation. Once you have identified your invalid assumptions and replaced them with more reasonable alternatives, you will invariably be able to reduce your anxiety and increase the potential for an assertive response. Because most nonassertive behavior is based on fears of reprisal or devaluation from another person, Ellis' (1973) irrational beliefs (see p. 158) are particularly relevant for consideration. If you have accepted the notion that disapproval will kill you (Belief 1), you will be extremely reluctant to express your opinions and wishes, to enter conflicts, to share feelings, and to engage others in encounters. If you have accepted the belief that you must be thoroughly competent in all contexts (Belief 2), you will, of course, apologize profusely for all your shortcomings and become anxious in situations that spotlight any of your less-than-perfect behaviors. You may also be resistant to assertive expression if you have a fear of hurting others, looking foolish, losing control, or being regarded as selfish or immoral.

Women, in particular, may have great difficulty engaging in assertive behavior. According to Transactional Analysis (Self-Change Technique 20), the female in our culture has been scripted to act in nonassertive ways. Early parental messages such as "A woman's place is in the home" or "You're only a girl" become reified into slogans for living that preempt assertive behavior. Try to identify any parental messages or injunctions that may inhibit your assertiveness. An analysis of ego states may reveal that your Adult is small and needs cultivating, while your Nurturant Parent, the tendency to rescue others by downgrading yourself, is overdeveloped and needs reducing. The decision you made at an earlier time to sacrifice your own needs and to be appreciated for your submissiveness may require reexamination and over-haul according to the procedures of direct decision therapy (Self-Change Technique 19).

AFFECTIVE METHODS

The primary affective obstacles to acting assertively are your anxiety and guilt about the potentially negative consequences of your assertive actions. Before you can develop direct emotional expressiveness, try to identify feelings you now experience when you fail to act assertively. Focusing may be helpful for this purpose (Self-Change Technique 4). Thereafter, self-induced relaxation (Self-Change Technique 1) or meditation (Self-Change Technique 2) can be used throughout the training process to facilitate new behavioral responses. These techniques can help you discriminate your anxiety level in problematic situations so that you can pause and relax totally before engaging in an assertive response.

Obviously, when you engage in any new risky behavior, you are likely to feel some anxiety. However, people experience bodily tension more often when they are not assertive than when they are assertive. This is because when you are unassertive, you are not acting on your feelings or impulses. Tension and anxiety occur most often as a function of incomplete or suppressed actions or statements in an interpersonal context. When you experience an increased pulse rate, a queasy stomach, a pounding heart, weak limbs, perspiration, blushing, and general fatigue, you are probably feeling anxious. These physiological fear reactions occur in anticipation of imagined, terrifying consequences and can be desensitized using relaxation methods.

Systematic desensitization (Self-Change Technique 3) can be used
to gradually attain confidence in more fear-inducing situations.
Construct a fear hierarchy for approaching confrontations that you
have been avoiding. Use fantasy and imagery to rehearse the
confrontation. For example, if you will be dealing with a hostile
relative, you can anticipate each response by desensitizing
yourself to each phase of the interaction: preparing for the
meeting, initiating the topic, rebutting the reply, insisting on your
position, and terminating the dialogue. Ask yourself what the

worst possible outcome might be and anticipate that. Note especially those statements from others that feed into your self-defeating pattern by yielding rationalizations for nonassertive behavior. Sometimes there are put-down sentences such as "If I were you . . . " or "Haven't you done this yet?" or "That's a stupid way to. . . . " With each successive step along the hierarchy, let the anxiety cue a relaxation response and then proceed to the next step.

The empty-chair fantasy technique (Self-Change Technique 5) can help put you in touch with the imagined reactions of others to your assertiveness. If you are shy about interacting with a special someone of the opposite sex, visualize that person in an empty chair and imagine his or her response to your initiating comments. Listen for your worst fears to materialize and respond calmly to them. Remember to relax. You can learn something about the underlying fears that keep you from acting assertively, while desensitizing yourself to imagined threats. It may be that your "top dog" is imagining the worst possible consequences, while your "bottom dog" wants to forge ahead. The fantasy dialogue may settle this conflict.

BEHAVIORAL METHODS

Sometimes a lack of assertiveness is a function of general timidity or reserve, and at other times specific behavioral deficits may be involved, such as the inability to make small talk or to initiate confrontations. Treatment depends to some extent on the type of deficit involved. With specific blocks, such as fearing ridicule or rejection or intimacy, it may be important to desensitize anxiety reactions first and then practice new behaviors. In part, the behavioral approach to encouraging assertiveness consists of breaking down complex behaviors into smaller units and then creating new, more assertive responses in increasingly threatening situations. The new responses are usually role played or rehearsed in the presence of supportive others prior to initiating them in the real world. Of course, it also helps if you can observe people who are assertive and whose responses can serve as models for you to practice. Try practicing more assertive verbal responses with a friend or in front of a mirror. Remember to maintain eye contact and to use a forceful yet moderate tone of voice. Overt behaviors that indicate a lack of assertion include a low speaking voice, lack of eye contact, slouching posture, disorganized or stuttering speech, and tense muscles.

The ultimate key to combatting nonassertiveness is action and practice. Begin with situations that are not overtly threatening and in which your chances for success are optimal. Practice making small talk. Casual comments, such as "Good morning" or "It looks like winter is on the way," are part of the process of mutual exploration between acquaintances. As you become comfortable and adept in the exchange of trivia, you can acquire increased skill and confidence in situations in which assertiveness is more crucial.

Move from desensitizing your fears in imagery (systematic desensitization) to using shaping and self-reinforcement principles to rehearse new behaviors that bridge the gap between low and high threat (Self-Change Technique 10). Begin with tasks at which you are relatively comfortable and increase the risk in very small steps. Practice expressing low-threat feelings such as complimenting a woman on her style of dress or a man on his choice of tie. Eventually these rehearsals will carry over to make a pronounced improvement in expressing other feelings. Difficulties in communicating warm, caring emotions directly and unequivocally are as common as problems in expressing anger and disappointment.

> Deliberately test yourself and set deadlines for your self-therapy. Ask a gas station attendant to wash your windshield, for example, after giving you gasoline. When you purchase only one item in the supermarket, ask if you may go to the front of the line. Return an item you just purchased that does not suit you and insist on getting your money back. Ask directions from a stranger on the street. Break into a group of strangers conversing at a social gathering. Experiment using assertive behavior with strangers and in commercial situations. Once you are comfortable with this behavior, you can safely become more open and direct with people with whom you have close and involved emotional relationships. Ensure that you have included appropriate rewards for yourself for meeting goals and improving performance.

DESC scripting (Bower & Bower, 1976) is a particular combination of behavioral and cognitive rehearsal for dealing assertively with interpersonal conflicts. This is a formal way of rewriting scenes that have not worked out well for you and in which you too often either yield, acting nonassertively, or fight, acting aggressively. In the first stage, *describe* the behaviors of others that are problematic for you. The second stage is *expressing* how you feel about that unwanted behavior. In the third step, *specify* the behavioral changes you might contract for with the other party to reach a more equitable outcome. Finally, note the *consequences* that you can provide for the other person that will enhance the likelihood of a negotiated solution.

Imagine, for instance, that your parents insist or assume that you will spend every holiday with them at their house and that you have thus far been unable to cope with their steamroller approach. Your DESC sequence might go like this:

1. *Describe:* "You are assuming that every holiday should be spent with you and the other relatives at your house."
2. *Express:* "When you do this, I feel overwhelmed. I believe

that, as an adult, with a family of my own, I have a right to have a voice in determining where I spend my holidays."

3. *Specify:* "I want you to stop insisting that it is my responsibility to spend my holidays in your home."

4. *Consequence:* "If you stop commenting on where you think I should spend the holidays, I would be happy to come to your home this year for either Thanksgiving or Christmas."

By writing the plan out first you create a clear picture of the way in which the discussion breaks down, an incentive toward making an assertive approach and the confidence to pursue it. It also gives you some idea of the probable outcome.

In carrying out the four steps, remember to describe the behavior as concretely as possible, avoiding generalizations by sticking to the specific situation. Express your feelings clearly and assertively rather than provoking the other person. A less satisfactory approach, for example, would be to yell "Stop being so bloody selfish! If you don't stop nagging, you'll never see me at your place again!" Try to focus on specifying the offending behavior rather than impugning the person or venting your hostility. Stay calm and positive and ask for small changes rather than grandiose overhauls. Be sure to indicate that you are willing to help reach an amicable solution. Increase the chances of success by rewarding the other person (coming over on some holiday if it seems reasonable to you). Punishment is recommended only when it appears necessary, when you are really willing to carry it out, and if it is appropriate to the offense. For instance, you could calmly assert that, if your parents continue their nagging harassment, you will not visit during any holiday this year.

Review your DESC sequence in preparation for using it in actual practice. Consistent with behavior-shaping principles, begin with a situation that is not too threatening. If you happen to meet up with a persistent opponent, try not to be immediately put off by his or her second line of attack, but maintain your own assertive stance. Smith (1975) suggests that automobile mechanics, notorious as the most difficult group to negotiate with successfully, are actually among the easiest people to deal with when you act assertively. Bear in mind that a sharp rise in tone of voice or an offensive attack may signal the other person's last desperate assault prior to yielding. Try to be sensitive to the other person's legitimate points. Although that person may act aggressively, persist with asserting your own demand by repeating your original point. Keep returning to your main theme ("I want my money back") instead of becoming defensive and thus aggressive or nonassertive.

The DESC script is similar to Lange and Jakubowski's (1976) use of "I" statements, which also involves four ingredients: making nonaccusatory descriptions of the other's behavior; describing the effects of the behavior on you; stating your own feelings; and stating your own preferences. For instance, if you want some help at home with babysitting, an assertive remark might be to say "When you fail to watch Timmy while I am studying, I do a poor job in my work because I have to attend to him. I am becoming irritated by this demand and would like to know what you will do to help me out with our child at those times."

An alternate response (Self-Change Technique 12) to becoming defensive or counterattacking when criticized is called "fogging" (Smith, 1975). In fogging, you agree with the basic principle or the valid components of the accusation or criticism, without yielding on your legitimate position. If your father accuses "You did a miserable job on that exam!" try a paradoxical and nondefensive response such as "That's true, I didn't do well on that exam," without going further and apologizing profusely or explaining yourself as if you were a justifiably convicted criminal. The friend who attacks by saying "I don't want you going out with John" might be told "I know you don't." In other words, sometimes an explanation just isn't called for. If you are in error, simply admit your mistake. Fogging is not meant to be used in an insincere, sarcastic way but openly and honestly as an assertive approach to coping with criticism. Remember that you are not obligated to share the other person's value system. It is perfectly reasonable to ask the person who criticizes your clothes what is particularly offensive about them. Such inquiries not only help to desensitize you to criticism but also invite the people you care about to explore their own value systems underlying their complaints.

The self-therapy strategy you select will depend somewhat on the extent to which your lack of assertiveness is a straightforward behavioral deficiency or an entrenched pattern of behavior maintained by avoiding particular situations that generate considerable anxiety. In the first instance, behavioral self-change techniques may be sufficient, but in the latter case the groundwork will have to be laid using cognitive and affective interventions. When minimal assertiveness is not effective or when strong personal feelings need to be shared, a full expression of anger may have to be disinhibited. For difficulties in expressing anger, the following sections may be helpful.

DEPRESSION

Depression is a universal disorder in which the emotions become a source of profound psychological distress. Once called "melancholia" and accurately described by Hippocrates in the fourth century B.C., depression has been recognized for centuries. Historical figures, notably Abraham Lincoln and Winston Churchill, have written vivid accounts of their own bouts with what Churchill called "the mad dogs of depression." Today, authorities estimate that 15% of the population of the United States exhibits significant symptoms of depression and that this figure is highest for people between 18 and 29 years of age (Secunda, Katz, Friedman, & Schuyler, 1973). We all have a common-sense understanding of this malady because we all become depressed at times; it goes with living in a world where things do not always work out the way we would like them to. Depression is in part the product of the collapse of an illusion. Indeed, depression may be part of our very humanness, the price we pay for confronting our own mortality. Depression becomes of clinical concern, however, when it is overly intense or when it does not abate with time.

Depression can be identified by symptoms operating on the affective, behavioral, and cognitive levels. On the affective level, when you become depressed, you feel low in mood, sad, dejected, discouraged, fatigued, irritable, and even guilty and angry. Behaviorally, you may withdraw from activities that were once satisfying and enjoyable and become slow or lethargic in action and speech. You may even become reclusive. You probably sleep poorly, have crying spells, and have no appetite or interest in sex. At the extreme, you may even flirt with suicide. On the cognitive level, you probably regard yourself as lacking some attribute you view as essential for happiness, and you are no doubt rather negativisitic about yourself and others. You may be very self-critical, thinking of yourself as helpless and worthless and of your position as pathetic and hopeless. Depression statements sound like "I can't get involved in anything," "I get fatigued and restless for no reason," "I feel like no one needs me anymore," and "I just feel empty and useless."

Bear in mind that depression can be caused by physiological problems such as biological or hormonal factors, where the primary treatment may best reside in the hands of a skilled professional who might recommend psychotropic drugs or hospitalization. One kind of depression, labeled "endogenous," is characterized by early morning waking, crying spells, weight loss, a perpetually downcast mood, obsessional thinking, and a general lack of pleasure in life. This syndrome, occurring most often during middle age and with a family history of depression, is best handled with professional consultation. However, most depression is situational; that is, it occurs as a result of some concrete loss, such as the death of a relative, the rupture of a close relationship, or a major disappointment. Self-change interventions can be useful to help combat situational depression and as supplemental therapy for more ongoing and chronic depression that may be either part of the personality structure or enmeshed in the secondary gains of interpersonal relationships.

BEHAVIORAL METHODS

A primary step to overcoming depression is to reverse your behavioral inertia as soon as possible. Most often depression is a response to some kind of loss. Consequently, you may see yourself as lacking some person, characteristic, or item that you consider necessary for your happiness. However, as you withdraw, you become lazier, reducing the number of positive reinforcers that are potentially available to you.

> Use the behavioral methods of self-observation, and make a list of possible reinforcers (Self-Change Technique 8). There must be some activities that you find pleasurable that are not self-destructive. Perhaps you enjoy listening to music, taking a walk, or going swimming. Maintain a daily written schedule of your activities. Label both the activities that you have to do and those that you enjoy doing. When using "Mastery and Pleasure Therapy" (Beck, 1967), check your behaviors by marking an "M" or a "P" beside each activity you perform to indicate its designation: mastery over something formidable, such as writing a few pages of a term paper or going to a meeting, or pleasure over an inherently enjoyable event, such as going out to dinner with a friend or treating yourself to a movie. Rate each activity on a scale from 1 to 5 according to how much mastery or pleasure you experience. Self-monitoring may seem boring or painful to you. However, it will probably help you to appreciate the relationship between specific behaviors and your depressive feelings and cognitions. As you track your M's and P's, you will probably also discover that there is some hope for lifting the fog of your depression. Use the P's as reinforcers, Premack style, to reward yourself for increasing M activities that are not as easily initiated.

Since the loss of reinforcers is so basic to states of depression, it is imperative to identify and seek out meaningful objects or activities. If you see yourself as unable to attain your goals, use your reinforcers to shape new behaviors (Self-Change Technique 10). If you cannot believe that there could be any potentially positive experiences in your current life, make a list of the reinforcers that you enjoyed in the past or that you might conceivably enjoy in the future. Monitor your ongoing behavior on an hourly basis just in case there are some worthwhile experiences you may have ignored or minimized in your depressed condition. Morita therapy, a form of psychotherapy indigenous to Japan, requires the depressed person to stay in bed for one week without any of the usual sources of reinforcements, including, of course, the attention of family members (Reynolds, 1976). After this period of social and physical deprivation, a period of physical work is prescribed, after which previously rewarding stimuli tend to be experienced as meaningful and relevant once again.

> Fight your behavioral inertia. Begin to initiate activities, even if you do not enjoy them at first. Remember that you can increase your low-base-rate behaviors by attending to the principles of self-reward (Self-Change Technique 10). Start by scheduling basic activities for yourself, including such elementary behaviors as getting up in the morning, eating balanced meals, doing your work, and interacting with others. Contract with yourself in the evening for the next day's activities and their reinforcement consequences. Since you are apt to be withdrawn and asocial when you feel depressed, start arranging modest tasks for yourself in such areas as conversation about nondepressive topics and participation in social activities. Reward yourself for success by covertly congratulating yourself and by using any overt reinforcers you can muster. In all likelihood you will be more able to overcome your inertia if you adhere to your schedule and reward yourself for each success. Gradually set challenges for yourself so that you can slowly begin to increase your rate of behavior. As you reinforce yourself each time you make progress toward your projected goal, you shape your behavior to become more outgoing, functional, and gratifying.

Remember that stimulus control is a potent behavior modifier (Self-Change Technique 9). Look for the stimulus cues associated with your depressive symptoms. If you stay in bed, you're not likely to accomplish much of anything. If you hide out alone in the house, there is no way you are going to be able to reignite defused relationships. If you can't stop worrying, schedule a time and place to worry a little each day. Specify a "worrying chair" and spend 30 minutes a day in it dutifully reviewing your problems and nothing else. You might even consider "blowing up" your worries to ludicrous proportions (Paradoxical Techniques, Self-Change Technique 13).

Since physical health plays such a critical role in stabilizing mental conditions, treat your body kindly. Although it may seem like your own worst enemy at the moment, exercise, eat right, and maintain personal hygiene. You can be sure that passivity will only feed a negative spiral of hopelessness and despair. Increased activity is not only a way to reacquaint yourself with the potential value of reinforcers. It is also a way to change your image of yourself from an incapable, worthless, ugly oaf to a functioning, worthwhile person.

An invaluable strategy for fighting depression is to look for alternate behaviors that are incompatible with your depressive symptoms (Self-Change Technique 12). One way to do this is to note activities that seem to be associated with those times when your mood is not depressed. These

FIGURE 5-1

Jogging has become a popular form of self-therapy. A few psychologists and physicians believe that running can lead to emotional breakthroughs by altering the hormonal composition of the body. Several therapists prescribe jogging as an adjunctive treatment for moderate depression. At the very least, jogging can serve as an alternate response technique to distract you from your more mundane woes and improve your general state of health.

activities can then become targets to increase. Distracting responses, such as going to a concert or indulging in a pleasant fantasy, may also be helpful alternate behaviors. Activity itself can serve as a distracting response by taking your attention away from your pain. By initiating action you may also find that other people will relate more positively to you.

It is difficult, of course, to change the way that others respond to you. One of the obstacles to overcoming your depressed state is that other people frequently do not understand your feelings and act in ways that merely exacerbate your problems. Friends and relatives may try to give you reassurance by saying "Things aren't so bad" and "You're okay" or by comforting and consoling you when you feel down. If their nurturant responses are helpful, that's fine. But too often such reassurance seems unrealistic and uncomprehending. It may be difficult for you to discern if your complaints are being met with genuine concern and interest or with placating responses intended to dismiss you when you are at your worst. Of course, even the warmest, most responsive people cannot tolerate a chronically depressed individual for very long. Yet because they are also genuinely concerned, it may be difficult for them to openly share their annoyance with you. As your pain grows, your listeners may find it more difficult to distinguish between your genuine confusion and need for assurance and your manipulations to get attention through your symptoms. If you find yourself in this position, try to be aware of the difficulty that others may have in dealing with you. Temper your interactions with as much nonsymptomatic verbal and nonverbal behavior as possible so that others do not give you phony nurturant responses. Avoid people and environments that are toxic for you or totally unresponsive to your needs. In short, try to analyze your interpersonal relationships so that you can restructure them to create more opportunities for pleasure and reinforcement.

COGNITIVE METHODS

One of the cognitive symptoms of depression is excessive self-blame. Blaming yourself for being imperfect is like giving yourself a report card and using the grade to determine whether you are a worthwhile human being. Although you may be tolerant and accept other people with all their faults, you are probably much harder on yourself. However, blaming yourself instead of changing your behavior is actually a tremendous conceit: it implies that you are not a fallible human being, that you are too perfect to allow yourself to fail, make mistakes, or handle defeat. Along with self-blame, there may be a heavy dose of self-pity, implying not only that you want your own way but also that it's an abject tragedy if you *don't* get your own way. In one sense, depression can be conceptualized as a problem of courage; the depressed individual becomes disillusioned with a previous way of being and is afraid to become fully involved in life. You may also believe that you have no control over things that happen to you, a phenomenon referred to as "learned helplessness" (Seligman, 1975). You may come to believe you are helpless and powerless. Passivity and loss of interest tend to accompany these beliefs.

> Cognitive self-therapy methods work by changing your conception of yourself as a loser. Try to identify your self-defeating, maladaptive thoughts (Cognitive Restructuring, Self-Change Technique 15). When you feel sad and discouraged, what internal messages do you hear? Do you tell yourself that it is a catastrophe when things don't work out the way you would like them to? Or do you believe that it is a dire necessity to be loved and approved unconditionally by every significant person in your life? Do you tell yourself that because Joe or Marsha is no longer interested in you, you are a worthless human being, incapable of maintaining a significant intimate relationship? Notice the ways in which you remorselessly criticize yourself. If other people spoke to you as you speak to yourself, would you accept their opinions as valid tenets for living, or would you suggest that they are assumptions to examine and consider? Would you despise someone else for making the same mistakes you make? Before you can effectively alter your own maladaptive thoughts, you must admit their irrationality and subjectivity to yourself. Listen for the "shoulds" you are using with yourself ("I should be able to shoulder this responsibility without flinching," "I should be able to earn more money," "I should be able to hold the man I want"). Who is the authority figure behind your "shoulds" (Linguistic Changes, Self-Change Technique 14)?

Genuinely depressed people typically maintain at least four false beliefs (Raimy, 1975):

1. The belief that they will be depressed forever;
2. The belief that no one understands the depth of their misery;
3. The belief that if they get any more depressed, they will lose their minds; and
4. The belief that, if they recover at all, recovery will take a long time and be incomplete.

If you are depressed, realize that these beliefs are not unusual but are as common as suicidal thoughts. They are misconceptions. Depressed people do improve. In fact, in one study (Rush, Beck, Kovacs, & Hollon, 1977), 79% of the depressives in an outpatient unit improved in an 11-week period of time with cognitive-therapy methods alone.

After you have identified your self-destructive cognitions, work on modifying them.

> Keep a record of your feelings, accompanying negative self-statements, and self-corrective thoughts (Beck, 1967). Try to identify the other components of your irrational reasoning, such as your use of overgeneralization ("I *always* lose this way," "Others *always* do better than I," "Things *never* work out for me") and dichotomous thinking ("I have to do well *or* I'm a failure," "He's either a hero *or* a son of a bitch"). Use problem solving to generate alternative explanations for depressing experiences when they occur, other than your usual self-abusive excuses (Self-Change Technique 17). Consider, for instance, that "He wasn't ready for a serious relationship" rather than "I must be a worthless partner." Use brainstorming to list all the alternative ways of interpreting the depressing event or the various steps you can take to make yourself feel better. Perhaps you can even view your depression as an opportunity to make significant life changes. After all, depression often occurs when events take an unexpected turn for the worse. Consequently, it may be time to reorient yourself and change directions, learning from your experiences.

Anticipate obstacles by engaging in cognitive rehearsal. Fantasize about the likely outcome or the obstacles to a particular set of behaviors. Imagine the consequences of phoning your mother-in-law when you are feeling depressed. Will she be supportive, or is she likely to inject some guilt-producing message into the conversation that will make you feel even more low and dejected? If you stay home today, will you really be able to accomplish all your goals? Will your sadness and grief be relieved by maintaining your deceased son's room as a shrine, or will doing so serve as a constant reminder of your loss, making it more difficult to renew your own life?

If your depressive thoughts become obsessive, you might try a more direct and dramatic technique like thought stopping to terminate them (Self-Change Technique 18). Practice associating the disruptive command "Stop!" with those indulgent and upsetting thoughts about, for example, your former lover being involved with someone else. A less abrupt interrupting phrase, such as "I'm going to think of something else now," may work as effectively. Consider combining thought stopping with the deliberate evocation of positive thoughts, such as "I didn't do such a bad job after all" or "Tomorrow is another day, and another chance." Since self-generated negative statements only prolong your depression, it stands to reason that positive self-statements can help you break your depressive pattern and reinforce a symptom-free state. Research by Hannum, Thoresen, and Hubbard (1974) attests to the value of this technique. Depressed women were asked to write six positive thoughts about themselves on index cards and then to carry the cards around with them. Whenever they felt especially depressed, they read the cards and rewarded themselves with a cigarette. Although any high-probability response other than a cigarette could be used, the low-probability act of reading an optimistic, positive statement was reinforced, and the women reported feeling less depressed.

From the perspective of Transactional Analysis (Self-Change Technique 20), the depressive's stance towards himself or herself and the world takes the form of "You're OK, I'm not–OK." The self-accusatory message you carry in your mind is derived from a series of early parental messages. These parental messages are introjected, or swallowed whole, and live on in your Critical Parent ego state. Your Parent demands and messages can trigger a "Kick Me" pattern, a behavioral sequence in which you set yourself up by subtly inviting misfortune and rejection, wondering later "Why does this always happen to me?" (Kemp, 1977). Whenever you are engaged in the "Kick Me" pattern, look to see if there is a self-destructive script involved. Examine the rationality of the internal message that you are "not-OK," and reduce the impact of your Parent. You may even have made a past decision to be depressed in order to elicit sympathy from others. Be aware that an old decision can be renegotiated (Direct Decision Therapy, Self-Change Technique 19), and you are not doomed to passively tumble into the same trap time and time again.

The treatment of depression in TA focuses on the need for strokes from others and from yourself. Strokes are interpersonal reinforcers or caring responses. They may be either verbal, such as praise, or physical, such as hugs and pats. The important issue is to be able to ask for, receive, and give strokes when the need arises. Let other people know what you want when you want it. Encourage yourself to want good things for yourself. Schedule pleasurable activities, and give yourself permission to ask for and receive the things you want. There is no limit to the number of physical and verbal strokes available to you, although people often act as if strokes were a scarce commodity. Self-stroking is valuable and important, too. Give yourself credit for small achievements. Brag a little. The Nurturant Parent you create for yourself may be better than any other around!

AFFECTIVE METHODS

Psychoanalytic writers suggest that depression is really anger turned inward against the self. Instead of directing the anger at a significant other, the depressed individual diverts it and punishes himself or herself. Some people behave as if any criticism or complaint will jeopardize the stability of their primary emotional relationship. They tend to see the needs and demands of the partner as more important than their own desires. In effect, their feelings of self-esteem are completely contingent on the relationship. As long as the relationship runs smoothly, they feel optimistic and energetic, but, if the relationship is threatened or terminated, they plunge to the depths of despair. In this case, the loss of the relationship also involves the loss of self-esteem and of powerful positive reinforcers. If you find yourself attaching this extreme value to a primary emotional relationship, you may be heading for depression, since you cannot defer to another's needs and wishes indefinitely and also maintain some sense of self-worth. Over time, the resentment you harbor will feed on your self-respect.

Use the focusing technique (Self-Change Technique 4) to try to get in touch with any feelings of anger you might be suppressing while you are depressed. Then discharge your rage in a safe environment (described in the next section on anger). For example, pound on a mattress in an isolated room and scream at the top of your lungs at the source of your frustration. This exercise is useful because it does not have the disadvantages, including the guilt, of yelling at and pounding people; mattresses can't fight back, and they don't suffer bruises and scars from the beatings they take.

When you are depressed, you may also be feeling ambivalent about some significant person in your life. This person is called a "trapper" because you give him or her the power to enrage and depress you (Raimy, 1975). You may deny any anger you feel toward your trapper because it seems to be unjustified. After all, you think, how can I be angry with a sacrificing mother or a gentle, considerate husband? Of course, you can! Remember that expressing rage in fantasy is completely different from expressing it in reality. Bioenergetic-release exercises and fantasy encounters are good for reducing depressive withdrawal and generating sufficient affective arousal to risk engaging in new assertive behaviors.

Depression is predictable following a significant loss through death or desertion. Since both sadness and anger are part of this grief reaction, it is perfectly appropriate to shed both the sadness through tears and the anger through verbal outbursts. Part of resolving your depressive grief reaction involves saying goodbye with finality to the person who has left you. Using the two-chair fantasy technique, address the person in an empty chair and share your parting thoughts and feelings (Self-Change Technique 5).

Since depression is associated with a severe depletion of energy, an outpouring of strong affect or emotion can help lift the depression. Increasing your intake of oxygen by breathing deeply also helps to build up energy when you feel depressed (Lowen, 1972). Although breathing does not cure depression, focusing regularly on your breathing cycles using meditation techniques can lead to increased vitality (Self-Change Technique 2).

Affective self-therapy techniques for depression also focus on redis-covering some positive feelings. It is important to recall pleasant events and seek new sources of gratification. One way to increase the appeal of activi-ties in order to counter the feelings of hopelessness that accompany the depressed state is by immersing yourself in a fantasy about the future (Self-Change Technique 5). Try a "time projection" (Lazarus, 1976).

> Sit back, close your eyes, and imagine some future time. You are
> not depressed; rather, you are enjoyably engaged in various
> rewarding activities. Try to actually see yourself participating in
> the activity and to experience the enjoyment of it. When you can
> master this step, push yourself to duplicate in reality what you
> experienced in fantasy. Since the near future may be too clouded
> with depressive affect, you should probably place your fantasy in
> the distant future and only gradually bring the fantasy closer to
> the present. The goal is to make yourself feel emotions that are
> incompatible with depression, such as joy, pleasure, or relaxation.
> If the fantasy stops feeling good or if you have no feelings at all,
> stop the exercise.

Finally, it is common for depressed people to also experience anxiety. Obsessive worries and apprehensions, lack of concentration, memory de-ficiencies, irritability, and insomnia are all fellow travelers on the depressive trip. You may need to inhibit your anxiety as you attempt to identify and pursue meaningful activities. For this purpose, relaxation strategies (Self-Change Technique 1) may be valuable.

ANGER

As a violent emotional response to provocation, anger is of particular concern in the context of maintaining harmony in our complex social sys-tem. Social violence is accelerating at an alarming rate, as reflected both in the criminal destruction of people and property in the city streets and in media representations of cops and robbers. It is epitomized by the glut of television programs and movies that accentuate the baser instincts of the human race. Many of us seem to need outlets for our anger without taking responsibility for it. The popularity of comedy based on abuse and injury attests to the affective relief found in aggression directed at someone else. Although anger seems to be a more or less unavoidable human response, it need not reach a totally destructive intensity. Experts disagree about whether anger and aggression are instinctual, unlearned responses or conditioned emotions acquired in development. Yet we all share the cautious hope that the expression of anger can be channeled and modified to maximize both the psychological and physical health of the individual and the welfare of society.

Anger as an affective response varies from mild annoyance to uncontrollable rage. On the whole, anger takes place when your expectations regarding other people and events are not met. You undoubtedly feel some of it whenever you are put down, humiliated, manipulated, taken advantage of, rejected, or unfairly criticized. If you deny these feelings to yourself by insisting that something "isn't worth getting angry about," you may be expressing anger indirectly and denying yourself the right to assert your needs. As mentioned in the previous section, people who have difficulty expressing negative feelings in direct, honest ways often have trouble expressing positive ones as well. In order to relate intimately and effectively with others, it is important to learn how to share *all* your feelings openly.

Novaco (1975) agrees that anger is a powerful emotional response to provocation that can serve a variety of functions, some frightening and some satisfying. Although intense feelings of anger may make it virtually impossible to carry out any deliberate and effective sequence of behavior, a certain amount of anger can actually stimulate and energize us. For example, the football coach exhorts the team to take the field and whip the opposition. Therapists often encourage the expression of anger in the marital relationship to keep the lines of communication open (Bach & Wyden, 1969). However, for many people the expression of anger serves as a defensive retort to feelings of helplessness and vulnerability. When it is not openly recognized and expressed, anger can debilitate you physiologically, by causing constipation, migraine, and various psychosomatic diseases, and psychologically, by destroying relationships and leading to feelings of guilt and depression. The issue, then, is to become comfortable with tolerable levels of anger (all of us become annoyed or irritated at times) without suffering from the crippling impact of anger when it is an automatic, uncontrollable response to provocation. It is important to note that true aggression, behavior that is meant to make the victim suffer, has little to do with anger since it is initiated for its own instrumental, reinforcing consequences.

Alexander Lowen (1967) maintains that all psychotherapy patients have reason to be angry as a consequence of experiencing frustrations in growing up that have led them to compromise their own wishes and desires for the sake of someone else's needs. Of course, by that standard, all people have reason to be angry. Some of us may become angry more often than we

INTEGRATING AFFECTIVE, BEHAVIORAL,
AND COGNITIVE METHODS

want to, either because there are lots of situations and cues in the environment that elicit anger responses or because anger has worked so effectively in meeting our needs. In such cases, the therapeutic goal may be to tone down the anger response and to develop new ways of handling provocative situations. On the other hand, those of us who rarely or never feel angry may need to become more acquainted with our feelings of anger.

There are some basic undesirable side effects of failing to acknowledge and express anger directly. For instance, essential hypertension, commonly known as chronic high blood pressure, is one particular syndrome that is believed to be related to difficulties with the expression of anger (Alexander, 1950). The potential hypertensive may be especially sensitive to anger-inducing cues and so becomes easily outraged. He or she may also have difficulty dealing directly and nonsubmissively with angry feelings and may consequently channel them inward. Over time, this can result in serious physical disabilities or even death. Figuratively speaking, the hypertensive's blood boils rather readily. He or she may need alternative ways to handle easily aroused rage. In fact, any number of bodily reactions, from headaches to stomach aches to back pains and fatigue, can become substitute responses for acute expressions of anger.

Somatic reactions are not the only indirect ways of manifesting anger. You may disguise your anger by labeling it disappointment or some other feeling. For example, you may say "I am disappointed in you." This kind of communication has the added payoff of inducing considerable guilt in the person with whom you are angry. Household martyrs are created in just this way. Or you may withdraw and refuse to talk to the person with whom you are angry. In extreme cases, this is labeled passive-aggressive behavior. The passive-aggressive person is difficult to pin down since he or she won't take responsibility for his or her feelings. Using sarcasm steadily and "forgetting" appointments or commitments also indirectly express anger.

There are numerous reasons why people respond in angry and aggressive ways. Some individuals are angry because they fear being powerless or taken advantage of; some overreact to current situations based on previous unpleasant experiences; some have a history of being stepped on through prior submissiveness and fear a repetition of that fate; some believe that only aggressive responses will be effective in any confrontation; and some simply do not have the skills for assertive confrontation. Moreover, anger and aggressiveness can be used to displace responsibility onto others or to manipulate others through fear. In most cases, however, the long-term consequences of habitual anger are largely negative. The angry, aggressive person tends to be distrusted and avoided and becomes increasingly vigilant for counterattack.

Affective, behavioral, and cognitive methods of self-change can all be used to modify anger. At the affective level, tension and agitation have come to be defined as the anger response; at the behavioral level, self-change techniques focus on the withdrawal and denial of the passive-aggressive individual or the antagonism and explosiveness of the easily angered individual; at the cognitive level, there are the distorted ways we perceive provocative situations and tell ourselves things that feed into our anger responses.

BEHAVIORAL METHODS

The first step in learning to control your anger and deal with it appropriately is to monitor your behavior in situations in which you tend to react with rage (Self-Change Technique 8). A number of the anger inventories available (Novaco, 1975) include situations such as the following:

> You lose your car keys.
> The barber cuts off too much hair.
> You are overcharged for a service.
> You are corrected or criticized for an error.
> Someone calls you a liar or a jerk.
> You are waiting in a restaurant without being served.
> You have been stood up for an appointment or date.
> You are being teased.
> You are held up on the highway by a slow car in front of you.
> You are being treated roughly by an opponent in an athletic
>   match.
> You lose a game.
> You see someone being cruel to animals.

This is only a sample of the various kinds of situations that can elicit anger in people. Imagine yourself in each situation. Would you feel your temperature rising in any of these instances? Try to imagine some other situations in which you might find yourself becoming angry. Proper diagnosis precedes any self-therapy treatment.

People do not need a "good reason" to get angry. Many of us tend to become angry when the circumstances may not seem to warrant it. Once you identify your feeling as anger, try to identify the source. Although you may find yourself shouting at the kids, the real source of your anger might very well be some other figure, such as your mother-in-law. It is especially common for us to displace our anger from powerful individuals or authority figures who can be intimidating or punitive onto innocent, more vulnerable persons. When the source of your anger is not a powerful, significant target, such as the government tax office or your boss, it might be someone to whom an expression of anger would generate guilt in you, such as your sick father or your generous but demanding mother.

Once you have identified the source and have an inkling about why you are angry, note how you handle it. Are your reactions realistic or are they out of proportion to the situation? Do your reactions seriously disturb both you and your relationships? Do you deny your anger and respond by being oversolicitously submissive? Do you express your anger indirectly and internalize it through headaches, eating, smiling, sleeping, drinking, withdrawing, or being depressed?

> In order to cope with excessive anger, try to become aware of
> your arousal early in the sequence. Once you notice the arousal of
> anger, you can use it as a cue for invoking alternate coping
> responses (Self-Change Technique 12). For example, gradually
> postpone your anger response. Count seconds before allowing
> yourself to become angry (Dyer, 1976). As you deliberately count
> seconds, you gradually increase your tolerance from 10 seconds to
> 20 seconds to 30 seconds before you act. In time, you can begin to
> overcome being victimized by crippling anger.

According to Bach and Wyden (1969), people who fight together stay together, as long as they fight properly and fairly. When couples can fight openly with each other, their affectionate lives improve, their sex lives improve, they raise children better, and they feel less guilty about their hostile emotions. Even the most mature and intimate of couples may need times to have it out with each other. But how do you channel aggressive, angry feelings into productive fighting?

Prior to any fight there are a number of issues to consider. Make certain that you are engaging in this fight for yourself rather than for someone else. Go into battle flying your own flag rather than the family crest or the gang's coat of arms. Be sure that you have a legitimate complaint and that you are not merely invested in hurting or humiliating your opponent. Be sure that you have a realistic appraisal of your position and that you have not merely overreacted. The quick triggering of a sensitive nerve in you may not really merit a full-scale engagement. Assess the price you will have to pay to make your point, ensuring that it will not be excessive. For example, your father-in-law may be too rigid to change and extremely sensitive to criticism, so that fighting with him about his misplacing your garden shears may not be worth the effort. Finally, assure yourself that you are prepared to be honest in this fight and that once you have vented your anger you will communicate some specific suggestion or demand to the other person. Once you have considered these issues and convinced yourself that they accurately describe your real motivations and feelings, you are set to engage in a fight with your opponent. Use the following behavioral techniques to guide the conduct of your fight (Bach & Wyden, 1969):

Announce your intention to fight before you actually engage your partner and dump your grievances. There are good times to fight and there are lousy times to fight. In bed before sex is not a good time to fight—unless you don't want to get involved in love making. And if that's the case, why not just say so? Try to choose a moment when you have both some space and opportunity. It may be best to make an appointment or date that is suitable to your partner. Another important point is to avoid gunnysacking—that is, letting fly with a hoard of stored-up complaints. There is no way your partner can usefully digest this information, and most fights about old issues tend to have negative outcomes. Stay with the current issue and refrain from commenting about your mother-in-law's weight or using similar extraneous ammunition. Be aware of your partner's "beltline," areas of vulnerability where he or she can be deeply injured. Don't drag in issues that can't be resolved, like the size of his penis or her breasts. State your anger and your complaint clearly: "I'm angry at you for criticizing my vocabulary in front of George and Ginny last night." Pause frequently for feedback. Indicate a willingness to listen. Try to repeat back what you heard every step along the way before replying. Don't merely parrot, but attempt to really express the essence of your partner's view: "What do you mean by that? I'll tell you how I heard it." Follow your anger with a specific request or demand: "I want you to stop criticizing me in front of our friends." At the end of the fight, summarize the resolution you have made so that there is true closure and neither of you leaves feeling unfinished or embittered.

The key to a fair fight is to realize that it is not a win/lose encounter in which one person is the victor and the other is the vanquished. Productive fights have only winners since the outcome provides an impetus for further growth, understanding, and intimacy in the relationship.

It has been pointed out (Mace, 1976) that Bach and Wyden's program of "marital fighting" is really an attempt to harmoniously solve conflicts without resorting to a spontaneous ventilation of anger and open fighting. The program is largely one of following clear rules for fair fighting and, as such, of obtaining stimulus control over your anger (Self-Change Technique 9).

Bach and his cotherapists (for example, Bach & Goldberg, 1974) claim that anger and aggression are part of intimacy in couples but that it is important that anger be expressed in constructive rather than hurtful ways. The "Vesuvius" is a paradoxical technique (Self-Change Technique 13) with stimulus control features that can be tried if it seems likely that you would otherwise vent your anger in ways that would embitter your partner and your children and harm relationships in the family.

Set aside a particular time, probably some time during the early evening hours, and obtain permission from your family to use the occasion to vent your pent-up frustrations. Schedule a few minutes each day and completely let loose in a loud, abusive way. This is a one-way explosion. Your family members must quietly accept your outburst and not interrupt or respond to it in any way.

This technique is especially appropriate if you have a tendency to allow your day's frustrations to build, only to have your anger set off by the first innocent gesture of your child, the first naive statement of your spouse, or the first clumsy move of your pet. If allowed to respond to your rage, your partner might escalate the battle into a full-scale "Who's afraid of Virginia Woolf" type of encounter. Or your partner might withdraw, become moody, and leave you with residual guilt. The Vesuvius is recommended as a ritual to be practiced whenever frustrations build, particularly during times of stress or crisis.

While parents have to cope with feeling anger toward each other, they also have to deal with their anger toward their children. When parents handle anger constructively, it can demonstrate love and concern. On the other hand, when parents view anger in the family as immoral, it will generate guilt and discomfort. By recognizing that you will occasionally become angry with your children and that you are entitled to these feelings without feeling guilt or shame, you can practice "anger without insult" (Ginott, 1971). In annoying situations describe clearly how you are affected ("I am angry with you!") and make this statement as strong as need be to reduce your own tension and warn your child. Most often you can stop at this point, since your directive to change his or her behavior will be clear. In situations where you feel angry suddenly, focus on describing what you observe, what you are feeling, and what needs to be done. If your son makes a mess of the living room, you might say "I get furious when I see games and food left on the floor. I want you to clean up this room immediately." Refrain from making personal insults ("You're a slob," "You're inconsiderate," "You never do anything to help"), and you will decrease the likelihood of a prolonged argument.

AFFECTIVE METHODS

Relaxation training (Self-Change Technique 1) is by far the most fundamental affective intervention in treating overwhelming feelings of anger. Once you have learned to identify anger cues, the stimulus cues that predictably elicit either full-blown anger responses or low-level feelings of irritation, relaxation techniques can lead to a diminution in the autonomic, or physiological, experience of anger. Muscle relaxation is usually used to replace a fear or anxiety response. However, anger is often initiated by fear. It may be a response to feeling threatened or vulnerable. Consequently, anger may no longer be necessary once the fear is removed (Rimm, de Groot, Boord, Heiman, & Dillow, 1971). Relaxation cues are valuable when high levels of anger arousal are particularly inappropriate. The impulsive person who must restrain himself or herself from telling off the boss or from slugging his or her mate needs a calming strategy. Since anger can disrupt complex motor performance, it must be minimized quickly and directly in some situations. Cue yourself to relax when the fellow in front of you is driving ten miles an hour below the speed limit. Inappropriate anger at this time might lead to some suicidal driving behavior, not to mention elevated blood pressure.

As you become aware of your anger and its latent intensity, use awareness techniques such as focusing (Self-Change Technique 4) to discover the origins of your sensitivity to particular situations and the original inhibitions on your anger. As you increase your understanding and control, you become more capable of dealing appropriately in the present with feelings that were previously mystifying and uncontrollable.

Most psychotherapists have learned to be comfortable with the full range of their clients' affective expressions, including rage and anger. Most of our parents were less comfortable with the extreme manifestations of our feelings. You can probably think of numerous times when your parents inhibited the direct expression of your rage while you were still a child. In fact, your kicking and screaming while in a rage was probably stifled by parental admonishments such as "Little girls don't yell" or "Big boys control themselves." Such early messages often lead to massive feelings of guilt and defensive denial when feelings of anger are stirred up in adulthood.

We speak about anger as if it were a tangible commodity within us. We say we are "filled with anger" or that we have "anger inside." In fact, these are linguistic metaphors. Feelings, including anger, are not really concrete entities residing in our bodies. They are labels describing a complex series of events involving emotional arousal, bodily reactions, and verbal labeling. When a current situation or a person "stirs up anger" within us, the event may in fact be triggering a memory, stored inside the nervous system for many years, that restimulates some old feelings. Catharsis does not really mean releasing old blocked emotions but remembering the original events with the concomitant feeling, communicating that feeling, and carrying out the vigorous bodily actions that may be part of "having" the feeling (Nichols & Zax, 1977).

Instead of denying your anger, it is important to express these feelings in nondestructive ways, ways that do not injure or interfere with the sanctity of another individual. Flooding (and implosive therapy) (Self-Change Technique 7) may be useful for this purpose.

> If you feel you are holding back from exploding with rage, seek out a private room and scream "No!" or "I won't!" at the top of your lungs. This kind of private explosion can be quite therapeutic, often resulting in feelings of calm and equanimity. Frequently, it provides you with the renewed ability to deal with the irritant in a rational, logical way that previously would have been impossible. You can also vent your negative feelings by coupling your private scream with a total bodily release. Take a tennis racket or a hard foam-rubber bat (called a "bataca") and pound the nearest bed, couch, or chair with it while yelling "Get off my back" or "I don't want to" (Lowen, 1967). Some of you may be afraid that, once you begin, this kind of outpouring of angry emotion will never end. Don't worry. Most people are very adept at setting their own limits, and the greater risk is that you may stop prematurely, just as the energy begins to build, and then leave the exercise in a more aroused state than when you began. You will find that, after several minutes of pounding and screaming, you will feel fatigued and depleted.

The movie "Network" illustrates the use of this technique at epidemic proportions. The television news commentator played by Peter Finch exhorts his audience to open their windows and yell into the streets "I'm mad as hell and I'm not going to take it anymore!" Obviously this kind of discharge does not solve problems in living in and of itself, but it does provide an outlet for people who are uncomfortable with their own anger and reluctant to express it directly.

If you are a person who is bubbling over with anger and aggressiveness, you can employ this rather harmless outlet instead of turning to destructive modes of aggression with regrettable consequences. In fact, a carefully crafted cathartic experience with verbal and physical release is a good initial prescription for most chronically angry people. Parents Anonymous, a self-help group for child-abusing parents, for instance, takes the stance that, when parents are tempted to bash and batter their kids, they should throw *anything* in the room but their child!

When you do know who is making you angry, use the Gestalt technique of placing that person in an empty chair and ventilating your feelings (Self-Change Technique 5). The key is to experience the sensation of your own anger in a safe setting where you can reevaluate your need to evade this emotion. In so doing, you may be able to relieve such diversionary symptoms as headaches or muscle tension and reenergize yourself for other, more adaptive purposes. As your feeling of anger increases, watch for sources of aggression that may not be directly related to your present situation. The present experience may be a recurrence of some past incident, so that part of your emotional discharge may be most appropriately directed—in fantasy—to parents or to other historical figures. If the per-

son you want to address is dead, do not be surprised to find a great deal of anger behind your grief. No one likes to be deserted or rejected. Try to express your affect fully. Be wary of bodily inhibition, weak, timid, or apologetic voice quality, and inappropriate laughter that may conceal rage. Increase the interactional aspects of your anger by playing the role of the other person (switching chairs) and using the provocative statements and accusations that you believe your target person might use.

Another fantasy approach to defusing destructive anger is the one of "self-reproach" (Bach & Goldberg, 1974).

Close your eyes and imagine all the events that occurred during the day that have made you angry with yourself: the time you smiled in a phony, placating way to a business rival; the second martini you are now ashamed of accepting at lunch; the client you forgot to call; the mistake you made in trying to fix the plumbing. Rather than store up this self-abuse and give yourself indigestion, headaches, or worse, scold yourself verbally; say "Dumb, dumb, dumb" to yourself, maybe adding a light slap to your own face, until you are no longer angry with yourself. Then stop and forgive yourself. Always try to end on a good note. Admit to yourself that you are an imperfect human like the rest of us. Claim the right to be wrong or dumb or stupid once in a while. Use this fantasy to get all the self-abuse out of your system so that you can carry on with a clean slate.

COGNITIVE METHODS

Although expressing anger in constructive ways is probably better than denying or suppressing it, it is also possible to reevaluate your need to be an angry person and begin to see yourself as a person who does not need to explode with anger. The reaction of anger is often predicated on the false belief that others should be more like you and should tailor their responses to meet your expectations (Cognitive Restructuring, Self-Change Technique 15). The value of cognitive reappraisal for anger is well illustrated by Albert Ellis' account of the time a stranger in a crowd stepped on his foot and he instantly became furious. When Ellis looked up, however, he realized that the offender was blind, and his anger quickly dissipated. The initial experience of anger is spontaneous and automatic. However, self-control strategies can be used to cue and convert anger, which has been triggered by frustration or fear, into productive problem solving rather than out-of-control, destructive discharge.

Try the following problem-solving method (Self-Change Technique 17) when you are angered by your lover, spouse, or partner (Mace, 1976): First, acknowledge your anger. State openly that you are becoming angry. Next, admit that your anger is inappropriate, given the present situation, and that you don't want to become angry. Finally, ask your partner for help in overcoming your problem. Work together to try to figure out why you are angry and to arrive at an alternative for dealing with it.

This technique may be especially helpful for people who are chronically angry whereas those who constantly suppress their anger may first need to vent it in controlled situations.

Some chronically angry people may need merely to temper and channel their anger without eliminating it completely. They may believe that, if they lost their anger, they would also lose their aggressiveness, which has proved to be valuable and even instrumental in their success both in the market place and in interpersonal relationships. These people need a set of interventions to help them manage provocations more effectively. Cognitive interventions can be used to translate provocation signals, giving them some other meaning. The easily angered individual may experience situations as threatening to his or her self-esteem and focus on the importance of vanquishing the opponent rather than completing the task. By changing the set from a personal assault to a task orientation the individual can channel anger in more productive ways. Since provocative comments or behaviors can dissuade the volatile person from sticking to a task at any point in the behavioral sequence, coping self-statements should be constructed for use as behavioral guides (Self-Instruction Training, Self-Change Technique 16).

Try the following self-instructive statements (Novaco, 1975):

Preparing for provocation:

This is going to upset me, but I know how to handle it.
I have the skill to control my anger.
Try not to take this too seriously.

Impact and confrontation:

Control yourself. Just relax.
I can be in control as long as I don't blow my cool.
Getting mad would serve no purpose.
Don't let him get to you now.

Coping with arousal:

Just take a deep breath and relax.
I'm getting a little angry. Time to stay with the task.
Don't get aggressive. Just take it easy.

Reflecting on the provocation:

When the conflict is unresolved:

No need to take it personally.
Just forget it. Don't let it mess up your job.
Next time it will go easier and I'll be better at it.

When the conflict is resolved:

Not so bad. It could have gone a lot worse.
Fine. I'm improving all the time.

Situations in which you feel provoked to anger are broken into a sequence consisting of a preparation stage preceding the confrontation, the point of confrontation, the stage at which control threatens to give way, and the period of time following the interaction, whether it is negotiated successfully or terminated unsuccessfully. It is easiest to inhibit impulsive responses when you begin early in the sequence, when the temptation to lose control is still of a low intensity.

Examine the negative beliefs that previously guided your behavior and elicited explosive outbursts of anger (for example, intolerance of someone's mistakes, a need to punish someone for past misdeeds, feelings of being taken advantage of) and trade them in for positive coping statements that diminish the chances for angry outbursts and help maintain task completion.

Rehearse the behavioral sequence in your imagination and by role playing to maximize your chance of applying it successfully in practice. It is important to identify those situations that are problematic for you. Record events that are particularly troublesome and anger-eliciting in an "anger diary." Write down the situation, the intensity of the affect, and the maladaptive coping style you now use, such as suppressing anger.

You can use problem-solving interventions (Self-Change Technique 17) by generating as many alternative approaches to anger-inducing situations as possible. Carry index cards around with you and specify each situation, the anger felt, its intensity, and your self-statements as they occur. This is particularly important if you are chronically angry or hypertensive, since you may literally be unaware of both the level of autonomic arousal you experience and the provoking situations that elicit your anger. The last step in the sequence is to reinforce yourself for progress in keeping anger to a minimum and maintaining your cool.

Anger takes many forms in transactional analysis (Self-Change Technique 20) and usually comes from the Child position. A temper tantrum by the Child is called a "racket," since the feelings of anger are more manipulative than real. The child may indulge himself or herself by collecting feelings of guilt, hurt, or resentment over time, storing them for eventual use in a self-righteous torrent of explosive anger and vindictiveness. Of course, anger may also be an honest fight for survival against restrictive forces or a legitimate grievance of the Adult against violence, personal abuse, starvation, or war.

If your anger is directed at yourself, try to listen for old parental messages or injunctions, particularly criticisms that originated with your parents and have now become part of your self-concept. This anger that you experience belongs in the past. Once you can sort out historical not–OK messages in your mind, you will be primed to express your anger at its source, usually some parental figure (Kemp, 1977). After you have used the affective self-change techniques to help you release your anger appropriately, you can begin to consider what it is that your Adult wants and stop looking for punishment from others so that you can become covertly angry and overtly hurt. Realize that your "wants" are legitimate and that you can forcefully state what you don't like. From a transactional-analysis perspective, this is part of resolving an "I Can't Control my Anger" life script.

INSOMNIA

Insomnia, the inability to obtain adequate sleep, is a widespread problem that is often amenable to self-management. The amount of sleep that people require is highly individualistic, and we now know that there are large variations in those individual differences. Some people may require eight or nine hours of sound sleep every night, whereas others seem to carry on vigorously and productively with considerably less. We have all suffered from insomnia at one time or another. Shift work, jet lag, physical illness, drugs, and personal crises can all make people unable to sleep. The form of the disorder also varies. One type of insomnia, known as "sleep-onset insomnia," refers to difficulty in falling asleep. For people with this problem, it may take 30 minutes or more to finally fall asleep. Others wake up frequently during the night, unable to maintain sleep once it is achieved. A third variety consists of early morning awakenings, waking up before you intend to and being unable to fall back to sleep.

One estimate reports that at least 30 million Americans are chronic insomniacs and that another 30 million have occasional difficulty in obtaining adequate sleep (Webb, 1975). The techniques offered in the ABC approach to self-change are useful when the insomnia is a result of psychological discomfort, such as the daily accumulation of tension that prevents sleep, napping during the day because of fatigue with a subsequent inability to sleep at night, and general discomfort generated by nagging worries or physical pains. The effects of self-therapy are greatest for moderate sleep disturbances and difficulties in falling asleep initially (Thoresen, Coates, Zarcone, Kirmil-Gray, & Rosenkind, 1978). The techniques are not useful for some kinds of insomnia that are based on physiological problems, such as nocturnal myoclonus, a disorder characterized by frequent leg twitches during the night that make it difficult to remain asleep, or sleep apnea, a rare disorder in which breathing ceases and the sleeper wakes up gasping for air.

At present the most prevalent self-management technique for problems in sleeping is the use of drugs. As a matter of fact, hypnotic medications are used so frequently that the average man, woman, and child in the United States takes about 50 doses of barbiturates in a single year! This might not be a problem were it not for the evidence suggesting that most pharmacological agents have a number of limitations and disadvantages. The general effectiveness of hypnotic drugs for inducing sleep at bedtime continues for only about two weeks (Kales & Kales, 1973). After this period of time a tolerance to the drugs develops so that they no longer have the desired effect. This information is not well advertised, however, so that people continue to use them and, in fact, go on believing that the hypnotic is responsible for each good night's sleep even though the drug has no effect at all. This placebo effect may prove to be a significant factor in continued drug use. Sleeping medications also create side effects for some people. Users often suffer from drowsiness the following day, thus encouraging the belief that sleep is actually deteriorating. For some, these drugs induce physical symptoms such as nausea or headache. Because many medications produce disruptions in physiological sleep cycles, such as a decrease in rapid eye movements (REM), for example, other symptoms develop when they are withdrawn. Drug deprivation can greatly increase REM frequency, sleeping difficulties, jitteriness and anxiety, or disturbing dreams and nightmares. Finally, barbiturate drugs that are prescribed for sleep induction are sometimes combined with alcohol with lethal effects. In short, it is undoubtedly more healthful to master affective, behavioral, and cognitive interventions than to rely on the continuous application of sleeping medications. If you can attribute your sleeping skill to yourself rather than to a pill, chances are increased that you will continue to fall and remain asleep without medication (Ribordy & Denny, 1977).

AFFECTIVE METHODS

The most frequently employed affective intervention to combat insomnia is some variant of deep muscle relaxation (Self-Change Technique 1). Chronic insomnia is often associated with heightened physiological

Puffer

arousal—such as tension, anxiety, or excitement, occurring before and during sleep. Relaxation and meditation techniques can be used to slow the system down and put the mind at ease, allowing sleep to come automatically. Too much effort and deliberate concentration have the paradoxical effect of making it more difficult to obtain sleep. Consequently, affective techniques such as deep muscle relaxation, autogenic training, self-hypnosis, meditation, and yoga can help reduce physiological activity and empty the mind of troublesome and interfering thoughts.

The quality of your sleep may be more important than the actual number of hours you spend lying in bed with your eyes closed.

> Take a warm bath or drink a glass of warm milk to help relax and slow you down before going to bed. Make sure that your surroundings are thoroughly relaxing. Take lots of time to luxuriate in preparing yourself for the night. Do not exercise actively immediately before bed, since this excites your system rather than relaxing it. Instead, practice progressive-relaxation exercises, autogenic exercises, breathing exercises, or yoga for a few minutes before lying down in bed. Continue to relax when you get into bed. Find a comfortable position in your bed (a firm mattress is optimal), and think pleasant, peaceful thoughts. Leave tomorrow's anticipated problems in another room.

Intersperse your self-instructions in progressive relaxation with suggestions that facilitate sleep. Say to yourself that your eyelids are growing heavier and heavier, that your entire body is becoming very, very relaxed, and that you are becoming sleepier and sleepier (Linde & Savary, 1974). Or you can count backward from ten as you focus on muscle relaxation, telling yourself that you will sink deeper and deeper with each number and that you will be asleep when you reach zero.

If you prefer to use meditation (Self-Change Technique 2) to relax, focus on your breathing. Concentrate your awareness on breathing in and out, in and out. Allow any extraneous thoughts to slip through your mind. Focusing on a single mental stimulus has also been shown to be effective in treating insomnia (Woolfolk, Carr-Kaffasan, McNulty, & Lehrer, 1976). If you are most comfortable with autogenic training (Self-Change Technique 1), concentrate on feeling your body become warm, feeling your body become heavy, then feeling your body become warm and heavy. These exercises can most easily precipitate sleep. If you use imagery (Self-Change Technique 5), imagine yourself relaxing in pleasant surroundings. Floating on water or on a cloud is especially good imagery for relaxation and sleep (Linde & Savary, 1974). Ahsen's eidetic-imagery approach can also be effective (Sheikh, 1976).

> Try to recall occasions in the past when you were very tired but had to refrain from giving in to sleep because of external demands that you stay awake. Perhaps you were listening to a guest speaker, preparing for an exam, performing on the job, or involved in a social activity. Imagine the past situation in as much detail as possible until you obtain a clear visual image of it. Concentrate on the image until it evokes the feelings of drowsiness that you had to ward off in the past. But this time you

don't have to comply with the demand to stay awake while your body is telling you to sleep. Disregard the demand to stay awake and allow yourself to doze off. Once you have located a specific image that works for you, conjure up that image whenever you find yourself lying in bed unable to sleep.

Systematic desensitization (Self-Change Technique 3) tends to be as effective as relaxation training for most insomniacs and even more effective for severe cases (Ribordy & Denny, 1977). To apply desensitization to sleeping behaviors, it is important to first become adept at relaxation. Next close your eyes and imagine lying in bed uncomfortably, unable to sleep. As soon as that image is clear, invoke the relaxation response. Establish a hierarchy of situations that keep you awake and practice the relaxation response in association with various modifications of the stimulus of lying in bed wide awake. Gradually, the cues that make you unable to sleep in your bed will begin to elicit feelings of relaxation and potentiate sleeping.

Dream work (Self-Change Technique 6) is appropriate if your sleep is inhibited by the apprehension of experiencing frightening dreams or if sleep is interrupted by nightmares or tension-arousing dreams. By recording your dreams and learning to understand and enjoy them, you can remove a potential interruption to a good night's sleep.

If your inability to sleep is associated with specific clinical syndromes such as depression or anxiety states, specific self-therapy interventions for insomnia may not be effective. You may have to deal directly with the issues that make sleep so difficult. Record your "mood" each night before you go to bed, using a five-point scale from feeling marvelous or relaxed to feeling very depressed or anxious. This kind of monitoring will allow you to gauge if depression is keeping you from sleep or if anxiety is the core issue. You may find that the self-therapy techniques that are useful for alleviating depression or specific anxiety-arousing preoccupations are more appropriate than direct interventions for insomnia. Interestingly, there are researchers who believe that depression may involve a disturbance in the normal 24-hour sleeping and waking cycle and that a night of deliberate sleeplessness can help to readjust the rhythm (Linde & Savary, 1974). This kind of "no sleep" therapy is recommended only for insomniacs who are also depressed.

BEHAVIORAL METHODS

From a behavioral point of view, your inability to sleep may be due to poor sleep habits that work against achieving a consistent circadian (daily) rhythm. Many people who have difficulty sleeping fail to establish a predictable schedule for sleeping and waking. They go to bed late some nights, early others, and nap in the early evening and are surprised that they take so long to doze off.

Simple self-monitoring of sleep (Self-Change Technique 8) can provide a measure of the amount of sleep you are actually obtaining (Jason, 1975). Insomniacs are notoriously unreliable at estimating how long it takes them to fall asleep, generally overestimating the length of time it takes them to doze off. They also tend to underestimate the number of hours they actually sleep during the night. For this reason, empirical studies on sleeping behavior make use of behavioral observations of sleep activity and physiological measures of the length of time spent in the various stages of sleep rather than the subjective estimates of the subjects. The first step in revising your sleep schedule is to determine your natural pattern.

> Keep a record of the length of time you take to fall asleep, the
> number of times you wake up, and the minutes you spend
> napping during the day on occasions when you have no
> important plans that will modify your natural rhythm. Keep a
> record of when you are sleepy and when you are awake to
> provide you with a guide for coordinating your schedule to
> accommodate your biological rhythm of sleeping and waking. The
> record will also offer you an index of change when you do
> improve and may actually lead to better sleep in and of itself.

Stimulus-control methods are integral to developing regularized sleep habits (Self-Change Technique 9). Benjamin Franklin is said to have believed that when he was unable to sleep it was because he was lying in a rumpled bed. Consequently he switched to a second, unrumpled bed whenever he could not sleep. Many such methods have become part of the folklore of coping with insomnia. Drinking hot cocoa, lining up the pillows in a specific order, setting a particular temperature in the room, having a glass of wine or beer, counting sheep, or taking two aspirin can all be effective—not because they are magic elixirs but because they help to routinize your pattern so that certain stimuli will lead to predictable responses (classical conditioning) and help promote a predictable biological pattern of sleeping. Establishing a routine seems to be the important ingredient.

The stimulus environment of the bedroom can influence sleep. The hardness or softness of the bed and the cold or warmth of the room can be important factors. Try to standardize them. Eliminate distractions that make sleep more difficult—light, noise, and stress. Too much alcohol before bed is not good, as it cuts short certain stages of sleep (REM sleep) that seem to be necessary for alert functioning during the day. Eliminate also behaviors that are incompatible with sleeping, such as watching television or worrying about the next day's concerns. In order to achieve stimulus control, try to restrict the behaviors associated with your bed and bedroom to sleep. Your bedroom may have become a stimulus associated with numerous extraneous activities that have nothing to do with sleeping, such as watching television, reading, worrying, or eating. You may wonder about your sex life if you restrict your bed to sleep only. Try to make the stimuli for sex and for sleeping a little different. Use candlelight and romantic music to create an atmosphere that is conducive to sex, but remove them when you are ready to sleep.

> Avoid the bedroom until you are sleepy. Lie down in your bed only when you intend to go to sleep. If you are unable to fall asleep in a short period of time (10 minutes is not an unreasonable time to fall asleep), get up and go into another room. Return to your bed only when you feel tired and believe that you can sleep. Set your alarm for the same time every morning and get up regardless of how many hours of sleep you have had or how difficult it is to rise (Bootzin & Nicassio, 1977). Don't cheat by taking naps in the afternoon and early evening. Dozing in the afternoon will make it more difficult for you to sleep at night.

Paradoxical techniques (Self-Change Technique 13) have been found to facilitate sleep (Ascher & Efran, 1978). Perhaps the most famous clinical example is Milton Erickson's case of an elderly gentleman suffering chronic insomnia (Haley, 1963). Erickson asked the client to choose the activity around the house that was most aversive to him. The client replied that scrubbing floors was most distasteful. He was thereupon instructed that, whenever he could not sleep, he was to get out of bed and scrub his floors. It did not take many nights of floor scrubbing before he succumbed to sleep very quickly! Since deliberate attempts to sleep sometimes make the situation worse rather than better, an alternative approach to dealing with insomnia is to give yourself the task of staying awake as long as possible. Engage in a task or keep track of your thoughts and feelings even if it means resisting the urge to sleep. You may find this task surprisingly difficult to achieve and end up falling asleep on the job!

COGNITIVE METHODS

Cognitive interventions are particularly useful for those cases in which insomnia is secondary to other problems. Preoccupations and worries can certainly compromise the amount of sleep you achieve. Although muscle relaxation may help reduce presleep tensions, it is not apt to decrease intrusive cognitions that delay the onset of sleep for many insomniacs. Any method that can reduce repetitive thinking and obsessing may thus be helpful in combatting insomnia. Problem solving (Self-Change

Technique 17) may help you to organize your worries into manageable units so that you will not need to devote precious sleeping time to extraneous thoughts.

With cognitive restructuring (Self-Change Technique 14) you can question the validity of a belief system that insists that something else is more vital than a good night's sleep, and with self-instruction training (Self-Change Technique 16) you can develop covert self-control by conditioning statements and behaviors that are incompatible with negative thoughts. If obsessional thoughts do persist, a more direct method such as thought stopping (Self-Change Technique 18) can be applied. Rimm (1973) prescribed thought stopping for a woman who habitually lay awake at night terrified that a man was hiding in her closet. In addition to checking the closet once before going to bed and then leaving the closet door open in order to extinguish her fear, she was instructed to repeat statements to herself silently to interrupt her obsessional thought sequence. The statements included rational alternatives such as "I really can take care of myself" and "There's no one there." These reassuring messages served to break up the thought pattern that had previously interfered with her sleep.

SUMMARY

For reasons that have previously been discussed, there is currently a trend in psychology to make the successful principles of the formal therapeutic relationship available to a broader population. By now you are familiar with 20 self-therapy techniques and how they can be applied for personal change and growth. Assertiveness, depression, anger, and insomnia are only representative examples of many common problems that can be modified, minimized, and eliminated using one or more of these interventions. The basic premise of this book has been that a comprehensive approach to self-therapy must consider the affective, the behavioral, and the cognitive dimensions. An approach that ignores coping with your feelings, getting your thinking straight, or amending your behavior is incomplete and less likely to be effective. It bears repeating that, although this book presents a foundation for effective problem definition and resolution, you may wish to consult original source material for a fuller elaboration of any given technique.

You may still have some questions regarding the application of self-change methods. The following answers provide more clarification:

1. *"How do I get started changing myself?"*

The commitment to self-change is undoubtedly the most important single step toward a successful self-therapy program or intervention. No matter how well versed you are in the principles and technology of self-therapy, you need to commit yourself to spending time and energy on a deliberate course of action in order to maximize your chances of making meaningful changes in your life. The first procedural step is to identify a particular problem—a feeling, a thought, an action—to work on. The more important your problem is to your self-image and psychological survival, the greater your commitment to apply the techniques is apt to be.

2. *"How do I know what techniques to choose?"*

The selection of interventions for your self-change program will depend to some extent on the nature of your problem. Read through the description of the techniques and get an idea of their focus and their applications. Consider whether you need to work primarily at the affective, the behavioral, or the cognitive level. Reject those techniques you would not be willing to carry out or that seem unamenable to your current living situation. Begin with one approach, and add additional techniques to build a total treatment package.

3. *"How do I know when a self-change method is working?"*

You'll know from changes in your mood and the realization of your target goals. The best way to demonstrate change to yourself is by determining a baseline, collecting data, and maintaining a running chart of your continued experience of your problems. As you work toward your goals, you'll be able to note your direction of movement and to appreciate small changes that are sometimes unnoticeable when your sights are ambitious and you are impatient for progress.

4. *"What do I do if a technique is not working?"*

First, be certain you are applying the technique correctly. Second, be sure you are giving the technique a fair chance. If at that point the approach is still not having an impact, you have a choice. On the one hand, you can always turn to another approach. No technique is universally effective. On the other hand, if you have conscientiously tried to apply the approaches described in this book and have consistently met with failure, this may be taken as a sign to consult with a professional who can offer direct intervention for your difficulty or provide guidance to refine your self-management approach. Professional consultation is always available when the going gets too tough and the recommended methods are not sufficient in promoting positive change.

5. *"How do I know when to terminate my self-change program?"*

Terminate your program whenever you like. Keep in mind, however, that a common mistake is not hanging on long enough to do justice to a technique. Even when you achieve a goal, it is advisable to maintain the intervention a little longer in order to ensure the permanence of the change. Many people find that self-change methods become not only tools to be used in time of need but a part of their personalities and ways of relating to people and the world. The methods can become part of you and can replace many maladaptive ways of coping. The more familiar and comfortable you become with the techniques you have selected, the more likely they are to become automatic responses to coping effectively and to becoming a more fulfilled individual.

REFERENCES

Alberti, R. E., & Emmons, M. L. *Your perfect right: A guide to assertive behavior* (2nd ed.). San Luis Obispo, Calif.: Impact Press, 1974.

Alexander, F. *Psychosomatic medicine.* New York: Norton, 1950.

Ascher, L. M., & Efran, J. S. Use of paradoxical intention in a behavioral program for sleep onset insomnia. *Journal of Consulting and Clinical Psychology,* 1978, 46(3), 547–550.

Bach, G. R., & Goldberg, H. *Creative aggression.* New York: Avon Books, 1974.

Bach, G. R. & Wyden, P. *The intimate enemy.* New York: Morrow, 1969.

Beck, A. T. *Depression.* Philadelphia: University of Pennsylvania, 1967.

Bootzin, R. R., & Nicassio, P. M. Behavioral treatments for insomnia. In M. Hersen, R. Eisler, & P. Miller (Eds.), *Progress in behavior modification* (Vol. 4). New York: Academic Press, 1977.

Bower, S. A., & Bower, G. H. *Asserting yourself.* Reading, Mass.: Addison-Wesley, 1976.

Dyer, W. W. *Your erroneous zones.* New York: Avon Books, 1976.

Eisler, R. M., Hersen, M., & Miller, P. M. Effects of modelling on components of assertive behavior. *Journal of Behavior Therapy and Experimental Psychiatry,* 1973, 4, 1–6.

Ellis, A. *Humanistic psychotherapy.* New York: McGraw-Hill, 1973.

Fensterheim, H., & Baer, J. *Don't say yes when you want to say no.* New York: Dell, 1975.

Ginnot, H. G. *Between parent and teenager.* New York: Avon Books, 1971.

Haley, J. *Strategies of psychotherapy.* New York: Grune & Stratton, 1963.

Hannum, J. W., Thoresen, C. E., & Hubbard, D. R., Jr. A behavioral study of self-esteem with elementary teachers. In M. J. Mahoney and C. E. Thoresen (Eds.), *Self-control: Power to the person.* Monterey, Calif.: Brooks/Cole, 1974.

Jason, L. Rapid improvement in insomnia following self-monitoring. *Journal of Behavior Therapy and Experimental Psychiatry*, 1975, *6*, 349–350.

Kales, A., & Kales, J. Recent advances in the diagnosis and treatment of sleep disorders. In G. Usden (Ed.), *Sleep research and clinical Practice.* New York: Brunner/Mazel, 1973.

Kemp, D. E. Curing "moral masochism." In M. James (Ed.), *Techniques in transactional analysis.* Reading, Mass.: Addison-Wesley, 1977.

Lange, A. J., & Jakubowski, P. *Responsible assertive behavior.* Champaign, Ill.: Research Press, 1976.

Lazarus, A. *Multi-modal behavior therapy.* New York: Springer, 1976.

Linde, S. M., & Savary, L. M. *The sleep book.* New York: Harper & Row, 1974.

Lowen, A. *The betrayal of the body.* New York: Collier Books, 1967.

Lowen, A. *Depression and the body.* Baltimore: Penguin, 1972.

Mace, D. R. Marital intimacy and the deadly love-anger cycle. *Journal of Marriage and Family Counseling*, 1976, *2*, 131–137.

Meichenbaum, D. *Cognitive-behavior modification.* New York: Plenum Press, 1977.

Nichols, M. P., & Zax, M. *Catharsis in psychotherapy.* New York: Gardner Press, 1977.

Novaco, R. *Anger control: The development and evaluation of an experimental treatment.* Lexington, Mass.: Heath & Co., 1975.

Raimy, V. *Misunderstanding of the self.* San Francisco: Jossey-Bass, 1975.

Rathus, S. A. A 30-item schedule for assessing assertive behavior. *Behavior Therapy,* 1973, *4,* 399–400.

Reynolds, D. *Morita psychotherapy.* Berkeley: University of California Press, 1976.

Ribordy, S. C., & Denny, D. R. The behavioral treatment of insomnia: An alternative to drug therapy. *Behavior Research and Therapy*, 1977, *15*, 39–50.

Rimm, D. C. Thought stopping and covert assertion in the treatment of phobias. *Journal of Consulting and Clinical Psychology*, 1973, *41*, 466–467.

Rimm, D. C., de Groot, J. C., Boord, P., Heiman, J., & Dillow, P. V. Systematic desensitization of an anger response. *Behavior Research and Therapy*, 1971, *9*, 273–280.

Rush, A. J., Beck, A. T., Kovacs, M., & Hollon, S. Comparative efficacy of cognitive therapy and imipramine in the treatment of depressed outpatients. *Cognitive Therapy and Research*, 1977, *1*, 17–37.

Schwartz, R., & Gottman, J. *A task analysis approach to clinical problems: A study of assertive behavior.* Unpublished manuscript, Indiana University, 1974.

Secunda, S. K., Katz, M. M., Friedman, R. J., & Schuyler, D. *Special report 1973—The depressive disorders.* Washington, D.C.: U.S. Government Printing Office, 1973.

Seligman, M.E.P. *Helplessness.* San Francisco: W. H. Freeman, 1975.

Sheikh, A. A. Treatment of insomnia through eidetic imagery: A new technique. *Perceptual and Motor Skills*, 1976, *43*, 994.

Smith, M. J. *When I say no, I feel guilty.* New York: Bantam Books, 1975.

Thoresen, C. E., Coates, T. J., Zarcone, V. P., Kirmil-Gray, K., & Rosenkind, M. R. Treating the complaint of insomnia: Self-management perspectives. In J. M. Ferguson and C. B. Taylor (Eds.), *Advances in behavioral medicine.* Englewood Cliffs, N.J.: Spectrum Publications, Inc. In press.

Webb, W. *Sleep: The gentle tyrant.* Englewood Cliffs, N.J.: Prentice-Hall, 1975.

Woolfolk, R., Carr-Kaffasan, L., McNulty, T., & Lehrer, P. Meditation training as a treatment for insomnia. *Behavior Therapy*, 1976, *7*, 359–365.

NAME INDEX

Ackerman, J. M., 135, 147
Adams, H., 14, 17
Adams, H. E., 85, 90
Adler, A., 113, 144
Agras, S. W., 46, 88, 116, 146
Ahsen, A., 237
Alberti, R. E., 202, 243
Alexander, F., 223, 243
Andrasik, K. A., 161, 162, 196
Arkowitz, H., 169, 196
Ascher, L. M., 240, 243
Ayllon, T., 117, 124, 144, 145
Axelrod, S., 129, 145
Azrin, N. H., 124, 138, 145

Bach, G. R., 145, 222, 225, 226, 230, 243
Baer, D. M., 104, 145
Baer, J., 203, 243
Bandler, R., 152, 154, 195
Bannister, G., Jr., 164, 195
Barber, T. X., 27, 88
Barlow, D. H., 46, 88
Barrett, B. H., 130, 145
Bayer, C. A., 129, 145
Beck, A. T., 150, 157, 159, 163, 196, 213, 217, 243, 244
Bedrosian, R., 12, 17
Beebe, J., III, 50, 51
Bellack, A. S., 109, 145
Bem, D. J., 11, 17

Benson, H., 25, 33, 85
Berne, E., 182, 184, 186, 189, 190, 196
Birchler, G. R., 128, 146
Blanchard, E. B., 28, 88
Bloomfield, H. H., 34, 88
Bodin, A., 144, 145
Boord, P., 228, 244
Bootzin, R. R., 240, 243
Bower, G. H., 209, 243
Bower, S. A., 209, 243
Brown, B. M., 164, 196
Budzynski, T. H., 28, 88
Bugle, C., 97, 147
Burchard, J. D., 130, 145

Cadwallader, T. C., 39, 88
Cameron, R., 167, 197
Carr-Kaffasan, L., 237, 244
Cassens, J., 50, 51
Cautela, J. R., 22, 88, 133, 145, 175, 176, 196
Chandhuri, H., 35, 88
Coates, T. J., 235, 244
Cohen, W., 39, 88
Cooper, K. H., 118, 145
Corlis, R. D., 55, 89
Cotter, L. H., 128, 145

Davidson, W. S., 128, 145
Davison, G. C., 26, 89
Dearborn, I. W., 121, 145

246
NAME INDEX

deGroot, J. C., 228, 244
Deikman, A., 36, 89
Dement, W., 73, 89
Denny, D. R., 235, 238, 244
Desoille, R., 57, 89
Dillow, P. V., 228, 244
Duncker, K., 173, 196
Dusay, J. M., 187, 196
Dussault, P., 124, 126, 147
Dyer, W. W., 225, 243
D'Zurilla, T., 171, 196

Ebbesen, E. B., 69, 90
Efran, J. S., 240, 243
Eisler, R. M., 203, 243
Ellis, A., 156, 158, 159, 160, 163, 196,
     206, 231, 243
Emery, G., 159, 196
Emmelkamp, P.M.G., 87, 89
Emmons, M. L., 202, 243
Enright, J. B., 80, 89
Erickson, M., 240

Faraday, A., 76, 77, 82, 89
Farber, L. H., 5, 17
Feather, B. W., 140, 145
Feldenkrais, M., 170, 196
Fensterheim, H., 203, 243
Ferster, C. B., 106, 113, 145
Fisch, R. I., 144, 147
Fisher, J., 118, 119, 146
Fishman, S. T., 45, 90
Frankl, V. E., 141, 143, 145
Franklin, B., 239
Frederiksen, L. W., 104, 105, 145
Freud, S., 5, 9, 20, 37, 72, 73, 89
Friedman, R. J., 212, 244

Gallwey, W. T., 170, 196
Garfield, P. L., 75, 89
Gelder, M. G., 128, 146
Gendlin, E. T., 50, 51, 52, 77, 89
Ginott, H. G., 227, 243
Girodo, M., 33, 89
Glasgow, R. E., 169, 196
Glass, C. R., 169, 196
Goldberg, H., 226, 230, 243

Goldfoot, D. A., 135, 146
Goldfried, M. R., 49, 89, 171, 196
Goldiamond, I., 106, 107, 111, 145
Goleman, D., 35, 89
Gottman, J. M., 169, 205, 206, 244
Goulding, R. L., 195, 196
Green, F. E., 28, 91
Greenberg, R., 73, 89
Greenleaf, E., 70, 89
Greenwald, H. M., 177, 178, 179, 180,
     181, 196
Grinder, J., 152, 154, 195
Groden, J., 22, 88

Hackman, A., 175, 196
Haley, J., 240, 243
Hall, R. V., 129, 145
Hannum, J. W., 177, 196, 219, 243
Hare-Mustin, R. T., 144, 145
Harper, R. A., 159, 196
Harris, D. E., 128, 146
Heiman, J., 228, 244
Hemingway, E., 103
Herbert, E. W., 104, 145
Hinkle, J. E., 30, 91
Hollon, S., 217, 244
Holmes, T. H., 7, 9, 17
Holroyd, K. A., 161, 162, 196
Homme, L. A., 117, 145
Horney, K., 4, 13, 17
Hubbard, D. R., Jr., 177, 196, 219, 243

Jacobson, E., 22, 90
Jakubowski, P., 210, 244
Jason, L., 239, 244
James, M., 182, 183, 187, 193, 197
Johnson, V. E., 48, 120, 134, 147
Jones, M. C., 94
Jongeward, D., 182, 197
Jung, C. G., 69, 73, 90

Kahler, T., 191, 192, 197
Kales, A., 235, 244
Kales, J., 235, 244
Kanfer, F. H., 14, 15, 16, 17, 93, 97,
     135, 145, 146
Kaplan, H. S., 120, 134, 146

SUBJECT INDEX